American Foreign Relations
Since 1898

Uncovering the Past: Documentary Readers in American History
Series Editors: Steven Lawson and Nancy Hewitt

The books in this series introduce students in American history courses to two important dimensions of historical analysis. They enable students to engage actively in historical interpretation, and they further students' understanding of the interplay between social and political forces in historical developments.

Consisting of primary sources and an introductory essay, these readers are aimed at the major courses in the American history curriculum, as outlined further below. Each book in the series will be approximately 225–50 pages, including a 25–30 page introduction addressing key issues and questions about the subject under consideration, a discussion of sources and methodology, and a bibliography of suggested secondary readings.

Published

Paul G. E. Clemens
The Colonial Era: A Documentary Reader

Sean Patrick Adams
The Early American Republic: A Documentary Reader

Stanley Harrold
The Civil War and Reconstruction: A Documentary Reader

Steven Mintz
African American Voices: A Documentary Reader, 1619–1877

Robert P. Ingalls and David K. Johnson
The United States Since 1945: A Documentary Reader

Camilla Townsend
American Indian History: A Documentary Reader

Steven Mintz
Mexican American Voices: A Documentary Reader

Brian Ward
The 1960s: A Documentary Reader

Nancy Rosenbloom
Women in Modern America Since 1880: A Documentary Reader

Jeremi Suri
American Foreign Relations Since 1898: A Documentary Reader

American Foreign Relations Since 1898

A Documentary Reader

Jeremi Suri

A John Wiley & Sons, Ltd., Publication

This edition first published 2010
© 2010 Blackwell Publishing Ltd except for editorial material and organization

Blackwell Publishing was acquired by John Wiley & Sons in February 2007. Blackwell's publishing program has been merged with Wiley's global Scientific, Technical, and Medical business to form Wiley-Blackwell.

Registered Office
John Wiley & Sons Ltd, The Atrium, Southern Gate, Chichester, West Sussex, PO19 8SQ, United Kingdom

Editorial Offices
350 Main Street, Malden, MA 02148–5020, USA
9600 Garsington Road, Oxford, OX4 2DQ, UK
The Atrium, Southern Gate, Chichester, West Sussex, PO19 8SQ, UK

For details of our global editorial offices, for customer services, and for information about how to apply for permission to reuse the copyright material in this book please see our website at www.wiley.com/wiley-blackwell.

The right of Jeremi Suri to be identified as the author of the editorial material in this work has been asserted in accordance with the Copyright, Designs and Patents Act 1988.

Library of Congress Cataloging-in-Publication Data

American foreign relations since 1898 : a documentary reader / edited by Jeremi Suri.
    p. cm. – (Uncovering the past)
  Includes bibliographical references and index.
  ISBN 978-1-4051-8448-9 (hardcover : alk. paper) – ISBN 978-1-4051-8447-2 (pbk. : alk. paper)
    1. United States–Foreign relations–20th century–Sources. 2. United States–Foreign relations–21st century–Sources. I. Suri, Jeremi.
E744.A53278 2010
973.91–dc22

                                                              2009043995

A catalogue record for this book is available from the British Library.

Set in 10/12.5pt Sabon by SPi Publisher Services, Pondicherry, India
Printed in Singapore by Ho Printing Singapore Pte Ltd

01 2010

Contents

List of Illustrations

Series Editors' Preface

Primary sources have become an essential component in the teaching of history to undergraduates. They engage students in the process of historical interpretation and analysis and help them understand that facts do not speak for themselves. Rather, students see how historians construct narratives that recreate the past. Most students assume that the pursuit of knowledge is a solitary endeavor; yet historians interact constantly with their peers, building upon previous research and arguing among themselves over the interpretation of documents and their larger meaning. The documentary readers in this series highlight the value of this collaborative creative process and encourage students to participate in it.

Each book in the series introduces students in American history courses to two important dimensions of historical analysis. They enable students to engage actively in historical interpretation, and they further students' understanding of the interplay among social, cultural, economic, and political forces in historical developments In pursuit of these goals, the documents in each text embrace a broad range of sources, including such items as illustrations of material artifacts, letters and diaries, sermons, maps, photographs, song lyrics, selections from fiction and memoirs, legal statutes, court decisions, presidential orders, speeches, and political cartoons.

Each volume in the series is edited by a specialist in the field who is concerned with undergraduate teaching. The goal is not to offer a comprehensive selection of material but to provide items that reflect major themes and debates; that illustrate significant social, cultural, political, and economic dimensions of an era or subject; and that inform, intrigue, and inspire undergraduate students. The editor of each volume has written an introduction that discusses the central questions that have occupied historians in this field and the ways in which historians have used primary sources to answer them. In addition, each introductory essay contains an explanation of the kinds of materials available to investigate a particular subject, the methods by which scholars analyze them, and the considerations that go into interpreting them. Each source selection is introduced by a short head note that gives students the necessary information and a context for understanding the document. Also, each section of the volume includes questions to guide student reading and stimulate classroom discussion.

Jeremi Suri's *American Foreign Relations Since 1898* offers an array of documents dealing with political, social, economic, and cultural aspects of the United States as an imperial power. This volume covers more than a century, during which the United States first rose as a player among global powers to its eventual predominance as the world's major superpower. This period ranges from the war of 1898 against Spain, the Forst and Second World Wars, the Cold War, and the War on Terror following September 11, 2001. Suri presents this history from multiple perspectives – government policymakers who shaped foreign policy, individuals and groups that protested against it, and foreign leaders who responded to it in both traditional and unexpected ways. These documents reflect the compiler's viewpoint that no single elite determined foreign policy, but rather that it reflected a variety of extra-governmental, non-governmental, and trans-national forces.

Suri's selections raise questions about the role of memory and culture in foreign affairs as well as about the notion of American exceptionalism within the rest of the world. He includes documents from the files of secretaries of state, provisions of treaties, sermons by religious leaders, lyrics of popular songs, a movie script, and newspaper accounts of foreign travels by heads of state. Suri provides an informative introduction to the vast literature on this period, and concise but rich head notes that locate specific documents in their larger context. The sources allow students to analyze the major international struggles engaged in by the United States from the late nineteenth to the early twenty-first century. From these selections, as well as the head notes and questions that accompany them, students will be better able to understand perhaps the most significant characteristic of the United States as a modern nation – its pre-eminent world presence – why and how it came to exist, and how long it will last.

Steven F. Lawson and Nancy A. Hewitt, Series Editors

Acknowledgments

Since 2001 my annual teaching load at the University of Wisconsin-Madison has included History 434: "The History of American Foreign Relations since 1898." Teaching this large lecture course has been a constant source of inspiration and excitement for me, and this book reflects that inspiration and excitement. These are documents that I have included in my lectures, assigned readings, class discussions, and examinations. I want to thank the thousands of students who have taken my courses for their enthusiasm, their encouragement, and their engagement with these materials. My students have been my teachers.

Peter Coveney at Blackwell first suggested this book to me. He patiently guided me through a series of extensive and very beneficial revisions. Deirdre Ilkson and Galen Smith helped me to bring the book to completion. Steven Lawson and Nancy Hewitt enthusiastically welcomed this book in their series, offering valuable suggestions. I am honored to be in their company.

I also want to thank Vanessa Walker for her help in assembling the materials for this book. She suggested crucial documents for inclusion, tracked down obscure information, and pushed me to make the book as useful as possible for a new generation of students. Vanessa will soon be a professor in her own right: I can't wait to watch her in action.

As always, I must close with a sincere appreciation for my family. My wife, Alison, is a model for the kind of citizenship I hope to encourage in my students. My children, Natalie and Zachary, embody the energy and optimism I hope to inspire in my students. I am very blessed in my family.

Source Acknowledgments

Charles Lindbergh, "New York to Paris," *We* (New York: Grosset and Dunlap, 1927), pp. 213–30. © 1927, renewed © 1955 by Charles A. Lindbergh. Used by permission of G. P. Putnam's Sons, a division of Penguin Group (USA) Inc.

Hamilton Fish Armstrong, *Peace and Counterpeace: From Wilson to Hitler, Memoirs of Hamilton Fish Armstrong* (New York: Harper & Row, 1971), pp. 535–9. © 1972 by Hamilton Fish Armstrong. Reprinted by permission of HarperCollins Publishers.

Barton J Bernstein, "Truman at Potsdam: His Secret Diary," *Foreign Service Journal* July/Aug. 1980, pp. 30–6. Reprinted with permission from the *Foreign Service Journal* (July/August 1980), the monthly magazine of the American Foreign Service Association.

James Melvin Washington (ed.), *A Testament of Hope: The Essential Writings and Speeches of Martin Luther King Jr.* (Washington, DC: HarperCollins, 1986), pp. 145–51. © 1960, Dr. Martin Luther King, Jr.; copyright renewed 1991, Coretta Scott King. Reprinted by arrangement with the Heirs to the Estate of Martin Luther King, Jr., c/o Writers House as agent for the proprietor, New York, NY.

"Dr. Strangelove, Or: How I Learned to Stop Worrying and Love the Bomb". Hawk Films Ltd, Shepperton Studios, Shepperton, Middlesex, Revised January 27, 1963. Scene 30 (30–1 to 30–7). Screenplay by Stanley Kubrick, Peter George and Terry Southern. © 1963, renewed 1991 Columbia Pictures Industries, Inc. Courtesy of Columbia Pictures.

Introduction

Foreign policy is about states, leaders, money, guns, and much more. Foreign policy is also about social movements, cultures, ideas, and images. Foreign policy represents the full range of relations between one society and its international counterparts – many of whom, like peace activists, have internal connections that evade the direct control of government leaders.

Adopting this broad framework, the present volume interrogates the range of American foreign relations from the late nineteenth century through the early twenty-first century. The documents presented are the tiny tip of a gargantuan archival iceberg containing the records of debates surrounding every development in American history during this period. Relevant and important documents include secret memos, personal letters, public speeches, newspaper articles, photographs, novels, songs, works of art, movies, and anything else that captures opinion, perspective, and sensibility about America and the world. A collected volume of this kind can only hint at the numerous historical treasures available in hidden places and before us in plain sight.

The words and images on the following pages probe the making (and unmaking) of foreign policy by diverse groups with diverse interests. They show the wide range of American power as well as its narrow limits. They show the promise of American democracy and the dark realities of its frequent distortion. This is a documentary record of the United States as a global actor that is short on heroics and villainy, and long on difficult choices with mixed results. This is a documentary record filled with fine-grained complexity, but few clear and easy answers.

The materials introduced in this volume are designed to serve three purposes. First, they highlight the range of diverse actors who have contributed to debates about American foreign policy – from presidents to protesters, students to singers. If nothing else, the scholarship of the last generation has opened the eyes of historians to the various non-state, sub-state, and even trans-state actors who influence – directly and indirectly – the most elite decision making.[1] Even figures as imposing as George Kennan and Henry Kissinger responded to the influences of foreign and domestic actors with far less recognized stature than their own.[2]

Second, the documents show the interrelation between policies in one moment (and one region) and another. They follow streams of thought, perceived "lessons of the past," and memories that condition responses to new threats and opportunities. Foreign policy is not made in neat theoretical vacuums, but in messy historical contexts that prevent perfectly "rational" decision making, even from hyper-rational thinkers. William Appleman Williams made this kind of analysis famous a half century ago when he pointed to the "tragedy" of Americans learning the wrong lessons from their continued international expansion.[3] John Lewis Gaddis, in contrast, has described the patterns of slow, but steady American reaction to foreign threats.[4] Although Williams and Gaddis have very different interpretations, they agree on the path dependence of US foreign policy – the inability of Americans to separate their judgments and decisions in the present from their prior experiences.[5]

Third, and perhaps most significant, the documents in this volume have inherent importance. Despite their diverse authors and forms of presentation, they were seen as significant in their own time. They moved people to action, sometimes in surprising ways. They mobilized citizens who had not been mobilized before. They were game-changers. Documents of this importance remain valuable long after their immediate moment because they explain change. They also highlight continuities in thought and action.

---

[1]   For an excellent survey of recent historical scholarship that makes this point, see Thomas W. Zeiler, "The Diplomatic History Bandwagon: A State of the Field," *Journal of American History*, 95 (March 2009), 1053–73.
[2]   See Anders Stephanson, *Kennan and the Art of Foreign Policy* (Cambridge, MA: Harvard University Press, 1989); Jeremi Suri, *Henry Kissinger and the American Century* (Cambridge, MA: Belknap Press of Harvard University Press, 2007).
[3]   William Appleman Williams, *The Tragedy of American Diplomacy*, enlarged edn. (New York: W. W. Norton, 1988).
[4]   John Lewis Gaddis, *Strategies of Containment: A Critical Appraisal of American National Security Policy during the Cold War*, revised edn. (New York: Oxford University Press, 2005).
[5]   On this point, see also Melvyn P. Leffler, *For the Soul of Mankind: The United States, the Soviet Union, and the Cold War* (New York: Hill and Wang, 2007).

More than anything else, foreign policy is a reflection of a society's efforts to master international transformation. This involves uncertainty and contestation, as well as national investment and collective risk-taking. No country has devoted more to these latter two endeavors over the last century than the United States. From John Hay to Martin Luther King, Jr., American ambition has left its mark on the nation's debates, its institutions, and its identity. Phrases like the "Open Door," "Wilsonianism," the "New Deal," and "Communist Containment" reflect the historical power of leadership and joint action in a self-consciously individualist nation. The documents in this volume testify to the constant reconstruction of American society both from without and within.[6]

These three themes – diversity, path dependence, and national mobilization – have deeply influenced scholarship on American foreign relations. Instead of asking "why the United States pursued foreign expansion in the twentieth century" and "who was responsible for this 'imperial' turn," historians now focus on the diverse military, political, social, and cultural pressures that made the projection of American power and interests so difficult to restrain. This is part of both the *internationalization* of what had been a much more American-centered approach to the subject, and the *diversification* of what had been a narrower understanding of power. Economic and military factors, of course, remain important, but the documents in this volume point to the role of other influences as well – strategic, ideological, racial, religious, and moral, among others. The "new" history of American expansion emphasizes multiple causes. It draws on primary sources from many foreign and domestic locales. It also highlights the different responses to power – including advocacy, acquiescence, avoidance, collaboration, and resistance – and the effects these varied forms of response exerted on policy.[7]

Similar points are in order for recent scholarship on the Cold War. Instead of asking "who started the Cold War" and "who was most responsible for its many horrors," scholars now assess the many military, political, social, and cultural pressures that made East–West conflict difficult to avoid. In the eyes of some historians, events after 1945 were a manifestation of a "security dilemma." Sincere efforts by the United States to defend itself against

---

[6] For a thoughtful set of essays on this phenomenon, see Thomas Bender (ed.), *Rethinking American History in a Global Age* (Berkeley, CA: University of California Press, 2002).
[7] For extended reflections on this topic, see Mathew Connelly, *Fatal Misconception: The Struggle to Control World Population* (Cambridge, MA: Belknap Press of Harvard University Press, 2008); Jeremi Suri, *Power and Protest: Global Revolution and the Rise of Détente* (Cambridge, MA: Harvard University Press, 2003).

perceived adversaries served to antagonize those same adversaries. Fears became self-fulfilling as one country's aggressive defense triggered another's aggressive defense. Especially in a nuclear age, the differences between defense and offense became difficult to discern. Through arms races, competitions for influence, and proxy wars, Cold War enemies continued to raise the stakes and dangers for one another. Less powerful societies suffered ever deeper (and bloodier) foreign intrusions, but they also benefited from new leverage as they became the highly desired dance partners for rich and powerful rivals.[8]

Even after the end of the Cold War, this dynamic still seems to drive much of American foreign policy. Leaders from George H. W. Bush and Bill Clinton to George W. Bush have emphasized toughness, overwhelming American power, and aggressive defense against emerging challenges. Although they have often chosen not to intervene in foreign conflicts (for example, the genocidal civil war in Rwanda), they have consistently expanded the range of American foreign commitments to forestall perceived threats and court potential allies. American citizens have devoted precious domestic resources to these growing international activities, and they reproduced a public rhetoric of security through displays of strength – sometimes even including torture of alleged terrorists. The rhetoric of "globalization" in the early twenty-first century was, more than anything else, a recognition of how far American influence now reached and how deeply this phenomenon transformed daily life – for better and for worse.[9]

The documents in this volume do not cover every event in this long history of American foreign relations. This is not a complete history, if such a thing exists. Rather, the diverse materials presented here are designed to elucidate long-standing thought patterns and habits of action. They point to turning points and change over time, but they also provide insights about continuities, cycles, and recurring tendencies. Every event is unique, but every unique event is set in a long history of comparable experiences. Above all, the documents in this volume have been chosen to encourage meditation on this historical tension: How did the trajectory of American society

---

[8]   See Melvyn P. Leffler, *A Preponderance of Power: National Security, the Truman Administration, and the Cold War* (Stanford, CA: Stanford University Press, 1992); John Lewis Gaddis, *The Cold War: A New History* (New York: Penguin, 2005); Vladislav Zubok, *A Failed Empire: The Soviet Union in the Cold War from Stalin to Gorbachev* (Chapel Hill, NC: University of North Carolina Press, 2007); Odd Arne Westad, *The Global Cold War: Third World Interventions and the Making of Our Times* (Cambridge: Cambridge University Press, 2005).

[9]   For a critical reflection on these developments, see Andrew Bacevich, *The Limits of Power: The End of American Exceptionalism* (New York: Metropolitan Books, 2008).

change at particular moments, how did it remain the same? When and how did leaders and citizens move society along a new path? What were the alternative paths – better and worse – not taken?

Answers to these difficult questions raise another set of important concerns. Was America "exceptional"? Was the twentieth century the "American century"? Did the United States fulfill – or at least endeavor to fulfill – a special mission in the world? The public rhetoric of American society and the sincere aspirations of many American citizens make these unavoidable topics of discussion.

This volume does not take an explicit position on each of these questions, but it does make a strong case for the distinctiveness of American power in this period. The mix of groups, interests, prejudices, and programs captured in the reprinted documents points to the *pluralism* of American society. No single "ruling class" made policy. No single creed controlled decisions. Instead, the choices of American society remained in constant flux, ever debated, contested, and compromised. Even during moments of apparent national unity – the Second World War and the Cold War – major issues remained unresolved and American policies continued to reflect compromises among contending parties. Pluralism, in this sense, surely has its echoes in other societies, but it is particularly prominent in the American record. Pluralism was the consistent backdrop for every decision recounted in the documents reprinted in this volume – even if particular decisions stand out for their peculiar insularity.

Pluralism, of course, does not imply equality for all groups and points of view. Although many diverse people contributed to the evolution of American foreign relations, in general certain figures mattered for policy outcomes more than others. The divisions between the empowered and the disempowered run, predictably, along race, class, ethnic, and gender lines. That is, however, only part of the story. Traditionally disempowered groups exerted leverage at recurring moments of war, domestic uncertainty, and foreign challenge. Marginal figures became central actors when they found a creative and cogent voice through popular culture or national politics that was difficult to dismiss. The pluralism of American foreign relations shifted with domestic society, but it never disappeared. In this sense, Americans were consistently inconsistent. This observation drove many more traditional foreign policy thinkers, especially Kennan and Kissinger, to despair. For them, American pluralism was disguised democratic provincialism.[10]

---

[10]   See footnote 2, above.

Pluralism, however, also had its cosmopolitan dimensions. The expanding international reach and penetration of American society contributed to the nation's personal and policy diversity, giving politics a powerful global inflection. Recent immigrants – European, Asian, African, Latin American – were both agents and targets of debates about national purpose. Alliances in war and peace framed deliberations about policy, as they also extended the range of American power. Most of all, the wealth and stature of the United States as a global power after 1898 – and then a superpower after 1945 – meant that Americans contended with a disorienting combination of entreaties for aid and warnings to stay at bay, often from different groups within the same society. American power meant that the nation could rarely remain aloof, or "neutral" in Woodrow Wilson's terms. The story of the United States in the twentieth century involves constant agonizing over tough choices in response to ever pressing international demands. Pluralism meant recurring debate and soul-searching. The "American century" was not easy.

The foreign relations of the United States were complex, contradictory, and generally far from consensual – at home or abroad. The documents in this volume are not presented to offer a single narrative, or any clear and obvious "lessons." Quite the contrary, a reading of the historical record opens our eyes to the difficult, unpredictable, and deeply human process by which American society interacts with the wider world. Abstract ideas and forces do not make American policy. Isolated individuals do not make decisions either. Instead, groups strive to understand the challenges and opportunities of their era; they plan, they react, and then they struggle to make sense of it all. That is the process revealed by the documents reprinted here. That is the process that also governs decision making in our present world.

This volume aims to be a useful history in examining the complex deliberations surrounding foreign policy. It asks the reader to empathize with diverse historical actors and interpret their endeavors. It begs the reader to bring this sensibility to other topics – historical and contemporary.

Chapter 1   War, Imperialism, Anti-Imperialism

1 Secretary of State, John Hay, Open Door Notes, 1899–1900

During the last decades of the nineteenth century politicians, missionaries, and businesspeople in Europe, Japan, and the United States looked enthusiastically to the "China market." This vast and densely populated society, teetering on the edge of collapse due to internal disunity and external pressures, offered the prospect of great riches for foreigners. By the 1890s Great Britain, France, Germany, Russia, Japan, and the United States, among other countries, had established "concession areas" in China where they exerted control over local events on the mainland. They had begun to carve up China, on the model of European imperialism in Africa. American Secretary of State, John Hay, recognized this dynamic. He feared that the imperial division of China would create new sources of international conflict, and also exclude the United States from full access to the society. In 1899 and 1900 he issued his two "Open Door Notes" to the other foreign powers in the hope of creating an alternative to traditional imperialism. Hay called for "equal and impartial trade" in China, shared development of Chinese infrastructure, and protections for foreign citizens under their national laws (extraterritoriality). Historians have long debated whether Hay's vision was a form of imperialism or an alternative to it. They have interrogated the ways in which Hay's advocacy of an "open door" contributed to America's rise as a dominant power in Asia at the start of the twentieth century.[1]

---

[1] See William Appleman Williams, *The Tragedy of American Diplomacy*, enlarged edn. (New York: W. W. Norton, 1988); Thomas Schoonover, *Uncle Sam's War of 1898 and the Origins of Globalization* (Lexington, KT: University Press of Kentucky, 2005); Robert L. Beisner, *From the Old Diplomacy to the New, 1865–1900* (New York: Harlan Davidson, 1986); Walter McDougall, *Promised Land, Crusader State: The American Encounter with the World Since 1776* (New York: Mariner Books, 1998).

FIRST OPEN DOOR NOTE

United States Secretary of State, John Hay, to US Ambassador to Britain, Joseph Choate, September 6, 1899. Similar notes were sent to Germany, France, Italy, Japan, and Russia.

SIR: The Government of Her Britannic Majesty has declared that its policy and its very traditions precluded it from using any privileges which might be granted it in China as a weapon for excluding commercial rivals, and that freedom of trade for Great Britain in that Empire meant freedom of trade for all the world alike. While conceding by formal agreements, first with Germany and then with Russia, the possession of "spheres of influence or interest" in China in which they are to enjoy special rights and privileges, more especially in respect of railroads and mining enterprises, Her Britannic Majesty's Government has therefore sought to maintain at the same time what is called the "open-door" policy, to insure to the commerce of the world in China equality of treatment within said "spheres" for commerce and navigation. This latter policy is alike urgently demanded by the British mercantile communities and by those of the United States, as it is justly held by them to be the only one which will improve existing conditions, enable them to maintain their positions in the markets of China, and extend their operations in the future. While the Government of the United States will in no way commit itself to a recognition of exclusive rights of any power within or control over any portion of the Chinese Empire under such agreements as have within the last year been made, it can not conceal its apprehension that under existing conditions there is a possibility, even a probability, of complications arising between the treaty powers which may imperil the rights insured to the United States under our treaties with China.

This Government is animated by a sincere desire that the interests of our citizens may not be prejudiced through exclusive treatment by any of the controlling powers within their so-called "spheres of interest" in China, and hope also to retain there an open market for the commerce of the world, remove dangerous sources of international irritation, and hasten thereby united or concerted action of the powers at Pekin[g] in favor of the administrative reforms so urgently needed for strengthening the Imperial Government and maintaining the integrity of China in which the whole western world is alike concerned. It believes that such a result may be greatly assisted by a declaration by the various powers claiming "spheres of interest" in China of their intentions as regards treatment of foreign trade therein. The present moment seems a particularly opportune one for informing Her Britannic Majesty's Government of the desire of the United States to see it make a formal declaration and to lend its support in obtaining similar declarations from the various powers claiming "spheres of influence" in China to the effect that each in its respective spheres of interest or influence –

First. Will in no wise interfere with any treaty port or any vested interest within any so-called "sphere of interest" or leased territory it may have in China.

Second. That the Chinese treaty tariff of the time being shall apply to all merchandise landed or shipped to all such ports as are within said "sphere of interest" (unless they be "free ports"), no matter to what nationality it may belong, and that duties so leviable [sic.] shall be collected by the Chinese Government.

Third. That it will levy no higher harbor dues on vessels of another nationality frequenting any port in such "sphere" than shall be levied on vessels of its own nationality, and no higher railroad charges over lines built, controlled, or operated within its "sphere" on merchandise belonging to citizens or subjects of other nationalities transported through such "sphere" than shall be levied on similar merchandise belonging to its own nationals transported over equal distances.

The recent ukase of His Majesty the Emperor of Russia, declaring the port of Ta-lien-wan open to the merchant ships of all nations during the whole of the lease under which it is to be held by Russia, removing as it does all uncertainty as to the liberal and conciliatory policy of that power, together with the assurances given this Government by Russia, justifies the expectation that His Majesty will cooperate in such an understanding as is here proposed, and our ambassador at the court of St. Petersburg has been instructed accordingly to submit the propositions above detailed to His Imperial Majesty, and ask their early consideration. Copy of my instruction to Mr. Tower is herewith inclosed [sic.] for your confidential information.

The action of Germany in declaring the port of Kiaochao a "free port," and the aid the Imperial Government has given China in the establishment there of a Chinese custom-house, coupled with the oral assurance conveyed the United States by Germany that our interests within its "sphere" would in no wise be affected by its occupation of this portion of the province of Shang-tung, tend to show that little opposition may be anticipated from that power to the desired declaration.

The interests of Japan, the next most interested power in the trade of China, will be so clearly served by the proposed arrangement, and the declaration of its statesmen within the last year are so entirely in line with the views here expressed, that its hearty cooperation is confidently counted on.

You will, at as early date as practicable, submit the considerations to Her Britannic Majesty's principal secretary of state for foreign affairs and request their immediate consideration. I inclose [*sic*.] herewith a copy of the instruction sent to our ambassador at Berlin bearing on the above subject.

I have the honor to be, etc.,

John Hay.

SECOND OPEN DOOR NOTE

Circular note of July 3, 1900, to the powers cooperating in China, defining the purposes and policy of the United States

In this critical posture of affairs in China it is deemed appropriate to define the attitude of the United States as far as present circumstances permit this to be done. We adhere to the policy initiated by us in 1857 of peace with the Chinese nation, of furtherance of lawful commerce, and of protection of lives and property of our citizens by all means guaranteed under extraterritorial treaty rights and by the law of nations. If wrong be done to our citizens we propose to hold the responsible authors to the uttermost accountability. We regard the condition at Pekin[g] as one of virtual anarchy, whereby power and responsibility are practically devolved upon the local provincial authorities. So long as they are not in overt collusion with rebellion and use their power to protect foreign life and property, we regard them as representing the Chinese people, with whom we seek to remain in peace and friendship. The purpose of the President, is as it has been heretofore, to act concurrently with the other powers; first, in opening up communication with Pekin[g] and rescuing the American officials, missionaries, and other Americans who are in danger; secondly, in affording all possible protection everywhere in China to American life and property; thirdly, in guarding and protecting all legitimate American interests; and fourthly, in aiding to prevent a spread of the disorders to the other provinces of the Empire and a recurrence of such disasters. It is of course too early to forecast the means of attaining this last result; but the policy of the Government of the United States is to seek a solution which may bring about permanent safety and peace to China, preserve Chinese territorial and administrative entity, protect all rights guaranteed to friendly powers by treaty and international law, and safeguard for the world the principle of equal and impartial trade with all parts of the Chinese Empire.

You will communicate the purport of this instruction to the minister for foreign affairs.

John Hay.

Source: *Papers Relating to the Foreign Relations of the United States*, 1899, pp. 129–30; *Ibid.*, 1900, p. 299.

Suggested Questions for Discussion:

1. How did the "Open Door" reflect long-standing American ideas about freedom and commerce?
2. How could the United States convince distant and powerful states to observe an "Open Door" in China?
3. Was John Hay's "Open Door" a form of imperialism?

2 President William McKinley, Account of his Decision to Occupy the Philippines, 1898

On April 29, 1898 the United States declared war on Spain, attacking its forces in both Cuba and the Philippines. Many Americans supported this war as a necessary effort to defeat a degenerate empire and protect American economic interests. The rapid retreat of Spanish authority in the Philippines forced Commodore (later Admiral) George Dewey, President William McKinley, and others to confront the question of future governance for this strategic archipelago. In a retrospective interview, McKinley described his initial desire to avoid a long-term American occupation of the Philippines, and his subsequent change of position. Under the provisions of the Treaty of Paris, signed by American and Spanish representatives on December 10, 1898, the United States asserted dominion over the Philippines.[2]

Hold a moment longer! Not quite yet, gentlemen! Before you go I would like to say just a word about the Philippine business. I have been criticized a good deal about the Philippines, but don't deserve it. The truth is I didn't want the Philippines, and when they came to us, as a gift from the gods, I did not know what to do with them. When the Spanish War broke out Dewey was at Hong Kong, and I ordered him to go to Manila and to capture or destroy the Spanish fleet, and he had to; because, if defeated, he had no place to refit on that side of the globe, and if the Dons were victorious they would likely cross the Pacific and ravage our Oregon and California coasts. And so he had to destroy the Spanish fleet, and did it! But that was as far as I thought then.

---

[2]   See Paul A. Kramer, *The Blood of Government: Race, Empire, the United States, and the Philippines* (Chapel Hill, NC: University of North Carolina Press, 2006); Lewis Gould, *The Presidency of William McKinley* (Lawrence, KA: University Press of Kansas, 1981); Brian McAllister Linn, *The Philippine War, 1899–1902* (Lawrence, KA: University Press of Kansas, 2000).

When I next realized that the Philippines had dropped into our laps I confess I did not know what to do with them. I sought counsel from all sides – Democrats as well as Republicans – but got little help. I thought first we would take only Manila; then Luzon; then other islands perhaps also. I walked the floor of the White House night after night until midnight; and I am not ashamed to tell you, gentlemen, that I went down on my knees and prayed Almighty God for light and guidance more than one night. And one night late it came to me this way – I don't know how it was, but it came: (1) That we could not give them back to Spain – that would be cowardly and dishonorable; (2) that we could not turn them over to France and Germany – our commercial rivals in the Orient – that would be bad business and discreditable; (3) that we could not leave them to themselves – they were unfit for self-government – and they would soon have anarchy and misrule over there worse than Spain's was; and (4) that there was nothing left for us to do but to take them all, and to educate the Filipinos, and uplift and civilize and Christianize them, and by God's grace do the very best we could by them, as our fellow-men for whom Christ also died. And then I went to bed, and went to sleep, and slept soundly, and the next morning I sent for the chief engineer of the War Department (our map-maker), and I told him to put the Philippines on the map of the United States (pointing to a large map on the wall of his office), and there they are, and there they will stay while I am President!

Source: General James Rusling's account of his interview with President William McKinley, printed two years after McKinley's assassination, in *The Christian Advocate*, January 22, 1903, 17. Reprinted in Daniel Schirmer and Stephen Rosskamm Shalom (eds.), *The Philippines Reader* (Boston, MA: South End Press, 1987), 22–3.

Suggested Questions for Discussion:

1. What were President McKinley's initial aims in ordering an attack on Spanish forces in the Philippines?
2. Why did American aims change after the fall of Spanish power?
3. Did the United States become a new imperialist in the Philippines?

3 The Platt Amendment, 1901

The United States formerly occupied the island of Cuba from December 1898 through May 1902. As part of the American preparations for Cuban independence, the US Congress passed the "Platt Amendment" (named for Senator Orville Platt, a Republican from Connecticut) in March 1901. The Platt Amendment dictated terms of independence for Cuba that ensured American domination of the island. The most significant and enduring provisions included: an American right of intervention; enforced sanitation to protect health and commerce; and American possession of military bases on Cuba – particularly the US naval base at Guantanamo Bay.[3]

Platt Amendment

Whereas the Congress of the United States of America, by an Act approved March 2, 1901, provided as follows:

Provided further, That in fulfillment of the declaration contained in the joint resolution approved April twentieth, eighteen hundred and ninety-eight, entitled "For the recognition of the independence of the people of Cuba, demanding that the Government of Spain relinquish its authority and government in the island of Cuba, and withdraw its land and naval forces from Cuba and Cuban waters, and directing the President of the United States to use the land and naval forces of the United States to carry these resolutions into effect," the President is hereby authorized to "leave the government and control of the island of Cuba to its people" so soon as a government shall have been established in said island under a constitution which, either as a part thereof or in an ordinance appended thereto, shall define the future relations of the United States with Cuba, substantially as follows:

I. That the government of Cuba shall never enter into any treaty or other compact with any foreign power or powers which will impair or tend to impair the independence of Cuba, nor in any manner authorize or permit any foreign power or powers to obtain by colonization or for military or naval purposes or otherwise, lodgment in or control over any portion of said island.

[3] See Luis A. Pérez, *Cuba Under the Platt Amendment, 1902–1934* (Pittsburgh, PA: University of Pittsburgh Press, 1986); Ada Ferrer, *Insurgent Cuba: Race, Nation, and Revolution, 1868–1898* (Chapel Hill, NC: University of North Carolina Press, 1999).

II. That said government shall not assume or contract any public debt, to pay the interest upon which, and to make reasonable sinking fund provision for the ultimate discharge of which, the ordinary revenues of the island, after defraying the current expenses of government shall be inadequate.

III. That the government of Cuba consents that the United States may exercise the right to intervene for the preservation of Cuban independence, the maintenance of a government adequate for the protection of life, property, and individual liberty, and for discharging the obligations with respect to Cuba imposed by the treaty of Paris on the United States, now to be assumed and undertaken by the government of Cuba.

IV. That all Acts of the United States in Cuba during its military occupancy thereof are ratified and validated, and all lawful rights acquired there under shall be maintained and protected.

V. That the government of Cuba will execute, and as far as necessary extend, the plans already devised or other plans to be mutually agreed upon, for the sanitation of the cities of the island, to the end that a recurrence of epidemic and infectious diseases may be prevented, thereby assuring protection to the people and commerce of Cuba, as well as to the commerce of the southern ports of the United States and the people residing therein.

VI. That the Isle of Pines shall be omitted from the proposed constitutional boundaries of Cuba, the title thereto being left to future adjustment by treaty.

VII. That to enable the United States to maintain the independence of Cuba, and to protect the people thereof, as well as for its own defense, the government of Cuba will sell or lease to the United States lands necessary for coaling or naval stations at certain specified points to be agreed upon with the President of the United States.

VIII. That by way of further assurance the government of Cuba will embody the foregoing provisions in a permanent treaty with the United States.

Source: "The Platt Amendment," in *Treaties and Other International Agreements of the United States of America, 1776–1949*, vol. 8, C. I. Bevans (ed.) (Washington, DC: United States Government Printing Office, 1971), pp. 1116–17.

Suggested Questions for Discussion:

1. How did the Platt Amendment limit Cuban independence?
2. Which American interests did the Platt Amendment serve most directly?
3. How did the Platt Amendment transform American foreign policy?

4 Jane Addams, Critique of American Militarism, 1902

During the last decades of the nineteenth century an international peace movement grew across the United States and Western Europe. Its advocates called upon states to abandon war and invest their resources in education, economic development, and social welfare. International peace advocates attacked the assumptions about struggle that underpinned Social-Darwinist thought, and they embraced a vision of cooperation and mutual benefit among societies. They also shared ideas across societies on the uses of Progressive domestic reform as a model and inspiration for international peace-making. Jane Addams, the famous founder of Hull House in Chicago, was a leading voice among these "progressive internationalists."[4]

THE NEWER IDEALS OF PEACE

An Address by Miss Jane Addams, of Hull House, Chicago, in the Hall, Monday, July 7, 1902.

Miss Jane Addams addressed a large audience in the Hall yesterday afternoon. The stenographic report follows:

At the opening of the Crystal Palace in 1851 which was to house the world's first exposition, a number of speeches were made on the present state of civilization. All of them in varying degree referred to the fact that war was a thing of the past. There had been no European war for the previous thirty years, following the Napoleonic upheaval, and it was assumed that the wars of the French Revolution and of Napoleon were sporadic and would not occur again. The speakers congratulated the world upon their arrival at a warless state. Only three years after that, the Crimean war began. During the next fifty years there were twelve great wars between white peoples, not including the wars in which one of the combatants was black or yellow. These wars began with the Crimean war in 1853, and included the second Boer war in 1899.

---

[4] See Alan Dawley, *Changing the World: American Progressives in War and Revolution* (Princeton, NJ: Princeton University Press, 2003); Daniel T. Rodgers, *Atlantic Crossings: Social Politics in a Progressive Age* (Cambridge, MA: Belknap Press of Harvard University Press, 1998); Jean Bethke Elshtain, *Jane Addams and the Dream of American Democracy* (New York: Basic Books, 2001).

One naturally is driven to speak on this changed point of view. We recall George Eliot's saying that we prepare ourselves for our deeds by our thoughts and ideals. If we look into our minds we will find that we have been preparing ourselves for this deed by allowing ourselves to think in a certain way, or perhaps by not taking care of our thoughts and expressions but allowing them to revert to a more primitive type. In someway or other the social ideal has changed between 1850 and 1900. We have lost faith in moral power. We believe moral life must be urged on by force, that only the moral issues backed by arms are the great issues. We may come to that in many ways, but let us admit that we have come to it. It was about the time that Darwin published his first book, which is the foundation for modern science and evolution. Darwin put great stress on the struggle for existence and the survival of the fittest, but he also emphasized mutual aid as a means of progress and survival. That solitary animal, the lion, that lives by struggling for food and destroying other life, is fast dying out, while animals that cooperate, such as the ant and the bee, are the ones that survive. All these things on the other side have been more or less ignored. Some scientists now claim that Darwin's work must be gone over again because the popular imagination seized on the things that pleased it for the moment, and emphasized that part of Darwin's teaching. It is only of late that the other side is being emphasized. We may say that this earlier idea is somewhat the result of scientific teaching and partly the result of the materialistic age. We love to talk about the great inventions of these fifty years. We have built up a mighty pedestal and on the top we have put the man with the hammer. Education and culture have come to be dependent on the man with the pedestal, and more or less he influences us all. What have we done with the higher ideals which the world seemed to have possessed fifty years ago?

You can go on and say that all the time there have been groups of people who have protested against warfare, that in nearly every civilized country there has been a small body of people who have said that warfare is a disgrace. The first line that has been worked is the appeal to pity and mercy. It is a question whether we could go on with war if we had not organized our hospitals and our Red Cross societies. Perhaps that appeal to pity has been something of an anodyne to our conscience. This voice has spoken out most clearly in two men. In Count Tolstoy, who in his picture of war almost makes one feel as if one had been through a campaign; not of waving of banners and all the rest of the trash we have associated with war, but as if one had been through a campaign with a common soldier, and dragged through all its sordidness and meanness. Then let us take [Vasily] Vereshchagin, who has portrayed war as it is, who has brought out the wretchedness and squalor of it all, and there we have two powerful appeals to pity and mercy. If we had to see it with our own eyes, we might question whether a moral cause is subserved by it all. In the end men must settle questions by reason. All war, then, has been so much wasted force ...

We can take the second line, the appeal to the sense of prudence, the line so largely taken in the Hague conference. A great Frenchman has estimated that a war costs as much as a university; that the men in the marine have a salary as large as that of the faculty of a large university. Do not let us destroy human life – it is too precious. Every child on the face of the earth represents someone's care and thought; why do we send him forth into the unknown over the pretext of some issue which he cannot change? Prudence is insisted on more by the French; but the Emperor William has of late been manifesting an interest in this side of the question. The Hague conference said, "Walk in the paths of arbitration."

Aside from this appeal to sympathy and to prudence, there is a third which is difficult to formulate; it is the appeal to the sense of human solidarity. Aside from the worth of human life, it is our business to aid human existence. If we are equal in the sight of the Lord, how can one set of men decide to do away with another set of men? There is sustenance for all the millions on the earth, but not unless we co-operate, which we cannot do so long as one sets itself up as superior. Here, too, the Russians seem beyond us. A highly educated Russian was visiting in this country. He made the remark that he did not feel that he was superior to any human being. Someone challenged his remark and said he was so learned that he surely must feel a difference between himself and a common criminal. "Of course, I am aware that I know more mathematics than most people, more than anyone in the world except two other men; I have a better trained mind, but that," he said, "has nothing to do with human equality. You talk about the 'common criminal.' I was once in a prison in France with a number of other political prisoners. There were also within the prison walls some criminals, and one of them a thief. I was angry, and felt a certain resentment at occupying a cell with this common thief. I was willing to suffer as a martyr for my political belief, but I was not willing to be put in a cell with a common thief. But this man was wiser than I, for he was able to escape and I was not. He was more clever than the prison guards, for he got out of the prison walls and yard. He was lying flat in a ditch waiting for darkness. He was lying there with his heart in his mouth, for he knew the guards were out looking for him, when he heard a peasant woman shriek that the house was on fire and their child was there in the upper story. She was hysterical and was doing nothing to save the child, but stood and shrieked to her husband for help. The man in the ditch without a moment's hesitation sprang from his hiding, rushed into the house, and brought down the child not into the arms of its mother but of the prison guards. He was marched back to prison and his sentence doubled. I do not believe I would have done that. With tears I apologized to him for my unkindly feeling toward him. I had blasphemed against our common nature, against the nobility which is common to all men, and to which, from time to time, men from the very lowest type arise. The one thing which I fear is this feeling of superiority and you always get it whenever you have a feeling of hatred."

Only through such feeling in regard to warfare could we get any approach to that equality which the world has dreamed of for so many years. When we look about us and see war everywhere, it seems that this feeling has been drugged. We do not speak of it, but it is there, and many of us believe it will yet assert itself.

If one goes back of these three: the appeal to the sense of pity, the appeal to prudence, and the sense of human solidarity, one will have to say that something has been the matter with the nature of the appeal or it would not have failed so completely. They are beginning to have another outlet – that of active labor and service, and all this does much to make war impossible. Let us take the civilian counterpart of the first one, the appeal to the sensibilities as related to the poor people – those who do the roughest work with their hands, wear the meanest clothes, whom we allow ourselves to feel a little differently towards. Lately there has been an attempt everywhere, in France, America and England, to appeal to the sensibilities on behalf of these people. I suppose we always think pre-eminently of Dickens as among the pioneer writers on these lines, and of Zola in France. In America we come to a long line of realistic novels dealing with life as a whole, and presenting people as they are, simply and truly. Certain words are almost dropping out of our vocabulary. When you know such a person even in literature, he has become individualized. We are dropping such hateful words as "slum," "the lower classes," because when we use them we think of fine people we have met to whom, after we know them, we could not possibly apply such terms.

There are economists who are beginning to assert very firmly that any nation that allows its people to be underfed and diseased is committing a great economic imprudence. Not only is the nation deprived of the wages and taxes of these people, but it is loading itself with a great lot of people who have to be cared for by the taxes of people more fortunate. More and more we hear that in the great world-struggle that that nation is going to go down which does not hold up a high standard of industrial labor; that the nation that allows child-labor is drawing on its capital; that the nation that allows its industrial people to go down is using up its future forces. Long and exhausting labor does this. A nation which can see that men in its working trades are used up at the age of thirty-four, and feels no responsibility about it, is a nation that is not using its forces well.

We come to the appeal to the sense of human solidarity. We talk of moral forces, and yet when we see such a force operating we are skeptical, and think there must be some self-seeking motive behind it. Under this head, of course, we might put all the educational efforts of government, and all those efforts which are trying to bring fullness of life to the humblest man. We could point to the old-age pensions in Germany, where people are taken care of after they are too old to care for themselves. We are getting rid of smallpox; and we are going to get rid of scarlet fever and many other diseases when we feel the same sense of responsibility for the community as for our own particular household. When we once surround human life with the same kind of heroism and admiration that we have surrounded war, we can say that this sense is having such an outlet that war will become impossible.

They say the temptation comes to every age to use an old moral standard and to fail to apply one to which to work up. It may be the new standard of life is at our hand, and if we fail to apply it we shall slip back to old standards, as apparently we have done in the last fifty years, which Prince Albert and his fellows thought were obsolete.

Source: *The Chautauqua Assembly Herald*, vol. 27, July 8, 1902. Reprinted in Allen F. Davis (ed.), *Jane Addams on Peace, War, and International Understanding, 1899–1932* (New York: Garland, Publishing, 1976), pp. 19–25.

Suggested Questions for Discussion:

1. What is Jane Addams' vision for a new kind of foreign policy?
2. How does she connect this foreign policy vision with domestic reforms?
3. Why does Jane Addams believe that her ideals are also "realistic"?

5 President Theodore Roosevelt, "Corollary" to the Monroe Doctrine, 1904

Theodore Roosevelt brought a sophisticated and expansive vision to the making of American foreign policy. In December 1904 he explained that the United States would play a more active and, at times, forceful role in world affairs to protect stability, trade, and "civilized mankind." In Latin America Roosevelt asserted a right of intervention to exclude other foreign powers, assure US interests, and promote good government. Later called the Roosevelt "Corollary," this aggressive posture of the United States in the Western Hemisphere transformed the Monroe Doctrine from a somewhat innocuous warning against new European colonialism in Latin America into a muscular claim of US "police" powers in the region. The Monroe Doctrine had little force behind it; the Roosevelt Corollary built on a modernizing American navy, army, and foreign service.[5]

Excerpted from Theodore Roosevelt's Annual Message to Congress, December 6, 1904

The steady aim of this Nation, as of all enlightened nations, should be to strive to bring ever nearer the day when there shall prevail throughout the world the peace of justice. There are kinds of peace, which are highly undesirable, which are in the long run as destructive as any war. Tyrants and oppressors have many times made a wilderness and called it peace. Many times peoples who were slothful or timid or shortsighted, who had been enervated by ease or by luxury, or misled by false teachings, have shrunk in unmanly fashion from doing duty that was stern and that needed self-sacrifice, and have sought to hide from their own minds their shortcomings, their ignoble motives, by calling them love of peace. The peace of tyrannous terror, the peace of craven weakness, the peace of injustice, all these should be shunned as we shun unrighteous war. The goal to set before us as a nation, the goal which should be set before all mankind, is the attainment of the peace of justice, of the peace which comes when each nation is not merely safe-guarded in its own rights, but scrupulously recognizes and performs its duty toward others. Generally peace tells for righteousness; but if there is conflict between the two, then our fealty is due first to the cause of righteousness. Unrighteous wars are common, and unrighteous peace is rare; but both should be shunned. The right of freedom and the responsibility for the exercise of that right can not be divorced. One of our great poets has well and finely said that freedom is not a gift that tarries long in the hands of cowards. Neither does it tarry long in the hands of those too slothful, too dishonest, or too unintelligent to exercise it. The eternal vigilance which is the price of liberty must be exercised, sometimes to guard against outside foes; although of course far more often to guard against our own selfish or thoughtless shortcomings.

If these self-evident truths are kept before us, and only if they are so kept before us, we shall have a clear idea of what our foreign policy in its larger aspects should be. It is our duty to remember that a nation has no more right to do injustice to another nation, strong or weak, than an individual has to do

---

[5] See John Morton Blum, *The Republican Roosevelt* (Cambridge, MA: Harvard University Press, 1977); Kristen Hoganson, *Fighting for American Manhood* (New Haven, CT: Yale University Press, 1998); Walter LaFeber, *The Panama Canal: The Crisis in Historical Perspective* (New York: Oxford University Press, 1978).

injustice to another individual; that the same moral law applies in one case as in the other. But we must also remember that it is as much the duty of the Nation to guard its own rights and its own interests as it is the duty of the individual so to do. Within the Nation the individual has now delegated this right to the State, that is, to the representative of all the individuals, and it is a maxim of the law that for every wrong there is a remedy. But in international law we have not advanced by any means as far as we have advanced in municipal law. There is as yet no judicial way of enforcing a right in international law. When one nation wrongs another or wrongs many others, there is no tribunal before which the wrongdoer can be brought. Either it is necessary supinely to acquiesce in the wrong, and thus put a premium upon brutality and aggression, or else it is necessary for the aggrieved nation valiantly to stand up for its rights. Until some method is devised by which there shall be a degree of international control over offending nations, it would be a wicked thing for the most civilized powers, for those with most sense of international obligations and with keenest and most generous appreciation of the difference between right and wrong, to disarm. If the great civilized nations of the present day should completely disarm, the result would mean an immediate recrudescence of barbarism in one form or another. Under any circumstances a sufficient armament would have to be kept up to serve the purposes of international police; and until international cohesion and the sense of international duties and rights are far more advanced than at present, a nation desirous both of securing respect for itself and of doing good to others must have a force adequate for the work which it feels is allotted to it as its part of the general world duty. Therefore it follows that a self-respecting, just, and far-seeing nation should on the one hand endeavor by every means to aid in the development of the various movements which tend to provide substitutes for war, which tend to render nations in their actions toward one another, and indeed toward their own peoples, more responsive to the general sentiment of humane and civilized mankind; and on the other hand that it should keep prepared, while scrupulously avoiding wrongdoing itself, to repel any wrong, and in exceptional cases to take action which in a more advanced stage of international relations would come under the head of the exercise of the international police. A great free people owes it to itself and to all mankind not to sink into helplessness before the powers of evil.

We are in every way endeavoring to help on, with cordial good will, every movement which will tend to bring us into more friendly relations with the rest of mankind. In pursuance of this policy I shall shortly lay before the Senate treaties of arbitration with all powers which are willing to enter into these treaties with us. It is not possible at this period of the world's development to agree to arbitrate all matters, but there are many matters of possible difference between us and other nations which can be thus arbitrated. Furthermore, at the request of the Interparliamentary Union, an eminent body composed of practical statesmen from all countries, I have asked the Powers to join with this Government in a second Hague conference, at which it is hoped that the work already so happily begun at The Hague may be carried some steps further toward completion. This carries out the desire expressed by the first Hague conference itself.

It is not true that the United States feels any land hunger or entertains any projects as regards the other nations of the Western Hemisphere save such as are for their welfare. All that this country desires is to see the neighboring countries stable, orderly, and prosperous. Any country whose people conduct themselves well can count upon our hearty friendship. If a nation shows that it knows how to act with reasonable efficiency and decency in social and political matters, if it keeps order and pays its obligations, it need fear no interference from the United States. Chronic wrongdoing, or an impotence which results in a general loosening of the ties of civilized society, may in America, as elsewhere, ultimately require intervention by some civilized nation, and in the Western Hemisphere the adherence of the United States to the Monroe Doctrine may force the United States, however reluctantly, in flagrant cases of such wrongdoing or impotence, to the exercise of an international police power. If every country washed by the Caribbean Sea would show the progress in stable and just civilization which with the aid of the Platt Amendment Cuba has shown since our troops left the island, and which so many of the republics in both Americas are constantly and brilliantly showing, all question of interference by this Nation with their affairs would be at an end. Our interests and those of our southern neighbors are in reality identical. They have great natural riches, and if within their borders the reign of law and justice obtains, prosperity is sure to come to them. While they thus obey the primary laws of civilized society they may rest assured that they will be treated by us in a spirit of cordial and helpful sympathy. We would interfere with them only in the last resort, and then only if it became evident that their inability or unwillingness to do justice at home and abroad had violated the rights of the United States or had invited foreign aggression to the detriment of the entire body of American nations. It is a mere truism to say that every nation, whether in America or anywhere else, which desires to maintain its freedom, its independence, must ultimately realize that the right of such independence can not be separated from the responsibility of making good use of it.

In asserting the Monroe Doctrine, in taking such steps as we have taken in regard to Cuba, Venezuela, and Panama, and in endeavoring to circumscribe the theater of war in the Far East, and to secure the open door in China, we have acted in our own interest as well as in the interest of humanity at large. There are, however, cases in which, while our own interests are not greatly involved, strong appeal is made to our sympathies. Ordinarily it is very much wiser and more useful for us to concern ourselves with striving for our own moral and material betterment here at home than to concern ourselves with trying to better the condition of things in other nations. We have plenty of sins of our own to war against, and under ordinary circumstances we can do more for the general uplifting of humanity by striving with heart and soul to put a stop to civic corruption, to brutal lawlessness and violent race prejudices here at home than by passing resolutions and wrongdoing elsewhere. Nevertheless there are occasional crimes committed on so vast a scale and of such peculiar horror as to make us doubt whether it is not our manifest duty to endeavor at least to show our disapproval of the deed and our sympathy with those who have suffered by it. The cases must be extreme in which such a course is justifiable. There must be no effort made to remove the mote from our brother's eye if we refuse to remove the beam from our own. But in extreme cases action may be justifiable and proper. What form the action shall take must depend upon the circumstances of the case; that is, upon the degree of the atrocity and upon our power to remedy it. The cases in which we could interfere by force of arms as we interfered to put a stop to intolerable conditions in Cuba are necessarily very few. Yet it is not to be expected that a people like ours, which in spite of certain very obvious shortcomings, nevertheless as a whole shows by its consistent practice its belief in the principles of civil and religious liberty and of orderly freedom, a people among whom even the worst crime, like the crime of lynching, is never more than sporadic, so that individuals and not classes are molested in their fundamental rights – it is inevitable that such a nation should desire eagerly to give expression to its horror on an occasion like that of the massacre of the Jews in Kishenef, or when it witnesses such systematic and long-extended cruelty and oppression as the cruelty and oppression of which the Armenians have been the victims, and which have won for them the indignant pity of the civilized world.

Source: *Congressional Record – Senate*, 58th Congress, Third Session, December 6, 1904, pp. 18–19.

Suggested Questions for Discussion:

1. How did Theodore Roosevelt define the aims of American foreign policy?
2. What did he define as the appropriate uses of military force?
3. What kind of relationship did he envision between the United States and the countries of Latin America?

Chapter 2   The Great War and Its Aftermath

1 George M. Cohan, "Over There," 1917

Soon after the United States entered the First World War in April 1917, Broadway composer George M. Cohan wrote a song that became one of the most popular war ballads in American history. "Over There" articulated a special American mission in the war – to bring liberty to the Old World and defeat the "Hun." This was not a traditional contest among nations, according to Cohan, but an opportunity for Americans to come together as a community, make collective sacrifice, and reform the world: "We'll be over, we're coming over, And we won't come back till it's over, Over there." The overwhelming popularity of Cohan's song indicates that President Woodrow Wilson's idealistic war rhetoric had deep resonance in popular culture and thought.[1]

"Over There"

Johnnie, get your gun,
Get your gun, get your gun,
Take it on the run,
On the run, on the run.
Hear them calling, you and me,
Every son of liberty.
Hurry right away,

[1] See David Kennedy, *Over Here: The First World War and American Society* (New York: Oxford University Press, 2004); John Milton Cooper, Jr., *Pivotal Decades: The United States, 1900–1920* (New York: W. W. Norton, 1992).

No delay, go today,
Make your daddy glad
To have had such a lad.
Tell your sweetheart not to pine,
To be proud her boy's in line.
(chorus sung twice)

Johnnie, get your gun,
Get your gun, get your gun,
Johnnie show the Hun
Who's a son of a gun.
Hoist the flag and let her fly,
Yankee Doodle do or die.
Pack your little kit,
Show your grit, do your bit.
Yankee to the ranks,
From the towns and the tanks.
Make your mother proud of you,
And the old Red, White and Blue.
(chorus sung twice)

Chorus
Over there, over there,
Send the word, send the word over there –
That the Yanks are coming,
The Yanks are coming,
The drums rum-tumming
Ev'rywhere.
So prepare, say a pray'r,
Send the word, send the word to beware.
We'll be over, we're coming over,
And we won't come back till it's over
Over there.

Source: http://www.firstworldwar.com/audio/overthere.htm (accessed August 20, 2008).

Suggested Questions for Discussion:

1. What made war in Europe such a patriotic calling for Americans in 1917?
2. How did George Cohan make abstract ideas about freedom and mission tangible for "ordinary" Americans?
3. Was George Cohan's song propaganda?

2 President Woodrow Wilson, Fourteen Points Address, 1918

President Woodrow Wilson refused to treat the Great War as just another military conflict between the world's most powerful states. He also refused to characterize American entry into the war as traditional politics. Instead, Wilson articulated a set of war aims that were designed to ensure that the "world be made fit and safe to live in" after what he anticipated would be the "culminating and final war for human liberty." Wilson's fourteen point "program" included open diplomacy, freedom of the seas, disarmament, national independence in eastern and southeastern Europe, and the foundations for a League of Nations.[2]

Address by the President of the United States, Woodrow Wilson, at a joint session of the two Houses of Congress, January 8, 1918

Gentlemen of the Congress, once more, as repeatedly before, the spokesmen of the Central Empires have indicated their desire to discuss the objects of the war and the possible bases of a general peace. Parleys have been in progress at Brest-Litovsk between Russian representatives and representatives of the Central Powers, to which the attention of all the belligerents has been invited for the purpose of ascertaining whether it may be possible to extend these parleys into a general conference with regard to terms of peace and settlement. The Russian representatives presented not only a perfectly definite statement of the principles upon which they would be willing to conclude peace, but also an equally definite programme of the concrete application of those principles. The representatives of the Central Powers, on their part, presented an outline of settlement which, if much less definite, seemed susceptible of liberal interpretation until their specific programme of practical terms was added. That programme proposed no concessions at all either to the sovereignty of Russia or the preferences of the populations with whose fortunes it dealt, but meant, in a word, that the Central Empires were to keep every foot of territory their armed forces had occupied – every province, every city, every point of vantage – as a permanent addition to

[2]   See Thomas J. Knock, *To End All Wars: Woodrow Wilson and the Quest for a New World Order* (Princeton, NJ: Princeton University Press, 1992); John Milton Cooper, Jr., *The Warrior and the Priest: Woodrow Wilson and Theodore Roosevelt* (Cambridge, MA: Belknap Press of Harvard University Press, 1983); Lloyd Ambrosius, *Wilsonianism: Woodrow Wilson and His Legacy in American Foreign Relations* (New York: Palgrave, 2002); Erez Manela, *The Wilsonian Moment: Self-Determination and the International Origins of Anticolonial Nationalism* (New York: Oxford University Press, 2007).

their territories and their power. It is a reasonable conjecture that the general principles of settlement which they at first suggested originated with the more liberal statesmen of Germany and Austria, the men who have begun to feel the force of their own peoples' thought and purpose, while the concrete terms of actual settlement came from the military leaders who have no thought but to keep what they have got. The negotiations have been broken off. The Russian representatives were sincere and in earnest. They cannot entertain such proposals of conquest and domination.

The whole incident is full of significance. It is also full of perplexity. With whom are the Russian representatives dealing? For whom are the representatives of the Central Empires speaking? Are they speaking for the majorities of their respective parliaments or for the minority parties, that military and imperialistic minority which has so far dominated their whole policy and controlled the affairs of Turkey and of the Balkan states, which have felt obliged to become their associates in the war? The Russian representatives have insisted, very justly, very wisely, and in the true spirit of modern democracy, that the conferences they have been holding with the Teutonic and Turkish statesmen should be held within open, not closed, doors, and all the world has been audience, as was desired. To whom have we been listening, then? To those who speak the spirit and intention of the Resolutions of the German Reichstag of the ninth of July last, the spirit and intention of the liberal leaders and parties of Germany, or to those who resist and defy that spirit and intention and insist upon conquest and subjugation? Or are we listening, in fact, to both, unreconciled and in open and hopeless contradiction? These are very serious and pregnant questions. Upon the answer to them depends the peace of the world.

But, whatever the results of the parleys at Brest-Litovsk, whatever the confusions of counsel and of purpose in the utterances of the spokesmen of the Central Empires, they have again attempted to acquaint the world with their objects in the war and have again challenged their adversaries to say what their objects are and what sort of settlement they would deem just and satisfactory. There is no good reason why that challenge should not be responded to, and responded to with the utmost candor. We did not wait for it. Not once, but again and again, we have laid our whole thought and purpose before the world, not in general terms only, but each time with sufficient definition to make it clear what sort of definitive terms of settlement must necessarily spring out of them. Within the last week Mr. Lloyd George has spoken with admirable candor and in admirable spirit for the people and Government of Great Britain. There is no confusion of counsel among the adversaries of the Central Powers, no uncertainty of principle, no vagueness of detail. The only secrecy of counsel, the only lack of fearless frankness, the only failure to make definite statement of the objects of war, lies with Germany and her Allies. The issues of life and death hang upon these definitions. No statesman who has the least conception of his responsibility ought for a moment to permit himself to continue this tragical and appalling outpouring of blood and treasure unless he is sure beyond a peradventure that the objects of the vital sacrifice are part and parcel of the very life of Society, and that the people for whom he speaks think them right and imperative as he does.

There is, moreover, a voice calling for these definitions of principle and of purpose which is, it seems to me, more thrilling and more compelling than any of the many moving voices with which the troubled air of the world is filled. It is the voice of the Russian people. They are prostrate and all but helpless, it would seem, before the grim power of Germany, which has hitherto known no relenting and no pity. Their power, apparently, is shattered. And yet their soul is not subservient. They will not yield either in principle or in action. Their conception of what is right, of what is humane and honorable for them to accept, has been stated with a frankness, a largeness of view, a generosity of spirit, and a universal human sympathy which must challenge the admiration of every friend of mankind; and they have refused to compound their ideals or desert others that they themselves may be safe. They call to us to say what it is that we desire, in what, if in anything, our purpose and our spirit differ from theirs; and I believed that the people of the United States would wish me to respond, with utter simplicity and frankness. Whether their present leaders believe it or not, it is our heartfelt desire and hope that some way may be opened whereby we may be privileged to assist the people of Russia to attain their utmost hope of liberty and ordered peace.

It will be our wish and purpose that the processes of peace, when they are begun, shall be absolutely open and that they shall involve and permit henceforth no secret understandings of any kind. The day of conquest and aggrandizement is gone by; so is also the day of secret covenants entered into in the interest of particular governments and likely at some unlooked-for moment to upset the peace of the world. It is this happy fact, now clear to the view of every public man whose thoughts do not still linger in an age that is dead and gone, which makes it possible for every nation whose purposes are consistent with justice and the peace of the world to avow now or at any other time the objects it has in view.

We entered this war because violations of right had occurred which touched us to the quick and made the life of our own people impossible unless they were corrected and the world secured once for all against their recurrence. What we demand in this war, therefore, is nothing peculiar to ourselves. It is that the world be made fit and safe to live in; and particularly that it be made safe for every peace-loving nation which, like our own, wishes to live its own life, determine its own institutions, be assured of justice and fair dealing by the other peoples of the world as against force and selfish aggression. All the peoples of the world are in effect partners in this interest, and for our own part we see very clearly that unless justice be done to others it will not be done to us. The program of the world's peace, therefore, is our program; and that programme, the only possible program, as we see it, is this:

I. Open covenants of peace, openly arrived at, after which there shall be no private international understandings of any kind but diplomacy shall proceed always frankly and in the public view.

II. Absolute freedom of navigation upon the seas, outside territorial waters, alike in peace and in war, except as the seas may be closed in whole or in part by international action for the enforcement of international covenants.

III. The removal, so far as possible, of all economic barriers and the establishment of an equality of trade conditions among all the nations consenting to the peace and associating themselves for its maintenance.

IV. Adequate guarantees given and taken that national armaments will be reduced to the lowest point consistent with domestic safety.

V. A free, open-minded, and absolutely impartial adjustment of all colonial claims, based upon a strict observance of the principle that in determining all such questions of sovereignty the interests of the populations concerned must have equal weight with the equitable claims of the government whose title is to be determined.

VI. The evacuation of all Russian territory and such a settlement of all questions affecting Russia as will secure the best and freest cooperation of the other nations of the world in obtaining for her an unhampered and unembarrassed opportunity for the independent determination of her own political development and national policy and assure her of a sincere welcome into the society of free nations under institutions of her own choosing; and, more than a welcome, assistance also of every kind that she may need and may herself desire. The treatment accorded Russia by her sister nations in the months to come will be the acid test of their good will, of their comprehension of her needs as distinguished from their own interests, and of their intelligent and unselfish sympathy.

VII. Belgium, the whole world will agree, must be evacuated and restored, without any attempt to limit the sovereignty which she enjoys in common with all other free nations. No other single act will serve as this will serve to restore confidence among the nations in the laws which they have themselves set and determined for the government of their relations with one another. Without this healing act the whole structure and validity of international law is forever impaired.

VIII. All French territory should be freed and the invaded portions restored, and the wrong done to France by Prussia in 1871 in the matter of Alsace-Lorraine, which has unsettled the peace of the world for nearly fifty years, should be righted, in order that peace may once more be made secure in the interest of all.

IX. A readjustment of the frontiers of Italy should be effected along clearly recognizable lines of nationality.

X. The peoples of Austria-Hungary, whose place among the nations we wish to see safeguarded and assured, should be accorded the freest opportunity of autonomous development.

XI. Rumania, Serbia, and Montenegro should be evacuated; occupied territories restored; Serbia accorded free and secure access to the sea; and the relations of the several Balkan states to one another determined by friendly counsel along historically established lines of allegiance and nationality; and international guarantees of the political and economic independence and territorial integrity of the several Balkan states should be entered into.

XII. The Turkish portions of the present Ottoman Empire should be assured a secure sovereignty, but the other nationalities which are now under Turkish rule should be assured an undoubted security of life and an absolutely unmolested opportunity of an autonomous development, and the Dardanelles should be permanently opened as a free passage to the ships and commerce of all nations under international guarantees.

XIII. An independent Polish state should be erected which should include the territories inhabited by indisputably Polish populations, which should be assured a free and secure access to the sea, and whose political and economic independence and territorial integrity should be guaranteed by international covenant.

XIV. A general association of nations must be formed under specific covenants for the purpose of affording mutual guarantees of political independence and territorial integrity to great and small states alike.

In regard to these essential rectifications of wrong and assertions of right we feel ourselves to be intimate partners of all the governments and peoples associated together against the Imperialists. We cannot be separated in interest or divided in purpose. We stand together until the end.

For such arrangements and covenants we are willing to fight and to continue to fight until they are achieved; but only because we wish the right to prevail and desire a just and stable peace such as can be secured only by removing the chief provocations to war, which this program does not remove. We have no jealousy of German greatness, and there is nothing in this program that impairs it. We grudge her no achievement or distinction of learning or of pacific enterprise such as have made her record very bright and very enviable. We do not wish to injure her or to block in any way her legitimate influence or power. We do not wish to fight her either with arms or with hostile arrangements of trade if she is willing to associate herself with us and the other peace-loving nations of the world in covenants of justice and law and fair dealing. We wish her only to accept a place of equality among the peoples of the world – the new world in which we now live – instead of a place of mastery.

Neither do we presume to suggest to her any alteration or modification of her institutions. But it is necessary, we must frankly say, and necessary as a preliminary to any intelligent dealings with her on our part, that we should know whom her spokesmen speak for when they speak to us, whether for the Reichstag majority or for the military party and the men whose creed is imperial domination.

We have spoken now, surely, in terms too concrete to admit of any further doubt or question. An evident principle runs through the whole program I have outlined. It is the principle of justice to all peoples and nationalities, and their right to live on equal terms of liberty and safety with one another, whether they be strong or weak. Unless this principle be made its foundation no part of the structure of international justice can stand. The people of the United States could act upon no other principle; and to the vindication of this principle they are ready to devote their lives, their honor, and everything that they possess. The moral climax of this the culminating and final war for human liberty has come, and they are ready to put their own strength, their own highest purpose, their own integrity and devotion to the test.

Source: *Congressional Record-Senate*, 65th Congress, 2nd Session, January 8, 1918, pp. 680–1.

Suggested Questions for Discussion:

1. Was Wilson's vision revolutionary?
2. Who was Wilson's audience?
3. Why did Wilson's ideas remain so influential decades later?

3 Senator Robert LaFollette, Opposition to President Wilson's War Message, 1917

Woodrow Wilson's war aims inspired strong opposition within the United States. Robert LaFollette, a Republican senator from Wisconsin, and one of the leading Progressive politicians in the country, actively campaigned against American participation in the war and the Versailles Treaty that followed the cessation of hostilities. LaFollette argued that American support for Great Britain and her allies impoverished the citizens of the United States, enriched selfish bankers (like J.P. Morgan), and unjustly harmed German civilians. LaFollette accused Great Britain of interfering with American commerce and he condemned the Wilson administration for repressing fair public debate. LaFollette's criticism of America's entry into the war echoed common themes of dissent in the United States during nearly every moment of foreign conflict.[3]

... Mr. President, many of my colleagues on both sides of this floor have from day to day offered for publication in the Record messages and letters received from their constituents. I have received some 15,000 letters and telegrams. They have come from forty-four states in the Union. They have been assorted according to whether they speak in criticism or commendation of my course in opposing war. Assorting the 15,000 letters and telegrams by states in that way, 9 out of 10 are an unqualified endorsement of my course in opposing war with Germany on the issue presented.

...

The poor, Sir, who are the ones called upon to rot in the trenches, have no organized power, have no press to voice their will upon this question of peace or war; but, oh, Mr. President, at some time they will be heard. I hope and I believe they will be heard in an orderly and a peaceful way. I think they may be heard from before long. I think, Sir, if we take this step, when the people today who are staggering under the burden of supporting families at the present prices of the necessaries of life find those prices multiplied, when they are raised 100 percent, or 200 percent, as they will be quickly, aye, sir, when beyond that those who pay taxes come to have their taxes doubled and again doubled to pay the interest on the nontaxable bonds held by [J.P.] Morgan and his combinations, which have been issued

[3]   See David Kennedy, *Over Here: The First World War and American Society* (New York: Oxford University Press, 2004); Nancy C. Unger, *Fighting Bob LaFollette: The Righteous Reformer* (Chapel Hill, NC: University of North Carolina Press, 2000); David P. Thelen, *Robert M. LaFollette and the Insurgent Spirit* (Boston, MA: Little, Brown, 1976).

to meet this war, there will come an awakening; they will have their day and they will be heard. It will be as certain and as inevitable as the return of the tides, and as resistless, too ...

In his message of April 2, the President said:

We have no quarrel with the German people it was not upon their impulse that their government acted in entering this war; it was not with their previous knowledge or approval.

Again he says:

We are, let me say again, sincere friends of the German people and shall desire nothing so much as the early reestablishment of intimate relations of mutual advantage between us.

At least, the German people, then, are not outlaws.

What is the thing the President asks us to do to these German people of whom he speaks so highly and whose sincere friend he declares us to be? Here is what he declares we shall do in this war. We shall undertake, he says –

The utmost practicable cooperation in council and action with the governments now at war with Germany, and as an incident to that, the extension to those governments of the most liberal financial credits in order that our resources may, so far as possible, be added to theirs.

"Practicable cooperation!" Practicable cooperation with England and her allies in starving to death the old men and women, the children, the sick and the maimed of Germany. The thing we are asked to do is the thing I have stated. It is idle to talk of a war upon a government only. We are leagued in this war, or it is the President's proposition that we shall be so leagued, with the hereditary enemies of Germany. Any war with Germany, or any other country for that matter, would be bad enough, but there are not words strong enough to voice my protest against the proposed combination with the Entente Allies.

When we cooperate with those governments, we endorse their methods; we endorse the violations of international law by Great Britain; we endorse the shameful methods of warfare against which we have again and again protested in this war; we endorse her purpose to wreak upon the German people the animosities which for years her people have been taught to cherish against Germany; finally, when the end comes, whatever it may be, we find ourselves in cooperation with our ally, Great Britain, and if we cannot resist now the pressure she is exerting to carry us into the war, how can we hope to resist, then, the thousand fold greater pressure she will exert to bend us to her purposes and compel compliance with her demands?

We do not know what they are. We do not know what is in the minds of those who have made the compact, but we are to subscribe to it. We are irrevocably, by our votes here, to marry ourselves to a non-divorceable proposition veiled from us now. Once enlisted, once in the co-partnership, we will be carried through with the purposes, whatever they may be, of which we now know nothing.

Sir, if we are to enter upon this war in the manner the President demands, let us throw pretense to the winds, let us be honest, let us admit that this is a ruthless war against not only Germany's Army and her Navy but against her civilian population as well, and frankly state that the purpose of Germany's hereditary European enemies has become our purpose.

Again, the President says "we are about to accept the gage of battle with this natural foe of liberty and shall, if necessary, spend the whole force of the nation to check and nullify its pretensions and its power." That much, at least, is clear; that program is definite. The whole force and power of this nation, if necessary, is to be used to bring victory to the Entente Allies, and to us as their ally in this war. Remember, that not yet has the "whole force" of one of the warring nations been used.

Countless millions are suffering from want and privation; countless other millions are dead and rotting on foreign battlefields; countless other millions are crippled and maimed, blinded, and dismembered; upon all and upon their children's children for generations to come has been laid a burden of debt which must be worked out in poverty and suffering, but the "whole force" of no one of the warring nations has yet been expended; but our "whole force" shall be expended, so says the President. We are pledged by the President, so far as he can pledge us, to make this fair, free, and happy land of ours the same shambles and bottomless pit of horror that we see in Europe today....

Will the President and the supporters of this war bill submit it to a vote of the people before the declaration of war goes into effect? Until we are willing to do that, it ill becomes us to offer as an excuse for our entry into the war the unsupported claim that this war was forced upon the German people by their government "without their previous knowledge or approval."

Who has registered the knowledge or approval of the American people of the course this Congress is called upon to take in declaring war upon Germany? Submit the question to the people, you who support it. You who support it dare not do it, for you know that by a vote of more than ten to one the American people as a body would register their declaration against it.

In the sense that this war is being forced upon our people without their knowing why and without their approval, and that wars are usually forced upon all peoples in the same way, there is some truth in the statement; but I venture to say that the response which the German people have made to the demands of this war shows that it has a degree of popular support which the war upon which we are entering has not and never will have among our people. The espionage bills, the conscription bills, and other forcible military measures which we understand are being ground out of the war machine in this country is the complete proof that those responsible for this war fear that it has no popular support and that armies sufficient to satisfy the demand of the Entente Allies cannot be recruited by voluntary enlistments....

I have constituents, American citizens, who organized a company and invested large sums of money in the purchase of ships to engage in foreign carrying. Several of their vessels plying between the United States and South America were captured almost in our own territorial waters, taken possession of by the British Government, practically confiscated, and put into her service or the service of her Admiralty. They are there today, and that company is helpless. When they appealed to our Department of State, they were advised that they might "file" their papers; and were given the further suggestion that they could hire an attorney and prosecute their case in the English Prize Court. The company did hire an attorney and sent him to England, and he is there now, and has been there for almost a year, trying to get some redress, some relief, some adjustment of those rights.

But those are individual cases. There are many others. All these violations have come from Great Britain and her allies, and are in perfect harmony with Britain's traditional policy as absolute master of the seas....

Source: *Congressional Record*, 65th Congress, 1st Session, April 2, 1917–October 6, 1917, pp. 223–36.

Suggested Questions for Discussion:

1. Who does LaFollette target as the people responsible for America's entrance into war?
2. Why does LaFollette oppose the war?
3. Why does LaFollette criticize Great Britain and sympathize with the citizens of Germany?

4 W. E. B. Dubois, Comments on the First World War, the Treaty of Versailles, and the Politics of Race, 1918

The First World War opened new avenues for international African and African-American activism. One of the most influential African-American figures of the early twentieth century, W. E. B. Dubois, played a powerful role mobilizing public opinion and negotiating with global leaders. He called upon Africans and African-Americans to join the "white" struggle against German militarism. After the defeat of Germany, he traveled to Paris and lobbied for self-determination and basic rights for non-white peoples. Dubois organized the first Pan-African Congress, fusing the demands for domestic civil rights in the United States with calls for national independence in the colonized territories of Asia and Africa. Dubois drew on international conditions to lobby for a global flattening of race hierarchies. He inspired generations of activists in Africa, Asia, Europe, and the United States.[4]

"Close Ranks," July 1918

This is the crisis of the world. For all the long years to come men will point to the year 1918 as the great Day of Decision, the day when the world decided whether it would submit to military despotism and an endless armed peace – if peace it could be called – or whether they would put down the menace of German militarism and inaugurate the United States of the World.

We of the colored race have no ordinary interest in the outcome. That which the German power represents today spells death to the aspirations of Negroes and all darker races for equality, freedom, and democracy. Let us, while this war lasts, forget our special grievances and close our ranks shoulder to shoulder with our own white fellow citizens and the allied nations that are fighting for democracy. We make no ordinary sacrifice, but we make it gladly and willingly with our eyes lifted to the hills.

Source: W. E. B. Du Bois, "Close Ranks," *The Crisis*, vol. 16, no. 3 (July 1918), p. 111.

---

[4]   See David Levering Lewis, *W. E. B. Du Bois*, vols. 1–2 (New York: Henry Holt, 1993, 2000); Kevin Gaines, *Uplifting the Race: Black Leadership, Politics, and Culture in the Twentieth Century* (Chapel Hill, NC: University of North Carolina Press, 1996); Brenda Gayle Plummer, *Rising Wind: Black Americans and US Foreign Affairs, 1935–1960* (Chapel Hill, NC: University of North Carolina Press, 1996); Penny Von Eschen, *Race Against Empire: Black Americans and Anticolonialism, 1937–1957* (Ithaca, NY: Cornell University Press, 1997).

"My Mission," May 1919

I went to Paris because today the destinies of mankind center there. Make no mistake as to this, my readers.

Podunk may easily persuade itself that only Podunk matters and that nothing is going on in New York. The South Sea Islander may live ignorant and careless of London. Some Americans may think that Europe does not count, and a few Negroes may argue vociferously that the Negro problem is a domestic matter, to be settled in Richmond and New Orleans.

But all these careless thinkers are wrong. The destinies of mankind for a hundred years to come are being settled today in a small room of the *Hotel Crillon* by four unobtrusive gentlemen who glance out speculatively now and then to Cleopatra's Needle on the Place de la Concorde.

You need not believe this if you do not want to. They do not care what you believe. They have the POWER. They are settling the world's problems and you can believe what you choose as long as they control the ARMIES and NAVIES, the world supply of CAPITAL and the PRESS.

Other folks of the world who think, believe and act – THIRTY-TWO NATIONS, PEOPLES and RACES, have permanent headquarters in Paris. Not simply England, Italy and the Great Powers are there, but all the little nations; not simply little nations, but little groups who want to be nations, like the Latts and Finns, the Armenians and Jugo-Slavs, Irish and Ukrainians. Not only groups, but races have come – Jews, Indians, Arabs and All-Asia. Great churches, like the Greek Orthodox and the Roman Catholic, are watching on the ground. Great organizations, like the American Peace Society, the League to Enforce Peace, the American Federation of Labor, the Woman's Suffrage Association and a hundred others are represented in Paris today.

In fine, not a single great, serious movement or idea in Government, Politics, Philanthropy or Industry in the civilized world has omitted to send and keep in Paris its Eyes and Ears and Fingers! And yet some American Negroes actually asked WHY I went to help represent the Negro world in Africa and America and the Islands of the Sea.

But why did I not explain my reasons and mission before going? Because I am not a fool. Because I knew perfectly well that any movement to bring the attention of the world to the Negro problem at this crisis would be stopped the moment the Great Powers heard of it. When, therefore, I was suddenly informed of a chance to go to France as a newspaper correspondent, I did not talk – I went.

What did I do when I got there? First, there were certain things that I did NOT do. I did not hold an anti-lynching meeting on the Boulevard des

Italiens. I would to God I could have, but I knew that France is still under martial law – *that no meeting can be held today in France, anywhere or at any time, without the consent of the Government; no newspaper can publish a line without the consent of the Censor and no individual can stay in France unless the French consent.*

But it did not follow that because I could not do everything I could do nothing. I first went to the American Peace Commission and said frankly and openly: "I want to call a Pan-African Congress in Paris." The Captain to whom I spoke smiled and shook his head. "Impossible," he said, and added: "The French Government would not permit it." "Then," said I innocently: "It's up to me to get French consent!" "It is!" he answered, and he looked relieved.

With the American Secret Service at my heels I then turned to the French Government. There are six colored deputies in the French Parliament and one is an under-secretary in the War Department. "Of course, we can have a Pan-African Congress," he said – "I'll see Clemenceau.": He saw Clemenceau, and there was a week's pause. Clemenceau saw Pichon, and there was another pause. Meantime, our State Department chuckled and announced that there would be no Congress and refused Negroes passports. England followed suit and refused to allow the Secretary of the Aborigines Protection Society even to visit Paris, while the South African natives were not allowed to sail.

But there are six Negroes in the French House and Clemenceau needs their votes. There were 280,000 black African troops in the war before whom France stands with uncovered head. The net result was that Clemenceau, Prime Minister of France, gave us permission to hold the Pan-African Congress in Paris.

What could a Pan-African Congress do? It could not agitate the Negro problem in any particular country, except in so far as that problem could be plausibly shown to be part of the problem of the future of Africa. The problem of the future of Africa was a difficult and delicate question before the Peace Conference – so difficult and so delicate that the Conference was disposed to welcome advice and co-operation.

If the Negroes of the world could have maintained in Paris during the entire sitting of the Peace Conference a central headquarters with experts, clerks and helpers, they could have settled the future of Africa at a cost of less than $10,000.

As it was the Congress cost $750. Yet with this meager sum a Congress of fifty-eight delegates, representing sixteen different Negro groups, was assembled. This Congress passed resolutions which the entire press of the world has approved, despite the fact that these resolutions had two paragraphs of tremendous significance to us:

Wherever persons of African descent are civilized and able to meet the tests of surrounding culture, they shall be accorded the same rights as their fellow citizens; they shall not be denied on account of race or color a voice in their own Government, justices before the courts and economic and social equality according to ability and desert.

Whenever it is proven that African natives are not receiving just treatment at the hands of any State or that any State deliberately excludes its civilized citizens or subjects of Negro descent from its body politic and cultural, it shall be the duty of the League of Nations to bring the matter to the attention of the civilized world.

Precisely the same principles are being demanded today by the Jews and the Japanese. And despite the enormous significance of these demands, Colonel House of the American Peace Commission received me and assured me that he wished these resolutions presented to the Peace Conference. Lloyd George wrote me that he would give our demands "his careful consideration." The French Premier offered to arrange an audience for the President and Secretary of the Conference. Portugal and Belgium, great colonial powers, offered complete co-operation.

The League for the Rights of Man, which freed Dreyfus, appointed a special commission to hear not only of the African, but the facts as to the American Negro Problem.

We got, in fact, the ear of the civilized world and if it had been possible to stay longer and organize more thoroughly and spread the truth – what might not have been accomplished?

As it was, we have organized the "Pan-African Congress" as a permanent body, with M. Diagne as president and myself as secretary, and we plan an international quarterly BLACK REVIEW to be issued in English, French and possibly in Spanish and Portuguese.

The world-fight for black rights is on!

Source: W. E. B. Du Bois, "My Mission," *The Crisis*, vol. 18 no. 1 (May 1919).

Suggested Questions for Discussion:

1. Why did Dubois encourage Africans and African-Americans to join the allied war against Germany?
2. What did Dubois hope to achieve by attending the Paris Peace Talks?
3. When Dubois wrote his articles for *The Crisis*, who was his audience?

5 Charles Lindbergh, Account of the First Solo Nonstop Airplane Flight Across the Atlantic Ocean, 1927

Charles Lindbergh was the greatest and most enduring international celebrity of the late 1920s. A child of the American Midwest and a drop-out from the University of Wisconsin, he became an early aircraft "barnstormer," traveling across the country. He also worked as a pilot for the United States Army Air Service and the Postal Service. Lindbergh's international fame came in May 1927, when he flew the first solo nonstop flight across the Atlantic Ocean, from New York to Paris. Lindbergh's flight, described in his endearing memoir We, *captured the imagination of technology enthusiasts, political activists, and foreign policy leaders. Lindbergh pointed to a future of easier international travel and commerce, but also growing capabilities for international destruction. Lindbergh would spend the rest of his long career writing and speaking, controversially, about these topics.[5]*

NEW YORK TO PARIS

At New York we checked over the plane engine and instruments, which required several short flights over the field. When the plane was completely inspected and ready for the trans-Atlantic flight, there were dense fogs reported along the coast and over Nova Scotia and Newfoundland, in addition to a storm area over the North Atlantic.

On the morning of May 19th, a light rain was falling and the sky was overcast. Weather reports from land stations and ships along the great circle course were unfavorable and there was apparently no prospect of taking off for Paris for several days at least. In the morning I visited the Wright plant at Paterson, New Jersey, and had planned to attend a theater performance in New York that evening. But at about six o'clock I received a special report from the New York Weather Bureau. A high pressure area was over the entire North Atlantic and the low pressure over Nova Scotia and New-foundland was receding. It was apparent that the prospects of the fog clearing up were as good as I might expect for some time to come. The North Atlantic should be clear with only local storms on the coast of Europe. The moon had just passed full and the percentage of days with

---

[5] See A. Scott Berg, *Lindbergh* (New York: Putnam, 1998); Robert Wohl, *The Spectacle of Flight: Aviation and the Western Imagination, 1920–1950* (New Haven, CT: Yale University Press, 2005).

fog over Newfoundland and the Grand Banks was increasing so that there seemed to be no advantage in waiting longer.

We went to Curtiss Field as quickly as possible and made arrangements for the barograph to be sealed and installed, and for the plane to be serviced and checked.

We decided partially to fill the fuel tanks in the hangar before towing the ship on a truck to Roosevelt Field, which adjoins Curtiss on the east, where the servicing would be completed. I left the responsibility for conditioning the plane in the hands of the men on the field while I went into the hotel for about two and one-half hours of rest; but at the hotel there were several more details which had to be completed and I was unable to get any sleep that night.

I returned to the field before daybreak on the morning of the twentieth. A light rain was falling which continued until almost dawn; consequently we did not move the ship to Roosevelt Field until much later than we had planned, and the take-off was delayed from daybreak until nearly eight o'clock.

At dawn the shower had passed, although the sky was overcast, and occasionally there would be some slight precipitation. The tail of the plane was lashed to a truck and escorted by a number of motorcycle police. The slow trip from Curtiss to Roosevelt was begun. The ship was placed at the extreme west end of the field heading along the east and west runway, and the final fueling commenced.

About 7:40 A.M. the motor was started and at 7:52 I took off on the flight for Paris.

The field was a little soft due to the rain during the night and the heavily loaded plane gathered speed very slowly. After passing the halfway mark, however, it was apparent that I would be able to clear the obstructions at the end. I passed over a tractor by about fifteen feet and a telephone line by about twenty, with a fair reserve of flying speed. I believe that the ship would have taken off from a hard field with at least five hundred pounds more weight.

I turned slightly to the right to avoid some high trees on a hill directly ahead, but by the time I had gone a few hundred yards I had sufficient altitude to clear all obstructions and throttled the engine down to 1750 R.P. M. I took up a compass course at once and soon reached Long Island Sound where the Curtiss Oriole with its photographer, which had been escorting me, turned back.

The haze soon cleared and from Cape Cod through the southern half of Nova Scotia the weather and visibility were excellent. I was flying very low, sometimes as close as ten feet from the trees and water.

On the three hundred mile stretch of water between Cape Cod and Nova Scotia I passed within view of numerous fishing vessels.

The northern part of Nova Scotia contained a number of storm areas and several times I flew through cloudbursts.

As I neared the northern coast, snow appeared in patches on the ground and far to the eastward the coastline was covered with fog.

For many miles between Nova Scotia and Newfoundland the ocean was covered with caked ice but as I approached the coast the ice disappeared entirely and I saw several ships in this area.

I had taken up a course for St. Johns, which is south of the great Circle from New York to Paris, so that there would be no question of the fact that I had passed Newfoundland in case I was forced down in the north Atlantic.

I passed over numerous icebergs after leaving St. Johns, but saw no ships except near the coast.

Darkness set in about 8:15 New York time and a thin, low fog formed through which the white bergs showed up with surprising clearness. This fog became thicker and increased in height until within two hours I was just skimming the top of storm clouds at about ten thousand feet. Even at this altitude there was a thick haze through which only the stars directly overhead could be seen.

There was no moon and it was very dark. The tops of some of the storm clouds were several thousand feet above me and at one time, when I attempted to fly through one of the larger clouds, sleet started to collect on the plane and I was forced to turn around and get back into clear air immediately and then fly around any clouds which I could not get over.

The moon appeared on the horizon after about two hours of darkness; then the flying was much less complicated.

Dawn came at about 1 A.M. New York time and the temperature had risen until there was practically no remaining danger of sleet.

Shortly after sunrise the clouds became more broken although some of them were far above me and it was often necessary to fly through them, navigating by instruments only.

As the sun became higher, holes appeared in the fog. Through one the open water was visible, and I dropped down until less than a hundred feet above the waves. There was a strong wind blowing from the northwest and the ocean was covered with white caps.

After a few miles of fairly clear weather the ceiling lowered to zero and for nearly two hours I flew entirely blind through the fog at an altitude of about 1500 feet. Then the fog raised and the water was visible again.

On several more occasions it was necessary to fly by instrument for short periods; then the fog broke up into patches. These patches took on forms of every description. Numerous shorelines appeared, with trees perfectly out-lined against the horizon. In fact, the mirages were so natural that, had I not been in mid-Atlantic and known that no land existed along my route, I would have taken them to be actual islands.

As the fog cleared I dropped down closer to the water, sometimes flying within ten feet of the waves and seldom higher than two hundred.

There is a cushion of air close to the ground or water through which a plane flies with less effort than when at a higher altitude, and for hours at a time I took advantage of this factor.

Also, it was less difficult to determine the wind drift near the water. During the entire flight the wind was strong enough to produce white caps on the waves. When one of these formed, the foam would be blown off, showing the wind's direction and approximate velocity. This foam remained on the water long enough for me to obtain a general idea of my drift.

During the day I saw a number of porpoises and a few birds but no ships, although I understand that two different boats reported me passing over.

The first indication of my approach to the European Coast was a small fishing boat which I first noticed a few miles ahead and slightly to the south of my course. There were several of these fishing boats grouped within a few miles of each other.

I flew over the first boat without seeing any signs of life. As I circled over the second, however, a man's face appeared, looking out of the cabin window.

I have carried on short conversations with people on the ground by flying low with throttled engine, shouting a question, and receiving the answer by some signal. When I saw this fisherman I decided to try to get him to point towards land. I had no sooner made the decision than the futility of the effort became apparent. In all likelihood he could not speak English, and even if he could he would undoubtedly be far too astounded to answer. However, I circled again and closing the throttle as the plane passed within a few feet of the boat I shouted, "Which way is Ireland?" Of course the attempt was useless, and I continued on my course.

Less than an hour later a rugged and semi-mountainous coastline appeared to the northeast. I was flying less than two hundred feet from the water when I sighted it. The shore was fairly distinct and not over ten or fifteen miles away. A light haze coupled with numerous local storm areas had prevented my seeing it from a long distance.

The coastline came down from the north, curved over towards the east. I had very little doubt that it was the southwestern end of Ireland but in order to make sure I changed my course towards the nearest point of land.

I located Cape Valentia and Dingle Bay, then resumed my compass course towards Paris.

After leaving Ireland I passed a number of steamers and was seldom out of sight of a ship.

In a little over two hours the coast of England appeared. My course passed over Southern England and a little south of Plymouth; then across the English Channel, striking France over Cherbourg.

The English farms were very impressive from the air in contrast to ours in America. They appeared extremely small and unusually neat and tidy with their stone and hedge fences.

I was flying at about a fifteen hundred foot altitude over England and as I crossed the Channel and passed over Cherbourg, France, I had probably seen more of that part of Europe than many native Europeans. The visibility was good and the country could be seen for miles around.

People who have taken their first flight often remark that no one knows what the locality he lives in is like until he has seen it from above. Countries take on different characteristics from the air.

The sun went down shortly after passing Cherbourg and soon the beacons along the Paris–London airway became visible.

I first saw the lights of Paris a little before ten P.M., or five P.M. New York time, and a few minutes later I was circling the Eiffel Tower at an altitude of about four thousand feet.

The lights of Le Bourget were plainly visible, but appeared to be very close to Paris. I had understood that the field was farther from the city, so continued out to the northeast into the country for four or five miles to make sure that there was not another field farther out which might be Le Bourget. Then I returned and spiralled [sic.] down closer to the lights. Presently I could make out long lines of hangars, and the roads appeared to be jammed with cars.

I flew low over the field once, then circled around into the wind and landed.

After the plane stopped rolling I turned it around and, started to taxi back to the lights. The entire field ahead, however, was covered with thousands of people all running towards my ship. When the first few arrived, I attempted to get them to hold the rest of the crowd back, away from the plane, but apparently no one could understand, or would have been able to conform to my request if he had.

I cut the switch to keep the propeller from killing some one, and attempted to organize an impromptu guard for the plane. The impossibility of any immediate organization became apparent, and when parts of the ship began to crack from the pressure of the multitude I decided to climb out of the cockpit in order to draw the crowd away.

Speaking was impossible; no words could be heard in the uproar and nobody apparently cared to hear any. I started to climb out of the cockpit, but as soon as one foot appeared through the door I was dragged the rest of the way without assistance on my part.

For nearly half an hour I was unable to touch the ground, during which time I was ardently carried around in what seemed to be a very small area, and in every position it is possible to be in. Everyone had the best of intentions but no one seemed to know just what they were.

The French military flyers very resourcefully took the situation in hand. A number of them mingled with the crowd; then, at a given signal, they placed my helmet on an American correspondent and cried: "Here is Lindbergh." That helmet on an American was sufficient evidence. The correspondent immediately became the center of attraction, and while he was being taken protestingly to the Reception Committee via a rather devious route, I managed to get inside one of the hangars.

Meanwhile a second group of soldiers and police had surrounded the plane and soon placed it out of danger in another hangar.

Source: Charles Lindbergh, *We* (New York: Grosset and Dunlap, 1927), pp. 213–30.

Suggested Questions for Discussion:

1. How did Lindbergh's flight embody the hopes for a new era of cooperation and prosperity?
2. How did Lindbergh's flight point to new international challenges and threats?
3. Who was Lindbergh's audience for his flight and his memoir?

6 The Kellogg–Briand Pact, 1928

Initially negotiated by American Secretary of State, Frank Kellogg, and French Foreign Minister, Aristide Briand, in 1928, the Kellogg–Briand Pact sought to build an international consensus against the use of war for foreign policy aims. Despite later appearances, this was not a naive endeavor. The signatories to the document appealed to what they perceived as an emerging democratic public opinion around the world. They believed that increased public activism against war would contribute to international peace. In place of traditional conflict, the signatories hoped to build a powerful body of international law.

At the time, the Kellogg–Briand vision drew wide support from domestic publics and national leaders. Fifteen countries signed the initial treaty, thirty-one additional countries pledged their adherence.[6]

Treaty between the United States and other Powers providing for the renunciation of war as an instrument of national policy. Signed at Paris, August 27, 1928; ratification advised by the Senate, January 16, 1929; ratified by the President, January 17, 1929; instruments of ratification deposited at Washington by the United States of America, Australia, Dominion of Canada, Czechoslovakia, Germany, Great Britain, India, Irish Free State, Italy, New Zealand, and Union of South Africa, March 2, 1929: By Poland, March 26, 1929; by Belgium, March 27 1929; by France, April 22, 1929; by Japan, July 24, 1929; proclaimed, July 24, 1929.

BY THE PRESIDENT OF THE UNITED STATES OF AMERICA.
A PROCLAMATION.

WHEREAS a Treaty between the President of the United States of America, the President of the German Reich, His Majesty the King of the Belgians, the President of the French Republic, His Majesty the King of Great Britain, Ireland and the British Dominions beyond the Seas, Emperor of India, His Majesty the King of Italy, His Majesty the Emperor of Japan, the President of the Republic of Poland, and the President of the Czecho-slovak Republic, providing for the renunciation of war as an instrument of national policy, was concluded and signed by their respective Plenipotentiaries at Paris on the twenty-seventh day of August, one thousand nine hundred and twenty-eight, the original of which Treaty, being in the English and the French languages, is word for word as follows:

THE PRESIDENT OF THE GERMAN REICH, THE PRESIDENT OF TIIE UNITED STATES OF AMERICA, HIS MAJESTY THE KING OF THE BELGIANS, THE PRESIDENT OF THE FRENCH REPUBLIC, HIS MAJESTY THE KING OF GREAT BRITAIN IRELAND AND THE BRITISH DOMINIONS BEYOND THE SEAS, EMPEROR OF INDIA, HIS MAJESTY THE KING OF ITALY, HIS MAJESTY THE EMPEROR OF

---

[6]   Robert H. Ferrell, *Peace in their Time: The Origins of the Kellogg–Briand Pact* (New Haven, CT: Yale University Press, 1952); Frank Costigliola, *Awkward Dominion: American Political, Economic, and Cultural Relations with Europe* (Ithaca, NY: Cornell University Press, 1984); Melvyn P. Leffler, *Elusive Quest: America's Pursuit of European Stability and French Security, 1919–1933* (Chapel Hill, NC: University of North Carolina Press, 1979).

JAPAN, THE PRESIDENT OF THE REPUBLIC OF POLAND THE PRESIDENT OF THE CZECHOSLOVAK REPUBLIC,

Deeply sensible of their solemn duty to promote the welfare of mankind;

Persuaded that the time has, come when a frank renunciation of war as an instrument of national policy should be made to the end that the peaceful and friendly relations now existing between their peoples may be perpetuated;

Convinced that all changes in their relations with one another should be sought only by pacific means and be the result of a peaceful and orderly process, and that any signatory Power which shall hereafter seek to promote its national interests by resort to war a should be denied the benefits furnished by this Treaty;

Hopeful that, encouraged by their example, all the other nations of the world will join in this humane endeavor and by adhering to the present Treaty as soon as it comes into force bring their peoples within the scope of its beneficent provisions, thus uniting the civilized nations of the world in a common renunciation of war as an instrument of their national policy; ...

Article I

The High Contracting Parties solemnly declare in the names of their respective peoples that they condemn recourse to war for the solution of international controversies, and renounce it, as an instrument of national policy in their relations with one another.

Article II

The High Contracting Parties agree that the settlement or solution of all disputes or conflicts of whatever nature or of whatever origin they may be, which may arise among them, shall never be sought except by pacific means.

Article III

The present Treaty shall be ratified by the High Contracting Parties named in the Preamble in accordance with their respective constitutional requirements, and shall take effect as between them as soon as all their several instruments of ratification shall have been deposited at Washington.

This Treaty shall, when it has come into effect as prescribed in the preceding paragraph, remain open as long as may be necessary for adherence by all the other Powers of the world. Every instrument evidencing the adherence of a Power shall be deposited at Washington and the Treaty shall immediately upon such deposit become effective as; between the Power thus adhering and the other Powers parties hereto.

It shall be the duty of the Government of the United States to furnish each Government named in the Preamble and every Government subsequently adhering to this Treaty with a certified copy of the Treaty and of every instrument of ratification or adherence. It shall also be the duty of the Government of the United States telegraphically to notify such Governments immediately upon the deposit with it of each instrument of ratification or adherence.

IN FAITH WHEREOF the respective Plenipotentiaries have signed this Treaty in the French and English languages both texts having equal force, and hereunto affix their seals.

DONE at Paris, the twenty-seventh day of August in the year one thousand nine hundred and twenty-eight.

[SEAL] GUSTAV STRESEMANN
[SEAL] FRANK B. KELLOGG
[SEAL] PAUL HYMANS
[SEAL] ARI BRIAND
[SEAL] CUSHENDUN
[SEAL] W. L. MACKENZIE KING
[SEAL] A. J. MCLACHLAN
[SEAL] C. J. PARR
[SEAL] J. S. SMIT
[SEAL] LIAM T. MACCOSGAIR
[SEAL] CUSHENDUN
[SEAL] G. MANZONI
[SEAL] UCHIDA
[SEAL] AUGUST ZALESKI
[SEAL] DR EDWARD BENES

Certified to be a true copy of the signed original deposited with the Government of the United States of America.
FRANK B. KELLOGG
Secretary of State of the United States of America

AND WHEREAS it is stipulated in the said Treaty that it shall take effect as between the High Contracting Parties as soon as all the several instruments of ratification shall have been deposited at Washington;

AND WHEREAS the said Treaty has been duly ratified on the parts of all the High Contracting Parties and their several instruments of ratification have been deposited with the Government of the United States of America, the last on July 24, 1929;

NOW THEREFORE, be it known that I, Herbert Hoover, President of the United States of America, have caused the said Treaty to be made public, to the end that the same and every article and clause thereof may be observed and fulfilled with good faith by the United States and the citizens thereof.

IN TESTIMONY WHEREOF, I have hereunto set my hand and caused the seal of the United States to be affixed.

DONE at the city of Washington this twenty-fourth day of July in the year of our Lord one thousand nine hundred and twenty-nine, and of the Independence of the United States of America the one hundred and fifty-fourth
HERBERT HOOVER
By the President:
HENRY L. STIMSON
Secretary of State
NOTE BY THE DEPARTMENT OF STATE
ADHERING COUNTRIES

When this Treaty became effective on July 24, 1929, the instruments of ratification of all of the signatory powers having been deposited at Washington, the following countries, having deposited instruments of definitive adherence, became parties to it:

Afghanistan
Albania
Austria-Hungary
Bulgaria
China
Croats and Slovenes
Cuba
Denmark
Dominican Republic
Egypt
Estonia
Ethiopia
Finland

Guatemala
Iceland
Kingdom of the Serbs
Latvia
Liberia
Lithuania
Netherlands
Nicaragua
Norway
Panama
Peru
Portugal
Rumania
Russia
Siam
Spain
Sweden
Turkey

Additional adhesions deposited subsequent to July 24, 1929. Persia, July 2, 1929; Greece, August 3, 1929; Honduras, August 6, 1929; Chile, August 12, 1929; Luxemburg, August 14, 1929; Danzig, September 11, 1929; Costa Rica, October 1, 1929; Venezuela, October 24, 1929.

Source: *US Statutes at Large, vol.* 46, Part 2, pp. 2343–8.

Suggested Questions for Discussion:

1. What were the enforcement mechanisms for the Kellogg–Briand Pact?
2. Why did the leaders of so many countries sign the document?
3. What role did international law and public opinion play in the document?

Chapter 3   The Great Depression, Fascist Fears, and Social Change in America

1 President Franklin D. Roosevelt, First Inaugural Address, 1933

President Franklin Roosevelt's first inaugural address laid out a broad domestic and international agenda for addressing the Great Depression – the greatest global economic crisis of the twentieth century. Pledging his administration to fast and wide-ranging action, Roosevelt famously explained that "the only thing we have to fear is fear itself." Roosevelt called for more government regulation of the economy, and expanded trade and consumption. Emphasizing the "interdependence" between societies, the President pledged the United States to a "good neighbor" policy that rejected war and intervention for shared work toward common interests. Roosevelt's response to the Great Depression had many dimensions, but it emphasized international openness and cooperation above all.[1]

I am certain that my fellow Americans expect that on my induction into the Presidency I will address them with a candor and a decision which the present situation of our Nation impels. This is preeminently the time to

---

[1] See Robert Dallek, *Franklin D. Roosevelt and American Foreign Policy, 1932–1945*, 2nd edn. (New York: Oxford University Press, 1995); Warren Kimball, *The Juggler: Franklin Roosevelt as Wartime Statesman* (Princeton, NJ: Princeton University Press, 1991); David M. Kennedy, *Freedom From Fear: The American People in Depression and War, 1929–1945* (New York: Oxford University Press, 1999); Anthony Badger, *FDR: The First Hundred Days* (New York: Hill and Wang, 2008).

speak the truth, the whole truth, frankly and boldly. Nor need we shrink from honestly facing conditions in our country today. This great Nation will endure as it has endured, will revive and will prosper. So, first of all, let me assert my firm belief that the only thing we have to fear is fear itself – nameless, unreasoning, unjustified terror which paralyzes needed efforts to convert retreat into advance. In every dark hour of our national life a leadership of frankness and vigor has met with that understanding and support of the people themselves which is essential to victory. I am convinced that you will again give that support to leadership in these critical days.

In such a spirit on my part and on yours we face our common difficulties. They concern, thank God, only material things. Values have shrunken to fantastic levels; taxes have risen; our ability to pay has fallen; government of all kinds is faced by serious curtailment of income; the means of exchange are frozen in the currents of trade; the withered leaves of industrial enterprise lie on every side; farmers find no markets for their produce; the savings of many years in thousands of families are gone.

More important, a host of unemployed citizens face the grim problem of existence, and an equally great number toil with little return. Only a foolish optimist can deny the dark realities of the moment.

Yet our distress comes from no failure of substance. We are stricken by no plague of locusts. Compared with the perils which our forefathers conquered because they believed and were not afraid, we have still much to be thankful for. Nature still offers her bounty and human efforts have multiplied it. Plenty is at our doorstep, but a generous use of it languishes in the very sight of the supply. Primarily this is because the rulers of the exchange of mankind's goods have failed, through their own stubbornness and their own incompetence, have admitted their failure, and abdicated. Practices of the unscrupulous money changers stand indicted in the court of public opinion, rejected by the hearts and minds of men.

True they have tried, but their efforts have been cast in the pattern of an outworn tradition. Faced by failure of credit they have proposed only the lending of more money. Stripped of the lure of profit by which to induce our people to follow their false leadership, they have resorted to exhortations, pleading tearfully for restored confidence. They know only the rules of a generation of self-seekers. They have no vision, and when there is no vision the people perish.

The money changers have fled from their high seats in the temple of our civilization. We may now restore that temple to the ancient truths. The measure of the restoration lies in the extent to which we apply social values more noble than mere monetary profit.

Happiness lies not in the mere possession of money; it lies in the joy of achievement, in the thrill of creative effort. The joy and moral stimulation of work no longer must be forgotten in the mad chase of evanescent profits. These dark days will be worth all they cost us if they teach us that our true destiny is not to be ministered unto but to minister to ourselves and to our fellow men.

Recognition of the falsity of material wealth as the standard of success goes hand in hand with the abandonment of the false belief that public office and high political position are to be valued only by the standards of pride of place and personal profit; and there must be an end to a conduct in banking and in business which too often has given to a sacred trust the likeness of callous and selfish wrongdoing. Small wonder that confidence languishes, for it thrives only on honesty, on honor, on the sacredness of obligations, on faithful protection, on unselfish performance; without them it cannot live.

Restoration calls, however, not for changes in ethics alone. This Nation asks for action, and action now.

Our greatest primary task is to put people to work. This is no unsolvable problem if we face it wisely and courageously. It can be accomplished in part by direct recruiting by the Government itself, treating the task as we would treat the emergency of a war, but at the same time, through this employment, accomplishing greatly needed projects to stimulate and re-organize the use of our natural resources.

Hand in hand with this we must frankly recognize the overbalance of population in our industrial centers and, by engaging on a national scale in a redistribution, endeavor to provide a better use of the land for those best fitted for the land. The task can be helped by definite efforts to raise the values of agricultural products and with this the power to purchase the output of our cities. It can be helped by preventing realistically the tragedy of the growing loss through foreclosure of our small homes and our farms. It can be helped by insistence that the Federal, State, and local governments act forthwith on the demand that their cost be drastically reduced. It can be helped by the unifying of relief activities which today are often scattered, uneconomical, and un-equal. It can be helped by national planning for and supervision of all forms of transportation and of communications and other utilities which have a def-initely public character. There are many ways in which it can be helped, but it can never be helped merely by talking about it. We must act and act quickly.

Finally, in our progress toward a resumption of work we require two safeguards against a return of the evils of the old order; there must be a strict supervision of all banking and credits and investments; there must be an end to speculation with other people's money, and there must be provision for an adequate but sound currency.

There are the lines of attack. I shall presently urge upon a new Congress in special session detailed measures for their fulfillment, and I shall seek the immediate assistance of the several States.

Through this program of action we address ourselves to putting our own national house in order and making income balance outgo. Our international trade relations, though vastly important, are in point of time and necessity secondary to the establishment of a sound national economy. I favor as a practical policy the putting of first things first. I shall spare no effort to restore world trade by international economic readjustment, but the emergency at home cannot wait on that accomplishment.

The basic thought that guides these specific means of national recovery is not narrowly nationalistic. It is the insistence, as a first consideration, upon the interdependence of the various elements in all parts of the United States – a recognition of the old and permanently important manifestation of the American spirit of the pioneer. It is the way to recovery. It is the immediate way. It is the strongest assurance that the recovery will endure.

In the field of world policy I would dedicate this Nation to the policy of the good neighbor – the neighbor who resolutely respects himself and, because he does so, respects the rights of others – the neighbor who respects his obligations and respects the sanctity of his agreements in and with a world of neighbors.

If I read the temper of our people correctly, we now realize as we have never realized before our interdependence on each other; that we can not merely take but we must give as well; that if we are to go forward, we must move as a trained and loyal army willing to sacrifice for the good of a common discipline, because without such discipline no progress is made, no leadership becomes effective. We are, I know, ready and willing to submit our lives and property to such discipline, because it makes possible a leadership which aims at a larger good. This I propose to offer, pledging that the larger purposes will bind upon us all as a sacred obligation with a unity of duty hitherto evoked only in time of armed strife.

With this pledge taken, I assume unhesitatingly the leadership of this great army of our people dedicated to a disciplined attack upon our common problems.

Action in this image and to this end is feasible under the form of government which we have inherited from our ancestors. Our Constitution is so simple and practical that it is possible always to meet extraordinary needs by changes in emphasis and arrangement without loss of essential form. That is why our constitutional system has proved itself the most superbly enduring political mechanism the modern world has produced. It has met every stress of vast expansion of territory, of foreign wars, of bitter internal strife, of world relations.

It is to be hoped that the normal balance of executive and legislative authority may be wholly adequate to meet the unprecedented task before us. But it may be that an unprecedented demand and need for undelayed action may call for temporary departure from that normal balance of public procedure.

I am prepared under my constitutional duty to recommend the measures that a stricken nation in the midst of a stricken world may require. These measures, or such other measures as the Congress may build out of its experience and wisdom, I shall seek, within my constitutional authority, to bring to speedy adoption.

But in the event that the Congress shall fail to take one of these two courses, and in the event that the national emergency is still critical, I shall not evade the clear course of duty that will then confront me. I shall ask the Congress for the one remaining instrument to meet the crisis – broad Executive power to wage a war against the emergency, as great as the power that would be given to me if we were in fact invaded by a foreign foe.

For the trust reposed in me I will return the courage and the devotion that befit the time. I can do no less.

We face the arduous days that lie before us in the warm courage of the national unity; with the clear consciousness of seeking old and precious moral values; with the clean satisfaction that comes from the stem performance of duty by old and young alike. We aim at the assurance of a rounded and permanent national life.

We do not distrust the future of essential democracy. The people of the United States have not failed. In their need they have registered a mandate that they want direct, vigorous action. They have asked for discipline and direction under leadership. They have made me the present instrument of their wishes. In the spirit of the gift I take it.

In this dedication of a Nation we humbly ask the blessing of God. May He protect each and every one of us. May He guide me in the days to come.

Source: *Public Papers and Addresses of Franklin D. Roosevelt*, vol. II (New York: Random House, 1938), pp. 11–16.

Suggested Questions for Discussion:

1. What were the key themes in Franklin Roosevelt's first inaugural address?
2. How did Roosevelt connect domestic and international issues?
3. What was Roosevelt's policy agenda?

2 Hamilton Fish Armstrong, Meeting with Adolf Hitler, 1933

In the aftermath of the First World War, a small group of American intellectuals, politicians, and businessman centered in New York formed what became a bipartisan foreign policy "establishment." Organized through the Council on Foreign Relations, publishing their views in the journal Foreign Affairs, *these men dominated the discussion of foreign policy in the United States from the 1920s to the 1960s. They exerted influence on every presidential administration during this period. Hamilton Fish Armstrong, the long-time editor of* Foreign Affairs, *was a key figure in this group. In April 1933 he was one of the first Americans to hold an extensive interview with the newly named German Chancellor, Adolf Hitler. Armstrong's prescient diary account of his meeting with the Führer, describes the zealotry, militancy, and seeming irrationality of Hitler. Armstrong was one of many observers who recognized as early as 1933 that the Nazis threatened "the wreck of a civilization" and "disaster for all the world."*[2]

Hitler's office at the Chancellery was filled with flowering plants, left from his birthday a week earlier. He greeted me with a slight bow from the waist. He was not in uniform and there was no Nazi salute. Instead, he shook hands and motioned me to a low round table on which reposed a pad with some headings in pencil. Evidently he was prepared with a speech. I sat opposite him, with [Ernst] Hanfstaengl on one side and Hans Thomsen on the other. Thomsen I had already met. He had been German Consul in Naples under the Fascists and had come easily to the belief that a similar movement in Germany was, as he put it, "obligatory." He and Putzi [nickname for Ernst Hanfstaengl] were to serve as interpreters, each, I suppose, to watch the other. Neither fulfilled the assignment very well, for when I asked an uncomfortable question both were reluctant to incur Hitler's displeasure by putting it to him in German. They undoubtedly knew, besides, that Hitler's format did not provide for interruptions.

In press photographs, Hitler usually posed, but evidently the gallery on this occasion was not large enough to make that worthwhile, or perhaps he thought simplicity was a better tack. At any rate, he looked me over calmly, without any of his usual grimaces. I was interested to find that he had rather

[2]   See Arnold A. Offner, *American Appeasement* (Cambridge, MA: Harvard University Press, 1969); Robert D. Schulzinger, *Wise Men of Foreign Affairs: The History of the Council on Foreign Relations* (New York: Columbia University Press, 1984); Jeremi Suri, "Hamilton Fish Armstrong, the 'American Establishment,' and Cosmopolitan Nationalism," *Princeton University Library Chronicle*, 63 (Spring 2002), 438–65.

nice, wide-open eyes, which dilated and became intense only when he was irritated. People disagreed as to their color; some said they were blue; Dorothy Thompson wrote later that they were gray; and Anthony Eden said in 1934 that they were pale and glaucous. My observation was that they were light brown with perhaps a greenish cast.

While he was talking he did not look at me but kept his eyes fixed on the upper distance, which made it seem as though he were in communication with God. He brought them down to me only when I tried to interject a remark or ask a question, and when that happened he looked surprised, as a clergyman might if interrupted in the middle of a sermon by someone in the congregation. He waited impatiently till the disturbance was over. His nose was large, with rather large nostrils. His general appearance was insignificant. Several small wrinkles around the eyes, particularly above, gave him an inquiring look which was misleading, for although I had come from the West where his policies had aroused such fierce antagonism he did not ask me a single question or by any remark or reference reveal that he was in the least concerned by what the world thought of him or of the position in which he had placed his country.

Without preliminary, then, Hitler began addressing me. He spoke quietly. Two or three times, however, he seemed to lose control. A few words at the start of a sentence about some indignity inflicted on Germany would suddenly carry his voice up to the breaking point, his eyes flashed and a wisp of hair fell down over his left eye in the way the whole world knew. The rocket went up with a whiz, then there was a splutter, he smoothed his hair and went on again comparatively calmly.

He started with a formal statement that Germany was for peace, noting that he had emphasized this in his very first pronouncements after coming into office. How could it be otherwise, he said, in a country which had eight million men out of work? This did not carry conviction, for I had learnt that statesmen always said their country wanted peace, and to prove it cited equally well either prosperity or bad times and unemployment. He went at length into the iniquities of Versailles but said that the moment had not come to rectify them. "We must look ahead; we must make a new Germany; we must consolidate our strength." All this was conventional stuff. The Polish frontier, he went on, was *unmöglich* und *unerträglich*, impossible and intolerable, and to accept it permanently was unthinkable, *absolut undenkbar*. How would Americans feel, he asked, if they were bound by a foreign Diktat that prevented them from having adequate troops while their neighbor Mexico, which bore the same cultural relationship to the United States as Poland did to Germany, had enormous armaments, was increasing those armaments and threatening the American frontier? "Poland holds a naked knife in her teeth," he said, clenching his teeth in demonstration, "and looks at us menacingly," glaring at me as though I were a regiment of Polish soldiers.

The question was rhetorical, but it seemed a good moment to arrest what had become a flood of words. I therefore answered that if the United States found itself in such a position of inferiority regarding Mexico, it would be grateful that it had a friendly country like Canada on the other frontier; whereas Germany had France on the other frontier. As neither interpreter liked the idea of translating that remark, I had to repeat it in my bad German. Hitler nodded vehemently in agreement, evidently thinking I had confirmed his argument. So I again asked Hanfstaengl to translate it, whereupon Hitler froze for a second with jaw set, then continued without comment.

It would have been much better, said Hitler, if Germany had been entirely bereft of soldiers by the Allies rather than allowed a miserable 100,000. That number was entirely useless to protect her frontiers, yet furnished her neighbors with an excuse to call her chauvinistic. This argument, he added, was one which he had not used before, and for a moment I thought he wanted a foreigner's reaction to it, but that was not the case, and he proceeded to ask, again of course rhetorically, whether the United States would consider that the peace of the world would be served if it scrapped its fleet? I interjected that it might be, if Britain and Japan did also. To this he paid no attention. Europe, he went on, was armed as it never had been before. This was the fault entirely of the Allies. For every soldier in the *Reichswehr* there were fifty in the armies of France, Poland, Czechoslovakia and Belgium. Again and again he repeated that if there was a clash it was the Allies who must bear the responsibility. "To say the contrary," he said vehemently, his voice rising and the lock of hair coming down menacingly over his eye, "is to say that a toothless rabbit would start a battle with a tiger."

Wasn't the present question, I asked, whether there would be sufficient time to agree on action to bring the German Army into a condition of more equality with neighboring armies before the situation deteriorated further? Both disarmament and treaty revision had seemed nearer six weeks ago than they were now. How soon could consideration begin of disarmament, not only as an end in itself but as one way of giving Germany equality? Hanfstaengl translated this, and Hitler made a reply, though he did not give an answer. Instead of commenting on what had become the most promising manner for Germany to achieve arms equality peacefully, he said that the bad *Stimmung* at the Disarmament Conference was not the result of any act of Germany's but of a deliberate plan by France to wreck it.

Everything being done at Geneva, he continued, was a "maneuver" and amounted to nothing but a "swindle." The mentality of 1919 was back again.

I protested that wars were not always made deliberately by governments or individuals but often came simply because things had been allowed to drift on a dangerous course. Could not Germany join to halt the drift? He disregarded the appeal and returned to Poland. To allow Poland to continue arming while Germany remained disarmed was a plot against Christian civilization. The world had two courses open to it – to accept Bolshevism or to stabilize nation states. On one side was acceptance of the disproportion of arms and the illogic of the present frontiers; on the other side was a determination to undo those wrongs. One course led to Bolshevism, the other to building defenses against Bolshevism by the strengthening of the system of nation states.

"We are armed today," said Hitler, "with spears, bows and arrows and swords. Does that condition represent a danger to the peace of the world? Or does the danger of war come from the vast arms possessed by Poland?" The answer, he concluded, was obvious, and the sooner the world recognized it the better for the world – he did not say for Germany, but for the world. "We have waited months and years for justice. To get it, we must rearm. We cannot and will not wait longer. The *sine qua non* of any agreement which Germany will join must be, at the very minimum, equality in arms."

Further generalizations followed, during which I found a chance to put a question to him about the national boycott of Jewish businesses on April 1, which had caused tremendous repercussions abroad. Would it be repeated? The world, I said, was following the campaign against German Jews with intense concern. Actually, I had taken his omission of any reference to the Jewish question as perhaps indicating, though in a negative way, that he might after all take some slight interest in foreign opinion. For the boycott had allegedly been staged in retaliation for foreign criticism of the Nazi persecution of the Jews, and threats were being made to repeat it if foreign criticism continued. Did Hitler's avoidance of the subject indicate indirectly that after all he was sensitive on the subject? I hoped to smoke him out. He ignored my question, and after a peroration to the effect that the Versailles Treaty was not binding because it had been entered into under duress he rose and solemnly bowed.

Hitler accompanied me to the door – a great compliment Putzi told me afterward. To pay him back for giving me a lecture rather than accepting a give-and-take of ideas, I thanked him for addressing me alone when usually he addressed sixty millions. The sarcasm he took as a compliment, said he had enjoyed what he miscalled our "animated talk" and again bowed slightly ...

Hitler had shied away from the suggestion that progressive disarmament by Germany's neighbors offered a way for her to acquire arms equality. This implied that he favored an opposite course of action. It materialized almost at once. Foreign Minister von Neurath announced that, regardless of the results of the Disarmament Conference, Germany would create a military and naval air force, arm with big guns and build up her manpower. And von Papen, trying to "keep up," made a belligerent speech at Munster aimed at strengthening the public determination to be satisfied with nothing less. "Mothers," he said, "must exhaust themselves to give life to children. Fathers must fight on the battlefield to secure the future of their sons." Plainly, Hitler was determined to have the means to acquire what he demanded, by blackmail or force, and to have it at once; and he had the support of a people in a feverish mood, ready to respond to his every call at whatever risk. The word pacifism had been struck from the German vocabulary.

What specifically, once he had the arms, did Hitler intend to achieve? He had itemized the list in many speeches, and even at this early stage it was a long one. He wanted the Polish Corridor and Silesia back from Poland, and Danzig back from its truancy as a Free State. He wanted *Anschluss* with Austria. He wanted Northern Schleswig back from Denmark, Memel back from Lithuania, Eupen and Malmédy back from Belgium and the former German colonies from their present possessors. It went without saying that he counted on getting back the Saar after the 1935 plebiscite. Alsace, for the moment, was being mentioned only indirectly, as when the Nazi Premier of Bavaria said at about the time of my visit that the Nazis would take an oath "never to rest or relax until the Rhine flows to the sea once more as Germany's river, not as Germany's frontier." In Hitler's words, "the revolution will only be complete when the entire German world is inwardly and outwardly formed anew." Since the Nazis never stopped proclaiming by radio and in the press and in textbooks for the children the right and duty to use force to attain Nazi demands, it could not be claimed that this program excluded a general European war.

It was not only the wreck of a civilization, then, that I had observed; it carried the threat of disaster for all the world. Yet as I left Berlin I speculated whether I might not be wrong, whether the current passions and violence might not be phenomena of a first era of revolutionary fervor only. Was there not the ghost of a chance that Hitler might modify the means he threatened to use to reach his promised goal? The German spirit had been purged at least in part of its pent-up store of hate and envy. Full legal and moral equality had been declared and the material evidence to support it would mount rapidly. Might Hitler decide, from his new vantage point of total power, total responsibility, that the cost of gaining his ends by war were too immeasurable and might be won instead by skillful diplomacy? There might be real reasons for caution. It was said that there were divisions in the party leadership, that Hitler sometimes had to hold back Goebbels and other especially reckless colleagues. There were rivalries between the secret police and the S. A., and, of course, between the S. A. and the *Reichswehr*, who still clung to the hope of controlling Germany's military future. Instead of laying plans to seize his requirements by force, might Hitler gradually revert to the methods of piecemeal revision exploited by his predecessors?

Nothing that I had heard or seen in Berlin really seemed to me to justify such a hope. And, even if the next to impossible did happen, was it conceivable that the world would accept it in good, faith? Would France believe in "a new Hitler" and make concessions to him which she had not been ready to make to a Stresemann and a Brüning? Everything in Hitler's make-up seemed to echo Lenin's dictum: "He who undertakes the storming of a fortress cannot refuse to continue the war after he has taken the fortress." Hitler had taken the old German fortress, and citizens who had not shouted "Sieg Heil!" had been beaten to their knees. In the little book which I wrote in the next few weeks I questioned most pessimistically both the hope that Hitler, armed, would draw back from the ultimate test of wills and the thesis of many that his reign would prove to be only a flash in the pan. A people had, in sober and awful truth, disappeared. I could not see the possibility of their rebirth as a part of Western civilization under Hitler or the possibility of their resurgence against him.

Source: Hamilton Fish Armstrong, *Peace and Counterpeace: Memoirs of Hamilton Fish Armstrong* (New York: Harper & Row, 1971), pp. 535–9.

Suggested Questions for Discussion:

1. Why did Hamilton Fish Armstrong find Adolf Hitler so threatening?
2. What were Hitler's aims, as described by Armstrong?
3. Why did Armstrong bring up the persecution of German Jews in his interview with Hitler?

3 Father Charles Coughlin, Radio attack on "Internationalism," 1931

During the 1930s Father Charles Coughlin, a Roman Catholic priest based in Detroit, became one of the most popular radio personalities in the country. His weekly broadcasts drew millions of listeners – perhaps more than listened to Roosevelt's famous "fireside chats." Coughlin attacked the internationalism represented by new immigrants, radical ideologies, and large corporations. Coughlin called for a return to traditional "patriotism" and Christian religion. Coughlin's demagogic rhetoric challenged Roosevelt's emphasis on international cooperation and Armstrong's attention to protecting "civilization" against groups like the Nazis. Coughlin echoed the populist anti-Semitic sentiments that animated Nazi propaganda.[3]

This evening's discourse deals with internationalism – a heresy which strikes at the root of patriotism and prosperity; and aims not at elevating all peoples to the standard of American living, but rather at the leveling of our standard to the common denominator of foreign misery.

Patriotism, my friends, holds the same relation between a citizen and his country as fidelity does between a man and his wife; as piety does between a child and its parent; as religion does between a creature and his Creator. It is a virtue by which a freed man so loves his country, its customs and ideals and constitution; is so enamored of its lakes and hills and rivers around which linger the sweet memories of bygone days; is so filled with devotion for the souls of those whose sacrifices have made home and its surroundings an immortal benediction, that he would die, if necessary, to defend that country where dwell these things because he loves it not equally with other countries – though they be mightier and more eminent – but more than all countries combined.

Patriotism and internationalism! The one born of Godliness and Christliness; the other, the offspring of atheism and greed!

Approximately one year ago there was occasion to discuss on the Golden Hour of the Little Flower the growth in our midst of the modern political and religious heresy called communism. At that time whoever made mention of this was considered to be a peddler of perils. Those were the days

---

[3]   See Alan Brinkley, *Voices of Protest: Huey Long, Father Coughlin, and the Great Depression* (New York: Alfred Knopf, 1982); Michael Kazin, *The Populist Persuasion: An American History* (New York: Basic Books, 1995); Donald Warren, *Radio Priest: Charles Coughlin: The Father of Hate Radio* (New York: Free Press, 1996).

when many of our great American industrialists, greedy for gold, were stumbling over themselves in their anxiety to sign contracts with the outlawed government of Soviet Russia. Whatever was said in disparagement either of sovietism or communism was regarded as inimical to the best interests of American commerce and finance ...

In the United States of America at this moment we have two separate kinds of radicals. To the first class belong those men who have sworn allegiance to the red flag of Russia and whose sole ambition is the overthrow of our government and the subjugation of our people. These unmolested revolutionists, in one sense, are to be congratulated because of their open honesty and straightforwardness.

The other class of radicals, who throw up their hands in unholy horror of the red flag, carry no card which proclaims their identity with the Third Internationale. Unlike their Russian cousins they do not preach sabotage, neither do they proclaim openly against religion nor scoff at patriotism. Both are desirous, however, of building up a world-wide rule of class ascendancy. Both are international. The former are less feared than the latter because, due to their power and their wealth, they are the greater menace to the American public's prosperity....

Undoubtedly, one of the first doctrines of communism is political internationalism. Alexander the Great was imbued with it when he desired to Persianize the entire world and wept by the banks of an oriental river because there were no more nations to conquer. So was Augustus Caesar. So was Napoleon whose secret ambition was to make the world his footstool and France his throne.

The most loathsome after-birth of the World War has been the revival of this internationalism which in its last analysis is nothing more than universal class rule. On the one hand the Soviet desires to control the entire world by the military arm of an enslaved laboring class. And on the part of certain captains of industry and finance there seems to be a determination to rule the universe through the agent of wealth.

If Russia established its Third Internationale, conservative Europe kept step with it in the establishment of a League of Nations. If Russia clumsily renounced its foreign obligations, the League of Nations adroitly accomplished the same thing through its establishment of a League Court which claims the authority to legislate for all its members on matters of immigration, of tariff and of other affairs of international character. This internationalism is a greater menace to our prosperity than is the type advocated by the Soviet....

My friends, this internationalism leads only to one thing. It means that the laboring class of this country will be reduced to the same status as that of the worn out European nations. Our ancestors came to these shores to be rid of the persecutions both financial and political and religious which were so common before the XVIII Century. Under brighter skies and with hearts filled with new hopes we and our forefathers built up a standard of living where poverty had practically ceased; where cheap charity was not required and where every man was guaranteed sufficient honest labor and such far-reaching opportunity for advancement that it surpassed the wildest dreams of the peasant class and the middle class of Europe. So today, we are on the verge through a decade of internationalistic philosophy of lowering our standards to meet those of war-torn Europe. The organized effort to accomplish this has been in no little sense responsible for the sadness and sorrow and misery in which we now find ourselves.

Near the close of our great Civil War, in reply to a letter from a friend in Illinois, President Lincoln is reported to have said: "Yes, we may all congratulate ourselves that the cruel war is nearing its close. It has cost a great amount of treasure and of blood. But I see in the near future, a crisis approaching that unnerves me and causes me to tremble for the safety of my country.

"As a result of the war, corporations have been enthroned and an era of corruption in high places will follow. The money power of the country will endeavor to prolong its reign by working upon the prejudices of the people until all wealth is aggregated in a few hands, and the Republic is destroyed. I feel at this moment more anxiety for the safety of my country than ever before, even in the midst of war. God grant that my suspicions may prove groundless."

Lest you are forgetful, Washington said: "The great rule of conduct for us, in regard to foreign nations, is, in extending our commercial relations, to have with them as little political connection as possible. So far as we have already formed engagements, let them be fulfilled with perfect good faith. Here let us stop."

It were high time to heed Lincoln's warning and Washington's advice that we refrain from entering into foreign entanglements – entanglements which throw patriotism to the four winds; which are bent on enthroning the basic principle of communism, and reducing the American common people to the status of a Persian peasant.

Ladies and gentlemen, the present depression has witnessed the reappearance of many old and well-known characters upon the stage of time. There is the banker who tells us of the decline and scarcity of gold in some quarters and the necessity on the part of America to reconstruct its balance. There is the professional business booster who charges it to a depressed psychology. And lastly, there is that type of statesman who blames it on the Russians.

Meanwhile, while words flow thick and fast the depression still remains with us. Meanwhile, at the very peak of it we are about to witness our Seventy-first Congress tomorrow enter upon, perhaps, a prolonged debate whether or not we shall practically sign away our national rights to the World Court of the League of Nations and be satisfied to become identified with Europe with our lisping voice which shall cry in the courts of its wilderness in vain.

Less care for internationalism and more care for national prosperity; less concern for the welfare of Europe and more concern for the welfare of our millions to whom are not given the opportunity of earning a livelihood is more palatable to the taste of the American people.

At this moment I have a mental picture of those wily scribes and pharisees who accosted Jesus Christ trying to catch Him in His speech. They were not forgetful of His beautiful sermon preached on the mountainside. They still remembered His Divine doctrine of charity. Thus, they thought within themselves that He Who preached the doctrine of the universal brotherhood of mankind would be quick to deny the virtue of patriotism.

"Is it lawful, therefore, to give tribute to Caesar?" was their question.

You remember the classic reply which confounded them all: "Render to God the things that are God's and to Caesar the things that are Caesar's."

Christianity, therefore, which insists that we love our fellowman whether he be Jew or Gentile, black or white, does not intimate for a moment that we shall jettison the cargo of our patriotism nor jeopardize the lastingness of our country.

In these days when approximately seventy-six million of our population hold no affiliation whatsoever to any church; in these days when religion has ceased to be an integral part in the lives of everyone of us, is it to be wondered at that the sound principles upon which a lesser virtue of patriotism was built should likewise be held in question?

In things spiritual let us be international. Let there be one God and Father, one faith and baptism and one spiritual domain under which every nation can live. But in things temporal let us render to Caesar the things that are his.

Source: *Father Coughlin's Radio Sermons, October 1930–April 1931, Complete* (Baltimore, MD: Knox and O'Leary, 1931), pp. 99–109.

Suggested Questions for Discussion:

1. How did Father Coughlin define patriotism?
2. Why did he condemn internationalism?
3. What role did religion play in Father Coughlin's rhetoric?

4 Charles Lindbergh, Speech to an America First Committee Meeting, 1941

By the autumn of 1940 Nazi Germany had conquered France and Hitler
appeared poised to force the collapse of Great Britain and its vast empire.
Many Americans, including President Franklin Roosevelt, began to
contemplate American military intervention in Europe to limit Nazi
aggression, and its long-term threat to American interests. Formed in
September 1940 at Yale University, the America First Committee mobilized
against this position. America First argued that the United States should stand
separate from Europe, avoiding any direct intervention in affairs across the
Atlantic. The famous American aviator, Charles Lindbergh, was one of
America First's most prominent and influential advocates.[4]

There are many viewpoints from which the issues of this war can be argued. Some are primarily idealistic. Some are primarily practical. One should, I believe, strive for a balance of both. But, since the subjects that can be covered in a single address are limited, tonight I shall discuss the war from a viewpoint which is primarily practical. It is not that I believe ideals are unimportant, even among the realities of war; but if a nation is to survive in a hostile world, its ideals must be backed by the hard logic of military practicability. If the outcome of war depended upon ideals alone, this would be a different world than it is today.

I know I will be severely criticized by the interventionists in America when I say we should not enter a war unless we have a reasonable chance of winning. That, they will claim, is far too materialistic a viewpoint. They will advance again the same arguments that were used to persuade France to declare war against Germany in 1939. But I do not believe that our American ideals, and our way of life, will gain through an unsuccessful war. And I know that the United States is not prepared to wage war in Europe successfully at this time. We are no better prepared today than France was when the interventionists in Europe persuaded her to attack the Siegfried Line....

I ask you to look at the map of Europe today and see if you can suggest any way in which we could win this war if we entered it. Suppose we had a large army in America, trained and equipped. Where would we send it to fight? The campaigns of the war show only too clearly how difficult it is to

[4]   See Justus D. Doenecke, *Storm on the Horizon: The Challenge to American Intervention,* *1939–1941* (New York: Rowman & Littlefield, 2000); Wayne S. Cole, *America First: The* *Battle Against Intervention, 1940–41* (Madison, WI: University of Wisconsin Press, 1953).

force a landing, or to maintain an army, on a hostile coast. Suppose we took our navy from the Pacific, and used it to convoy British shipping. That would not win the war for England. It would, at best, permit her to exist under the constant bombing of the German air fleet. Suppose we had an air force that we could send to Europe. Where could it operate? Some of our squadrons might be based in the British Isles; but it is physically impossible to base enough aircraft in the British Isles alone to equal in strength the aircraft that can be based on the continent of Europe.

I have asked these questions on the supposition that we had in existence an army and an air force large enough and well enough equipped to send to Europe; and that we would dare to remove our navy from the Pacific. Even on this basis, I do not see how we could invade the continent of Europe successfully as long as all of that continent and most of Asia is under Axis domination. But the fact is that none of these suppositions are correct. We have only a one-ocean navy. Our army is still untrained and inadequately equipped for foreign war. Our air force is deplorably lacking in modern fighting planes.

When these facts are cited, the interventionists shout that we are defeatists, that we are undermining the principles of Democracy, and that we are giving comfort to Germany by talking about our military weakness. But everything I mention here has been published in our newspapers, and in the reports of congressional hearings in Washington. Our military position is well known to the governments of Europe and Asia. Why, then, should it not be brought to the attention of our own people?

I say it is the interventionist in America, as it was in England and in France, who gives comfort to the enemy. I say it is they who are undermining the principles of Democracy when they demand that we take a course to which more than eighty percent of our citizens are opposed. I charge them with being the real defeatists, for their policy has led to the defeat of every country that followed their advice since this war began. There is no better way to give comfort to an enemy than to divide the people of a nation over the issue of foreign war. There is no shorter road to defeat than by entering a war with inadequate preparation. Every nation that has adopted the interventionist policy of depending on some one else for its own defense has met with nothing but defeat and failure.

When history is written, the responsibility for the downfall of the democracies of Europe will rest squarely upon the shoulders of the interventionists who led their nations into war uninformed and unprepared. With their shouts of defeatism, and their disdain of reality, they have already sent countless thousands of young men to death in Europe. From the campaign of Poland to that of Greece, their prophecies have been false and their policies have failed. Yet these are the people who are calling us defeatists in America today. And they have led this country, too, to the verge of war.

There are many such interventionists in America, but there are more people among us of a different type. That is why you and I are assembled here tonight. There is a policy open to this nation that will lead to success – a policy that leaves us free to follow our own way of life, and to develop our own civilization. It is not a new and untried idea. It was advocated by Washington. It was incorporated in the Monroe Doctrine. Under its guidance, the United States became the greatest nation in the world. It is based upon the belief that the security of a nation lies in the strength and character of its own people. It recommends the maintenance of armed forces sufficient to defend this hemisphere from attack by any combination of foreign powers. It demands faith in an independent American destiny. This is the policy of the America First Committee today. It is a policy not of isolation, but of independence; not of defeat, but of courage. It is a policy that led this nation to success during the most trying years of our history, and it is a policy that will lead us to success again.

We have weakened ourselves for many months, and still worse, we have divided our own people by this dabbling in Europe's wars. While we should have been concentrating on American defense, we have been forced to argue over foreign quarrels. We must turn our eyes and our faith back to our own country before it is too late. And when we do this, a different vista opens before us. Practically every difficulty we would face in invading Europe becomes an asset to us in defending America. Our enemy, and not we, would then have the problem of transporting millions of troops across the ocean and landing them on a hostile shore. They, and not we, would have to furnish the convoys to transport guns and trucks and munitions and fuel across three thousand miles of water. Our battleships and submarines would then be fighting close to their home bases. We would then do the bombing from the air, and the torpedoing at sea. And if any part of an enemy convoy should ever pass our navy and our air force, they would still be faced with the guns of our coast artillery, and behind them, the divisions of our army.

The United States is better situated from a military standpoint than any other nation in the world. Even in our present condition of unpreparedness, no foreign power is in a position to invade us today. If we concentrate on our own and build the strength that this nation should maintain, no foreign army will ever attempt to land on American shores. . . .

The time has come when those of us who believe in an independent American destiny must band together, and organize for strength. We have been led toward war by a minority of our people. This minority has power. It has influence. It has a loud voice. But it does not represent the American people. During the last several years, I have traveled over this country, from one end to the other. I have talked to many hundreds of men and women, and I have had letters from tens of thousands more, who feel the same way as you and I. Most of these people have no influence or power. Most of them have no means of expressing their convictions, except by their vote which has always been against this war. They are the citizens who have had to work too hard at their daily jobs to organize political meetings. Hitherto, they have relied upon their vote to express their feelings; but now they find that it is hardly remembered except in the oratory of a political campaign. These people – the majority of hard-working American citizens are with us. They are the true strength of our country. And they are beginning to realize, as you and I, that there are times when we must sacrifice our normal interests in life in order to insure the safety and the welfare of our nation.

Such a time has come. Such a crisis is here. That is why the America First Committee has been formed – to give voice to the people who have no newspaper, or newsreel, or radio station at their command; to the people who must do the paying, and the fighting, and the dying, if this country enters the war.

Source: available at: www.pbs.org/wgbh/amex/lindbergh/filmmore/reference/primary/firstcommittee.html.

Suggested Questions for Discussion:

1. Why did Lindbergh argue that the United States was unprepared for war in 1941?
2. Why did Lindbergh believe that some Americans advocated military intervention in Europe?
3. What were the foreign policy aims of the America First Committee?

5 The Atlantic Charter, 1941

With German armies occupying most of the European continent, British Prime Minister, Winston Churchill, and American President, Franklin Delano Roosevelt, secretly met in August 1941 at sea, off the cost of Newfoundland. The United States supported British military activities against Germany, but Washington remained officially "neutral." In their joint declaration – later called the "Atlantic Charter" – Churchill and Roosevelt pledged their countries to a series of common aims in the defeat of Nazi Germany. They echoed Woodrow Wilson's emphasis on free trade, self-determination, disarmament,

*and international cooperation. They also added a commitment to work
together so that "men in all the lands may live out their lives in freedom from
fear and want." This expansive agenda provided a dynamic foundation for
Anglo-American postwar planning.*[5]

Joint Statement by President Franklin Delano Roosevelt and Prime Minister Winston Churchill, August 14, 1941

The President of the United States and the Prime Minister, Mr. Churchill, representing His Majesty's Government in the United Kingdom, have met at sea.

They have been accompanied by officials of their two Governments, including high ranking officers of their Military, Naval and Air Services

The whole problem of the supply of munitions of war, as provided by the Lease-Lend Act, for the armed forces of the United States and for those countries actively engaged in resisting aggression has been further examined.

Lord Beaverbrook, the Minister of Supply of the British Government, has joined in these conferences. He is going to proceed to Washington to discuss further details with appropriate officials of the United States Government. These conferences will also cover the supply problems of the Soviet Union.

The President and the Prime Minister have had several conferences They have considered the dangers to world civilization arising from the policies of military domination by conquest upon which the Hitlerite Government of Germany and other Governments associated therewith have embarked, and have made clear the steps which their countries are respectively taking for their safety in the face of these dangers.

They have agreed upon the following joint declaration:

The President of the United States of America and the Prime Minister, Mr. Churchill, representing His Majesty's Government in the United Kingdom, being met together, deem it right to make known certain common principles in the national policies of their respective countries on which they base their hopes for a better future for the world.

First, their countries seek no aggrandizement, territorial or other.

Second, they desire to see no territorial changes that do not accord with the freely expressed wishes of the peoples concerned.

---

[5]   See Elizabeth Borgwardt, *A New Deal for the World: America's Vision for Human Rights* (Cambridge, MA: Belknap Press of Harvard University Press, 2005); David M. Kennedy, *Freedom From Fear: The American People in Depression and War, 1929–1945* (New York: Oxford University Press, 1999); Theodore Wilson, *The First Summit: Roosevelt and Churchill at Placentia Bay, 1941*, rev. edn. (Lawrence, KA: University Press of Kansas, 1991).

Third, they respect the right of all peoples to choose the form of government under which they will live; and they wish to see sovereign rights and self-government restored to those who have been forcibly deprived of them.

Fourth, they will endeavor, with due respect for their existing obligations, to further the enjoyment by all states, great or small, victor or vanquished, of access, on equal terms, to the trade and to the raw materials of the world which are needed for their economic prosperity.

Fifth, they desire to bring about the fullest cooperation between all nations in the economic field, with the object of securing, for all improved labor standards, economic advancement, and social security.

Sixth, after the final destruction of the Nazi tyranny, they hope to see established a peace which will afford to all nations the means of dwelling in safety within their own boundaries, and which will afford assurance that all the men in all the lands may live out their lives in freedom from fear and want.

Seventh, such a peace should enable all men to traverse the high seas and oceans without hindrance.

Eighth, they believe that all of the nations of the world, for realistic as well as spiritual reasons, must come to the abandonment of the use of force. Since no future peace can be maintained if land, sea, or air armaments continue to be employed by nations which threaten, or may threaten, aggression outside of their frontiers, they believe, pending the establishment of a wider and permanent system of general security, that the disarmament of such nations is essential. They will likewise aid and encourage all other practicable measures which will lighten for peace-loving peoples the crushing burden of armaments.

Franklin D. Roosevelt
Winston S. Churchill

Source: Samuel Rosenman (ed.), *Public Papers and Addresses of Franklin D. Roosevelt*, vol. 10 (Washington, DC: US Government Printing Office, 1938–50), p. 314.

Suggested Questions for Discussion:

1. How did the Atlantic Charter echo Wilson's Fourteen Points?
2. How did it differ from the Fourteen Points?
3. Why was the Atlantic Charter threatening to the sustenance of the British Empire in the eyes of many observers?

Chapter 4   The Second World War

1 Lawrence T. Kagawa, the Internment of Japanese-Americans, 1942

After the Japanese attack on Pearl Harbor and the American declaration of war, President Roosevelt authorized numerous infringements on domestic liberty for the sake of national security. On February 19, 1942 Roosevelt signed Executive Order 9066, ordering the War Department to remove American citizens of Japanese descent by force from their homes and temporarily resettle them in government supervised concentration camps. The US Army interned nearly 120,000 Japanese-American citizens, mostly from the West Coast, for more than three years. In 1988 the United States government finally apologized for this act of wartime injustice, and offered restitution to the internees and their relatives. The letter excerpted below from a Japanese-American, Lawrence T. Kagawa, captures the disorientation and anger felt by loyal American citizens forcibly relocated and interned by the federal government. Kagawa worked for a large American life insurance company in Honolulu, Hawaii at the outbreak of war. The US government transferred him and his family to an internment camp at Camp McCoy in Wisconsin. Hawaii did not have representation in Congress at the time, so Kagawa writes to his non-voting congressional "delegate," Samuel W. King.[1]

---

[1] See Greg Robinson, *By Order of the President: FDR and the Internment of Japanese Americans* (Cambridge, MA: Harvard University Press, 2001); Roger Daniels, *Prisoners Without Trial: Japanese Americans in World War II* (New York: Hill and Wang, 1993); California Historical Society, *Only What We Could Carry: The Japanese American Internment Experience* (San Francisco, CA: Heyday Books, 2000).

March 12, 1942
L. T. Kagawa
Camp McCoy
Sparta, Wisconsin

My dear Delegate King:

Will you pardon my writing you a personal letter when are so busy and the country needs you most.

You will notice from the above address that I am detained in the camp now, transferred from our beloved city, Honolulu.

As you know, Mr. King, I am always and have been a good American citizen and I am still [a] good American in my heart. I don't know why I am detained. If I am detained here because of my dual citizenship then it is no fault of mine. [The] Constitution gave me the absolute sacred right as American citizen upon my birth … If I am allowed to say, this is the time for unity and every well thinking American's responsibility is to uphold the principle of democracy and liberty which we Americans treasure most. I have preached and lead [sic.] all those years among my race of American citizens to know and understand the spirit of our country and after declared war, I wrote so many letters including my brother at Tulane University to stand by and give our life to American [sic.]. I wrote so many letters to the fact that our beloved America is standing on the crossroad to defend American democracy[,] and the American citizen of Japanese descent should give their life to defend the country, not only from the standpoint of American citizen but this is the time and only chance to show our absolute loyalty to the country so that the next generation of our race will be accepted as fine Americans without prejudice or suspicion.

I still believe the above stated reason and pray for fair play on the part of other American[s] and praying every day for my freedom so that I'll be able to serve the country properly because we owe as much to the American.

As to my character and ability please refer to Occidental Life Insurance Company of Los Angeles, Calif. The entire officers of the company are my business personal associates for many years.
Thank you for your kind consideration, I remain.

Lawrence T. Kagawa

Suggested Questions for Discussion:

1. How did Lawrence Kagawa define his citizenship?
2. How did he understand his internment?
3. What does his experience tell us about the effects of the Second World War on American democracy?

2 President Franklin Roosevelt and Soviet Marshal Josef Stalin at the Tehran Conference, 1943

After the anticipated destruction of the fascist militaries in Europe and Asia, what would the postwar world look like? How would the allied powers govern the postwar international system? As the United States, Great Britain, and the Soviet Union struggled to defeat their enemies, in late 1943 they began to plan for the future. Meeting in Tehran, President Franklin Roosevelt, Prime Minister Winston Churchill, and Marshal Josef Stalin discussed their security interests and their postwar expectations. Roosevelt proposed the creation of a worldwide organization, the "United Nations." In this conversation between Roosevelt and Stalin, the President outlines his proposal for an "Executive Committee" of powerful nations within the United Nations, and the separate creation of an organization composed of the "Four Policemen" – the United States, Great Britain, the Soviet Union, and China. Stalin offers tepid support for the United Nations, but expresses his skepticism about the Four Policemen. The Soviet leader emphasizes his fears of a resurgent postwar German threat and his preference for regional security organizations.[2]

NOVEMBER 29, 1943, 2: 45 P.M., Tehran.

Present:
US President Franklin Roosevelt, Soviet Marshal Josef Stalin, Charles Bohlen (US translator), and Valentin Berezhkov (Soviet translator)

THE PRESIDENT ... said the question of a post war organization to preserve peace had not been fully explained and dealt with and he would like to

---

[2]   See Robert Dallek, *Franklin D. Roosevelt and American Foreign Policy, 1932–1945*, 2nd edn. (New York: Oxford University Press, 1995); Warren Kimball, *The Juggler: Franklin Roosevelt as Wartime Statesman* (Princeton, NJ: Princeton University Press, 1991); Vladislav Zubok, *A Failed Empire: The Soviet Union in the Cold War from Stalin to Gorbachev* (Chapel Hill, NC: University of North Carolina Press, 2007); Geoffrey Roberts, *Stalin's Wars: From World War to Cold War, 1939–1953* (New Haven, CT: Yale University Press, 2007).

discuss with the Marshal the prospect of some organization based on the United Nations.

THE PRESIDENT then outlined the following general plan:

(1) There would be a large organization composed of some 35 members of the United Nations which would meet periodically at different places, discuss and make recommendations to a smaller body.

MARSHAL STALIN inquired whether this organization was to be world-wide or European, to which the President replied, world-wide.

THE PRESIDENT continued that there would be set up an executive committee composed of the Soviet Union, the United States, United Kingdom and China, together with two additional European states, one South American, one Near East, one Far Eastern country, and one British Dominion. He mentioned that Mr. Churchill did not like this proposal for the reason that the British Empire only had two votes. This Executive Committee would deal with all non-military questions such as agriculture, food, health, and economic questions, as well as the setting up of an International Committee. This Committee would likewise meet in various places.

MARSHAL STALIN inquired whether this body would have the right to make decisions binding on the nations of the world.

THE PRESIDENT replied, yes and no. It could make recommendations for settling disputes with the hope that the nations concerned would be guided thereby, but that, for example, he did not believe Congress of the United States would accept as binding a decision of such a body. THE PRESIDENT then turned to the third organization which he termed "The Four policemen," namely, the Soviet Union, the United States, Great Britain, and China. This organization would have the power to deal immediately with any threat to the peace and any sudden emergency which requires this action. He went on to say that in 1935, when Italy attacked Ethiopia, the only machine in existence was the League of Nations. He personally had begged France to close the Suez Canal, but they instead referred it to [the] League which disputed the question and in the end did nothing. The result was that the Italian Armies went through the Suez Canal and destroyed Ethiopia. THE PRESIDENT pointed out that had the machinery of the Four Policemen, which he had in mind, been in existence, it would have been possible to close the Suez Canal. THE PRESIDENT then summarized briefly the idea that he had in mind.

MARSHAL STALIN said that he did not think that the small nations of Europe would like the organization composed of the Four Policemen. He said, for example, that a European state would probably resent China having the right to apply certain machinery to it. And in any event, he did not think China would be very powerful at the end of the war. He suggested as a possible alternative, the creation of a European or a Far Eastern Committee and a European or a Worldwide organization. He said that in the European Commission there would be the United States, Great Britain, the Soviet Union and possibly one other European state.

THE PRESIDENT said that the idea just expressed by Marshal Stalin was somewhat similar to Mr. Churchill's idea of a Regional Committee, one for Europe, one for the Far East, and one for the Americas. Mr. Churchill had also suggested that the United States be a member of the European Commission, but he doubted if the United States Congress would agree to the United States' participation in an exclusively European Committee which might be able to force the dispatch of American troops to Europe.

THE PRESIDENT added that it would take a terrible crisis such as at present before Congress would ever agree to that step.

MARSHAL STALIN pointed out that the world organization suggested by the President, and in particular the Four Policemen, might also require the sending of American troops to Europe.

THE PRESIDENT pointed out that he had only envisaged the sending of American planes and ships to Europe, and that England and the Soviet Union would have to handle the land armies in the event of any future threat to the peace. He went on to say that if the Japanese had not attacked the United States he doubted very much if it would have been possible to send any American forces to Europe. THE PRESIDENT added that he saw two methods of dealing with possible threats to the peace. In one case if the threat arose from a revolution or developments in a small country, it might be possible to apply the quarantine method, closing the frontiers of the countries in question and imposing embargoes. In the second case, if the threat was more serious, the four powers, acting as policemen, would send an ultimatum to the nation in question and if refused, [it] would result in the immediate bombardment and possible invasion of that country.

MARSHAL STALIN said that yesterday he had discussed the question of safe-guarding against Germany with Mr. Churchill and found him optimistic on the subject in that Mr. Churchill believed that Germany would not rise again. He, Stalin, personally thought that unless prevented, Germany would completely [recover] within 15 to 20 years, and that therefore we must have something more serious than the type of organization proposed by the President. He pointed out that the first German aggression had occurred in 1870 and then 42 [sic.] years later in the 1st World War, whereas only 21 years elapsed between the end of the last war and the beginning of the present. He added that he did not believe the period between the revival of German strength would be any longer in the future and therefore he did not consider the organizations outlined by the President were enough.

He went on to say that what was needed was the control of certain strong physical points either within Germany along German borders, or even farther away, to insure that Germany would not embark on another course of aggression. He mentioned specifically Dakar as one of those points. He added that the same method should be applied in the case of Japan and that the islands in the vicinity of Japan should remain under strong control to prevent Japan's embarking on a course of aggression.

He stated that any commission or body which was set up to preserve peace should have the right to not only make decisions but to occupy such strong points against Germany and Japan.

THE PRESIDENT said that he agreed 100% with Marshal Stalin.

MARSHAL STALIN then stated he still was dubious about the question of Chinese participation.

THE PRESIDENT replied that he had insisted on the participation of China in the 4 Power Declaration at Moscow not because he did not realize the weakness of China at present, but he was thinking farther into the future and that after all China was a nation of 400 million people, and it was better to have them as friends rather than as a potential source of trouble.

THE PRESIDENT, reverting to Marshal Stalin's statements as to the ease of converting factories, said that a strong and effective world organization of the 4 Powers could move swiftly when the first signs arose of the beginning of the conversion of such factories for warlike purposes.

MARSHAL STALIN replied that the Germans had shown great ability to conceal such beginnings.

THE PRESIDENT accepted Marshal Stalin's remark. He again expressed his agreement with Marshal Stalin that strategic positions in the world should be at the disposal of some world organization to prevent a revival of German and Japanese aggression.

Source: *Foreign Relations of the United States: The Conferences at Cairo and Tehran, 1943*. (Washington DC: US Government Printing Office, 1961), pp. 529–33.

Suggested Questions for Discussion:

1. What purposes would the United Nations serve, according to Franklin Roosevelt?
2. What role would the Four Policemen play, according to Roosevelt?
3. How did Josef Stalin's fears of a resurgent postwar Germany challenge Roosevelt's proposals?

3 Dwight Eisenhower, the Liberation of Nazi Concentration Camps, 1945

Citizens of the United States and other allied countries received information about the Holocaust during the Second World War, but detailed knowledge of German atrocities remained limited. In April 1945 American military leaders gained first-hand access to the Nazi concentration camps. For men like General Dwight Eisenhower who had extensive personal experience with the horrors of war, the "bestiality" of German mass killings was without precedent. Eisenhower reported his sickness at the corpses, the suffering, and the indignities inflicted on millions of Jews and other innocent victims: "The things I saw beggar description."[3]

General Dwight Eisenhower to General George Marshall
April 15, 1945
Secret

... On a recent tour of the forward areas in First and Third Armies, I stopped momentarily at the salt mines to take a look at the German

[3] See David S. Wyman, *The Abandonment of the Jews: America and the Holocaust, 1941–1945* (New York: Pantheon, 1984); Peter Novick, *The Holocaust in American Life* (Boston, MA: Houghton Mifflin, 1999).

treasure. There is a lot of it. But the most interesting – although horrible – sight that I encountered during the trip was a visit to a German internment camp near Gotha. The things I saw beggar description. . . .

I encountered three men who had been inmates and by one ruse or another had made their escape. I interviewed them through an interpreter. The visual evidence and the verbal testimony of starvation, cruelty and bestiality were so overpowering as to leave me a bit sick. In one room, where [there] were piled up twenty or thirty naked men, killed by starvation, [General] George Patton would not even enter. He said he would get sick if he did so. I made the visit deliberately, in order to be in position to give *first-hand* evidence of these things if ever, in the future, there develops a tendency to charge these allegations merely to "propaganda."

General Dwight Eisenhower to General George Marshall
April 19, 1945
Secret – For Eyes Only

We continue to uncover German concentration camps for political prisoners in which conditions of indescribable horror prevail. I have visited one of these myself and I assure you that whatever has been printed on them to date has been understatement. If you would see any advantage in asking about a dozen leaders of Congress and a dozen prominent editors to make a short visit to this theater in a couple of C-54's, I will arrange to have them conducted to one of these places where the evidence of bestiality and cruelty is so overpowering as to leave no doubt in their minds about the normal practices of the Germans in these camps. I am hopeful that some British individuals in similar categories will visit the northern area to witness similar evidence of atrocity.

Source: *Papers of Dwight David Eisenhower, The War Years: IV*, Alfred D. Chandler (ed.) (Baltimore, MD: The Johns Hopkins Press, 1970), pp. 2614–16, 2621.

Suggested Questions for Discussion:

1. What did General Dwight Eisenhower see?
2. How did it affect him?
3. How did Eisenhower convey his feelings to General George Marshall?

4 President Harry Truman, Diary Entries on the Potsdam Conference and his Decision to Drop the Atomic Bombs on Japan, 1945

In July 1945 President Harry Truman traveled to Berlin for the last of the allied war conferences, in the Potsdam suburb of the German capital. Truman witnessed the destruction of Berlin and the suffering of the German people. He also commented on what he perceived as Russian cruelty in victory. Truman met extensively with Winston Churchill and Josef Stalin to discuss a variety of issues. The President encouraged Soviet entry into the continuing war against Japan. He also attempted to build a cooperative relationship with Stalin in Europe. During Truman's visit to Berlin, on July 16, 1945 the secret American "Manhattan Project" detonated the first atomic bomb in Alamogordo, New Mexico. Truman planned for the use of the new "terrible bomb" against Japan to bring the final defeat of that nation.[4]

President Truman's Private Diary

Berlin, July 16, 1945

... [W]e went to Berlin and saw absolute ruin. Hitler's folly. He overreached himself by trying to take in too much territory. He had no morals and his people backed him up. Never did I see a more sorrowful sight, nor witness retribution to the nth degree.

The most sorrowful part of the situation is the deluded Hitlerian populace. Of course the Russians have kidnapped the able bodied and I suppose have made involuntary workmen of them. They have also looted every house left standing and have sent the loot to Russia. But Hitler did the same thing to them.

It is the Golden Rule in reverse – and it is not an uplifting sight. What a pity that the human animal is not able to put his moral thinking into practice!

We saw old men, old women, young women, children from tots to teens carrying packs[,] pushing carts, pulling carts, evidently ejected by the conquerors and carrying what they could of their belongings to nowhere in particular.

---

[4]   See Andrew J. Rotter, *Hiroshima: The World's Bomb* (Oxford: Oxford University Press, 2008); Michael J. Hogan (ed.), *Hiroshima in History and Memory* (New York: Cambridge University Press, 1996); Campbell Craig and Sergey S. Radchenko, *The Atomic Bomb and the Origins of the Cold War* (New Haven, CT: Yale University Press, 2008).

I thought of Carthage, Baalbec [Baalbek], Jerusalem, Rome, Atlanta, Peking, Babylon, Nineveh; – Scipio, Rameses II, Titus, Hermann, Sherman, Genghis Khan, Alexander, Darius the Great – but Hitler only destroyed Stalingrad – and Berlin. I hope for some sort of peace – but I fear that machines are ahead of mortals by some centuries and when mortals catch up perhaps there'll [be] a reckoning – who knows?

Berlin, July 17, 1945

Just spent a couple of hours with Stalin. Joseph Davies [former American ambassador to Russia] called on [Ivan] Maisky [Assistant Foreign Minister] and made the date last night for noon today. Promptly a few minutes before twelve I looked up from the desk and there stood Stalin in the doorway. I got to my feet and advanced to meet him. He put out his hand and smiled. I did the same [and] we shook. I greeted [Soviet Foreign Minister Vyacheslav] Molotov and the interpreter and we sat down. After the usual polite remarks we got down to business. I told Stalin that I am no diplomat but usually said yes or no to questions after hearing all the arguments. It pleased him. I asked him if he had the agenda for the meeting. He said he had and that he had some more questions to present. I told him to fire away. He did and it is dynamite – but I have some dynamite too which I am not exploding right now. He wants to fire Franco [Spain's dictator], to which I wouldn't object and divide up the Italian colonies and other mandates, some no doubt that the British have. Then he got on the Chinese situation [and] told us what agreements had been reached and what was in abeyance. Most of the big points are settled. He'll be in the Jap War on August 15th. Fini Japs when that comes about. We had lunch and talked socially[,] put on a real show drinking toasts to everyone[,] then had pictures made in the backyard. I can deal with Stalin. He is honest – but smart as hell.

Berlin, July 18, 1945

Went to lunch with P.M. [Prime Minister Winston Churchill] at 1:30 [and] walked around to British Headquarter. Met at the gate by Mr. Churchill. Guard of honor drawn up. Band played Star Spangled banner. Inspected Guard and went in for lunch. P.M. & I ate alone. Discussed Manhattan [atomic bomb] (it is a success). Decided to tell Stalin about it. Stalin had told P.M. of telegram from Jap Emperor [actually from the Foreign Secretary] asking for peace. Stalin also read his answer to me. It was satisfactory. Believe Japs will fold before Russia comes in.

I am sure they will when Manhattan appears over their homeland. I shall inform Stalin about it at opportune time. Stalin's luncheon was a most satisfactory meeting. I invited him to come to the US. Told him I'd send the Battleship *Missouri* for him if he'd come. He said he wanted to cooperate with the US as we had cooperated in war but it would be harder. Said he was grossly misunderstood in US and I was misunderstood in Russia. I told him that we each could help to remedy that situation in our home countries and that I intended to try with all I had to do my part at home. He gave me a most cordial smile and said he would do as much in Russia.

We then went to the conference and it was my job to present the Ministers proposed agenda. There were three proposals [on peace machinery, a Control Commission for Germany, and the Polish Question] and I banged them through in short order, much to the surprise of Mr. Churchill. Stalin was very much pleased. Churchill was too after he recovered. I'm not going to stay around this terrible place all summer just to listen to speeches. I'll go home to the Senate for that....

Berlin, July 25, 1945

We met at 11 A.M. today. That is Stalin, Churchill and the US president. But I had a most important session with Lord [Louis M.] Mountbatten and General [George C.] Marshall before that. We have discovered the most terrible bomb in the history of the world. It may be the fire destruction prophesied in the Euphrates Valley Era, after Noah and his fabulous Ark.

Anyway we think we have found the way to cause a disintegration of the atom. An experiment in the New Mexican desert was startling – to put it mildly. Thirteen pounds of the explosive caused the complete disintegration of a steel tower 60 feet high, created a crater 6 feet deep and 1200 feet in diameter, knocked over a steel tower ½ mile away and knocked down men 10,000 yards away. The explosion was visible for more than 200 miles and audible for 40 miles and more.

The weapon is to be used against Japan between now and August 10th. I have told the Sec. of War Mr. [Henry L.] Stimson to use it so that military objectives and soldiers and sailors are the target and not women and children. Even if the Japs are savages, ruthless, merciless and fanatic, we as the leader of the world for the common welfare cannot drop this terrible bomb on the old Capital [Kyoto] or the new [Tokyo].

He & I are in accord. The target will be a purely military one and we will issue a warning statement [the Potsdam Declaration] asking the Japs to surrender and save lives. I'm sure they will not do that, but we will have given them the chance. It is certainly a good thing for the world that Hitler's crowd or Stalin's did not discover this atomic bomb. It seems to be the most terrible thing ever discovered, but it can be made the most useful.

Source: Barton J Bernstein, "Truman at Potsdam: His Secret Diary," *Foreign Service Journal* July/Aug. 1980, pp. 30–6.

Suggested Questions for Discussion:

1.   How did Harry Truman view postwar Germany and Russia?
2.   How did Truman understand the power of the atomic bomb?
3.   How did Truman intend to use the atomic bomb?

5   The Atomic Mushroom Cloud Over Nagasaki, 1945

On August 9, 1945 the United States dropped the second atomic bomb, this time on the Japanese city of Nagasaki. The first bomb, dropped three days earlier on Hiroshima, marked the first use of atomic weapons in war. With the second bombing observers recognized that the awesome destruction of these warheads challenged traditional concepts of war. The United States possessed what some called an "absolute weapon" that could kill tens of thousands (later millions) from the air. The military and political uses of this capability remained uncertain and highly contested throughout the early Cold War. The mushroom cloud image of the Nagasaki bomb became an icon for the power, the destruction, and the danger of the atomic age.[5]

---

[5]   See Bernard Brodie (ed.), *The Absolute Weapon: Atomic Power and World Order* (New York: Harcourt Brace, 1946); Sean L. Malloy, *Atomic Tragedy: Henry L. Stimson and the Decision to Use the Bomb Against Japan* (Ithaca, NY: Cornell University Press, 2008); Campbell Craig and Sergey Radchenko, *The Atomic Bomb and the Origins of the Cold War* (New Haven, CT: Yale University Press, 2008).

Figure 4.1   The Atomic Mushroom Cloud over Nagasaki, 1945 © PA Photos/ AP Photo/USAF.

Source: US Department of Defense Photo, available at: http://media-2.web.britannica.com/eb-media/42/112542–004–59879F6D.jpg (accessed June 1, 2009).

Suggested Questions for Discussion:

1. Why did the mushroom cloud become a symbol of fear and danger?
2. What effect did it have that this image of the atomic bomb was separated from images of the destruction on the ground and the wider war?
3. How do you think this image influenced popular culture?

Chapter 5   The Early Cold War

1 George F. Kennan, "Long Telegram" on the Soviet Union, 1946

An obscure American foreign service officer stationed in Moscow at the time, in February 1946 George Kennan penned the most influential telegram of the post-1945 years. Kennan offered a simple and compelling explanation of Soviet behavior, rooted in a combination of traditional Russian expansionism and Marxist–Leninist fears of foreign capitalist adversaries. Kennan called for increased American attention to the Soviet threat, but he also counseled against an overreaction. Rejecting wistful hopes of peace and dire warnings of war, Kennan advocated a determined policy of American firmness that would force Soviet leaders to restrain themselves. The United States should use its strength to deter bad behavior. American military, economic, and political vigor would, according to Kennan, create an internal crisis within the Soviet Union, leading to the long-term disintegration of communism. These general propositions became the foundation for debates and applications of communist "containment" as the central strategic principle for American foreign policy in the Cold War.[1]

---

1 See John Lewis Gaddis, *Strategies of Containment: A Critical Appraisal of American National Security Policy during the Cold War*, rev. edn. (New York: Oxford University Press, 2005); Melvyn P. Leffler, *A Preponderance of Power: National Security, the Truman Administration, and the Cold War* (Stanford, CA: Stanford University Press, 1992); Wilson D. Miscamble, *George F. Kennan and the Making of American Foreign Policy, 1947–1950* (Princeton, NJ: Princeton University Press, 1992).

US Chargé d'Affaires in the Soviet Union (George Kennan) to the Secretary of State

SECRET

Moscow, February 22, 1946

... At bottom of Kremlin's neurotic view of world affairs is traditional and instinctive Russian sense of insecurity. Originally, this was insecurity of a peaceful agricultural people trying to live on vast exposed plain in neighborhood of fierce nomadic peoples. To this was added, as Russia came into contact with economically advanced West, fear of more competent, more powerful, more highly organized societies in that area. But this latter type of insecurity was one which afflicted rather Russian rulers than Russian people; for Russian rulers have invariably sensed that their rule was relatively archaic in form fragile and artificial in its psychological foundation, unable to stand comparison or contact with political systems of Western countries. For this reason they have always feared foreign penetration, feared direct contact between Western world and their own, feared what would happen if Russians learned truth about world without or if foreigners learned truth about world within. And they have learned to seek security only in patient but deadly struggle for total destruction of rival power, never in compacts and compromises with it.

It was no coincidence that Marxism, which had smoldered ineffectively for half a century in Western Europe, caught hold and blazed for first time in Russia. Only in this land which had never known a friendly neighbor or indeed any tolerant equilibrium of separate powers, either internal or international, could a doctrine thrive which viewed economic conflicts of society as insoluble by peaceful means. After establishment of Bolshevist regime, Marxist dogma, rendered even more truculent and intolerant by Lenin's interpretation, became a perfect vehicle for sense of insecurity with which Bolsheviks, even more than previous Russian rulers, were afflicted. In this dogma, with its basic altruism of purpose, they found justification for their instinctive fear of outside world, for the dictatorship without which they did not know how to rule, for cruelties they did not dare not to inflict, for sacrifice they felt bound to demand. In the name of Marxism they sacrificed every single ethical value in their methods and tactics. Today they cannot dispense with it. It is [a] fig leaf of their moral and intellectual respectability. Without it they would stand before history, at best, as only the last of that long succession of cruel and wasteful Russian rulers who have relentlessly forced [their] country on to ever new heights of military power in order to guarantee external security of their internally weak regimes. This is why Soviet purposes [will] most always be solemnly clothed in trappings of Marxism, and why no one should underrate importance of dogma in Soviet affairs. Thus Soviet leaders are driven [by] necessities of their own past and present position to put forward which [apparent omission] outside world as evil, hostile and menacing, but as bearing within itself germs of creeping disease and destined to be wracked with growing internal convulsions until it is given final Coup de grace by rising power of socialism and yields to new and better world. This thesis provides justification for that increase of military and police power of Russian state, for that isolation of Russian population from outside world, and for that fluid and constant pressure to extend limits of Russian police power which are together the natural and instinctive urges of Russian rulers. Basically this is only the steady advance of uneasy Russian nationalism, a centuries old movement in which conceptions of offense and defense are inextricably confused. But in new guise of international Marxism, with its honeyed promises to a desperate and war torn outside world, it is more dangerous and insidious than ever before.

It should not be thought from above that Soviet party line is necessarily disingenuous and insincere on [the] part of all those who put it forward. Many of them are too ignorant of outside world and mentally too dependent to question self-hypnotism, and who have no difficulty making themselves believe what they find it comforting and convenient to believe. Finally we have the unsolved mystery as to who, if anyone, in this great land actually receives accurate and unbiased information about outside world. In atmosphere of oriental secretiveness and conspiracy which pervades this Government, possibilities for distorting or poisoning sources and currents of information are infinite. The very disrespect of Russians for objective truth – indeed, their disbelief in its existence – leads them to view all stated facts as instruments for furtherance of one ulterior purpose or another. There is good reason to suspect that this Government is actually a conspiracy within a conspiracy; and I for one am reluctant to believe that Stalin himself receives anything like an objective picture of outside world. Here there is ample scope for the type of subtle intrigue at which Russians are past masters. Inability of foreign governments to place their case squarely before Russian policy makers – extent to which they are delivered up in their relations with Russia to good graces of obscure and unknown advisors whom they never see and cannot influence – this to my mind is [the] most disquieting feature of diplomacy in Moscow, and one which Western statesmen would do well to keep in mind if they would understand nature of difficulties encountered here....

In summary, we have here a political force committed fanatically to the belief that with US there can be no permanent *modus vivendi* that it is desirable and necessary that the internal harmony of our society be disrupted, our traditional way of life be destroyed, the international authority of our state be broken, if Soviet power is to be secure. This political force has complete power of disposition over energies of one of world's greatest peoples and resources of world's richest national territory, and is borne along by deep and powerful currents of Russian nationalism. In addition, it has an elaborate and far flung apparatus for exertion of its influence in other countries, an apparatus of amazing flexibility and versatility, managed by people whose experience and skill in underground methods are presumably without parallel in history. Finally, it is seemingly inaccessible to considerations of reality in its basic reactions. For it, the vast fund of objective fact about human society is not, as with us, the measure against which outlook is constantly being tested and re-formed, but a grab bag from which individual items are selected arbitrarily and tendenciously to bolster an outlook already preconceived. This is admittedly not a pleasant picture. Problem of how to cope with this force in [is] undoubtedly greatest task our diplomacy has ever faced and probably greatest it will ever have to face. It should be point of departure from which our political general staff work at present juncture should proceed. It should be approached with same thoroughness and care as solution of major strategic problem in war, and if necessary, with no smaller outlay in planning effort. I cannot attempt to suggest all answers here. But I would like to record my conviction that problem is within our power to solve – and that without recourse to any general military conflict. And in support of this conviction there are certain observations of a more encouraging nature I should like to make:

(1) Soviet power, unlike that of Hitlerite Germany, is neither schematic nor adventuristic. It does not work by fixed plans. It does not take unnecessary risks. Impervious to logic of reason, and it is highly sensitive to logic of force. For this reason it can easily withdraw – and usually does when strong resistance is encountered at any point. Thus, if the adversary has sufficient force and makes clear his readiness to use it, he rarely has to do so. If situations are properly handled there need be no prestige-engaging showdowns.

(2) Gauged against Western World as a whole, Soviets are still by far the weaker force. Thus, their success will really depend on degree of cohesion, firmness and vigor which Western World can muster. And this is factor which it is within our power to influence.

(3) Success of Soviet system, as form of internal power, is not yet finally proven. It has yet to be demonstrated that it can survive supreme test of

successive transfer of power from one individual or group to another. Lenin's death was first such transfer, and its effects wracked Soviet state for 15 years. After Stalin's death or retirement will be second. But even this will not be final test. Soviet internal system will now be subjected, by virtue of recent territorial expansions, to series of additional strains which once proved severe tax on Tsardom. We here are convinced that never since termination of civil war have mass of Russian people been emotionally farther removed from doctrines of Communist Party than they are today. In Russia, party has now become a great and – for the moment – highly successful apparatus of dictatorial administration, but it has ceased to be a source of emotional inspiration. Thus, internal soundness and permanence of movement need not yet be regarded as assured.

(4) All Soviet propaganda beyond Soviet security sphere is basically negative and destructive. It should therefore be relatively easy to combat it by any intelligent and really constructive program.

For those reasons I think we may approach calmly and with good heart problem of how to deal with Russia. As to how this approach should be made, I only wish to advance, by way of conclusion, following comments:

(1) Our first step must be to apprehend, and recognize for what it is, the nature of the movement with which we are dealing. We must study it with same courage, detachment, objectivity, and same determination not to be emotionally provoked or unseated by it, with which doctor studies unruly and unreasonable individual.

(2) We must see that our public is educated to realities of Russian situation. I cannot over-emphasize importance of this. Press cannot do this alone. It must be done mainly by Government, which is necessarily more experienced and better informed on practical problems involved. In this we need not be deterred by [ugliness] of picture. I am convinced that there would be far less hysterical anti-Sovietism in our country today if realities of this situation were better understood by our people. There is nothing as dangerous or as terrifying as the unknown. It may also be argued that to reveal more information on our difficulties with Russia would reflect unfavorably on Russian–American relations. I feel that if there is any real risk here involved, it is one which we should have courage to face, and sooner the better. But I cannot see what we would be risking. Our stake in this country, even coming on heels of tremendous demonstrations of our friendship for Russian people, is remarkably small. We have here no investments to guard, no actual trade to lose, virtually no citizens to protect, few cultural contacts to preserve. Our only stake lies in what we hope rather than what

we have; and I am convinced we have better chance of realizing those hopes if our public is enlightened and if our dealings with Russians are placed entirely on realistic and matter-of-fact basis.

(3) Much depends on health and vigor of our own society. World communism is like malignant parasite which feeds only on diseased tissue. This is point at which domestic and foreign policies meets Every courageous and incisive measure to solve internal problems of our own society, to improve self-confidence, discipline, morale and community spirit of our own people, is a diplomatic victory over Moscow worth a thousand diplomatic notes and joint communiqués. If we cannot abandon fatalism and indifference in face of deficiencies of our own society, Moscow will profit – Moscow cannot help profiting by them in its foreign policies.

(4) We must formulate and put forward for other nations a much more positive and constructive picture of sort of world we would like to see than we have put forward in past. It is not enough to urge people to develop political processes similar to our own. Many foreign peoples, in Europe at least, are tired and frightened by experiences of past, and are less interested in abstract freedom than in security. They are seeking guidance rather than responsibilities. We should be better able than Russians to give them this. And unless we do, Russians certainly will.

(5) Finally we must have courage and self-confidence to cling to our own methods and conceptions of human society. After all, the greatest danger that can befall us in coping with this problem of Soviet communism, is that we shall allow ourselves to become like those with whom we are coping.

Source: http://www.gwu.edu/~nsarchiv/coldwar/documents/episode-1/kennan.htm (accessed August 20, 2008).

Suggested Questions for Discussion:

1.   How did George Kennan describe the sources and goals of Soviet foreign policy?
2.   How did Kennan advise American leaders to respond?
3.   Why did Kennan's advice become so influential in postwar America?

2   The Truman Doctrine, 1947

Civil war in Greece and instability in Turkey contributed to postwar fears of Soviet expansionism close to the Mediterranean Sea and the Middle East. Great Britain had formerly exerted strong anti-communist influence in these regions, but it no longer had the resources to maintain these commitments. In

*a powerful address to Congress in March 1947, President Harry Truman
called upon the United States to assert itself more forcefully in Greece and
Turkey, sending extensive aid to groups resisting the Soviet Union. In his
description of growing communist threats and his commitment of American
resources to "support free peoples," the President articulated what became
known as the "Truman Doctrine" – a broad American inclination to intervene
on the side of anti-communist groups around the world.*[2]

---

*President Harry S. Truman's address before a joint session
of Congress, March 12, 1947*

... I am fully aware of the broad implications involved if the United States
extends assistance to Greece and Turkey, and I shall discuss these implications with you at this time.

One of the primary objectives of the foreign policy of the United States is
the creation of conditions in which we and other nations will be able to work
out a way of life free from coercion. This was a fundamental issue in the war
with Germany and Japan. Our victory was won over countries which sought
to impose their will, and their way of life, upon other nations. ...

At the present moment in world history nearly every nation must choose
between alternative ways of life. The choice is too often not a free one.

One way of life is based upon the will of the majority, and is distinguished
by free institutions, representative government, free elections, guarantees of
individual liberty, freedom of speech and religion, and freedom from political oppression.

The second way of life is based upon the will of a minority forcibly imposed
upon the majority. It relies upon terror and oppression, a controlled press and
radio, fixed elections, and the suppression of personal freedoms.

I believe that it must be the policy of the United States to support free
peoples who are resisting attempted subjugation by armed minorities or by
outside pressures.

I believe that we must assist free peoples to work out their own destinies
in their own way.

---

[2] See Bruce Kuniholm, *The Origins of the Cold War in the Near East: Great Power Conflict
and Diplomacy in Iran, Turkey, and Greece* (Princeton, NJ: Princeton University Press, 1980);
John Lewis Gaddis, *Strategies of Containment: A Critical Appraisal of American National
Security Policy during the Cold War*, new edn. (New York: Oxford University Press, 2005);
Melvyn P. Leffler, *A Preponderance of Power: National Security, the Truman Administration,
and the Cold War* (Stanford, CA: Stanford University Press, 1992); Arnold Offner, *Another
Such Victory: President Truman and the Cold War, 1945–1953* (Stanford, CA: Stanford
University Press, 2002).

I believe that our help should be primarily through economic and financial aid which is essential to economic stability and orderly political processes.

The world is not static, and the status quo is not sacred. But we cannot allow changes in the status quo in violation of the Charter of the United Nations by such methods as coercion, or by such subterfuges as political infiltration. In helping free and independent nations to maintain their freedom, the United States will be giving effect to the principles of the Charter of the United Nations.

It is necessary only to glance at a map to realize that the survival and integrity of the Greek nation are of grave importance in a much wider situation. If Greece should fall under the control of an armed minority, the effect upon its neighbor, Turkey, would be immediate and serious. Confusion and disorder might well spread throughout the entire Middle East.

Moreover, the disappearance of Greece as an independent state would have a profound effect upon those countries in Europe whose peoples are struggling against great difficulties to maintain their freedoms and their independence while they repair the damages of war.

It would be an unspeakable tragedy if these countries, which have struggled so long against overwhelming odds, should lose that victory for which they sacrificed so much. Collapse of free institutions and loss of independence would be disastrous not only for them but for the world. Discouragement and possibly failure would quickly be the lot of neighboring peoples striving to maintain their freedom and independence.

Should we fail to aid Greece and Turkey in this fateful hour, the effect will be far reaching to the West as well as to the East.

We must take immediate and resolute action.

I therefore ask the Congress to provide authority for assistance to Greece and Turkey in the amount of $400,000,000 for the period ending June 30, 1948. In requesting these funds, I have taken into consideration the maximum amount of relief assistance which would be furnished to Greece out of the $350,000,000 which I recently requested that the Congress authorize for the prevention of starvation and suffering in countries devastated by the war.

In addition to funds, I ask the Congress to authorize the detail of American civilian and military personnel to Greece and Turkey, at the request of those countries, to assist in the tasks of reconstruction, and for the purpose of supervising the use of such financial and material assistance as may be furnished. I recommend that authority also be provided for the instruction and training of selected Greek and Turkish personnel.

Finally, I ask that the Congress provide authority which will permit the speediest and most effective use, in terms of needed commodities, supplies, and equipment, of such funds as may be authorized.

If further funds, or further authority, should be needed for purposes indicated in this message, I shall not hesitate to bring the situation before the Congress. On this subject the Executive and Legislative branches of the Government must work together.

Source: *Public Papers of President Harry S. Truman*, 1947 (Washington, DC: US Government Printing Office, 1963), pp. 176–80.

Suggested Questions for Discussion:

1. How did Harry Truman define the threat of communism?
2. What kind of American response did Truman advocate?
3. How did the Truman Doctrine differ from the advice in Kennan's Long Telegram?

3 Assistant Secretary of State, Dean Rusk, the "Loss" of China, 1950

By October 1949 the Chinese Communist Party, led by Mao Zedong, had taken control of mainland China. For many observers, this ominous development signaled a grave threat. Communism appeared to be the wave of the future, at least in Asia. Communist regimes now controlled the two largest Eurasian countries. In addition, the Soviet Union had detonated its first atomic bomb, and it appeared poised to challenge American military capabilities in Germany, Japan, and other key strategic areas. The United States had refrained from any direct intervention against the Chinese Communist Revolution in the late 1940s, and it also withdrew its forces from the Korean peninsula. In May 1950, then Assistant Secretary of State, Dean Rusk, echoed widespread concerns about perceived American weakness and communist advances. In anticipation of what later became known as the "domino theory," Rusk argued that the United States had to take a strong stand in Formosa (Taiwan) to show communist and non-communist observers that Washington would not allow Soviet-sponsored expansion to continue. Less than one month after Rusk wrote his memo, the North Korean invasion of South Korea forced the United States to react to the very threats that the Assistant Secretary had described.[3]

---

[3]   See Robert L. Beisner, *Dean Acheson: A Life in the Cold War* (New York: Oxford University Press, 2006); Chen Jian, *Mao's China and the Cold War* (Chapel Hill, NC: University of North Carolina Press, 2000); Warren I. Cohen, *America's Response to China*, 4th edn. (New York: Columbia University Press, 2000).

Draft memorandum by the Assistant Secretary of State for Far Eastern Affairs Dean Rusk to the Secretary of State Dean Acheson

Top Secret

May 30, 1950

The United States faces a new and critical period in its world position.

The loss of China to Communists who, it now seems, will work in Asia as junior partners of Soviet Communism has had tremendous repercussions throughout the world. It has marked a shift in the balance of power in favor of Soviet Russia and to the disfavor of the United States.

While that *basic fact* is generally accepted, no one is yet quite sure as to the *precise extent* to which that power relationship has been shifted. Throughout the world, in Europe, the Mediterranean, the Middle East, Asia and the Pacific, governments and peoples are intently watching for the next move which will provide a measure of the extent of the power shift, so that they can orient their own policies accordingly.

The barometer most closely watched is that which seems to measure the judgment of the United States itself as to its present power and position in the world. If our conduct indicates a continuing disposition to fall back and allow doubtful areas to fall under Soviet Communist control, then many nations will feel confirmed in the impression already drawn from the North Atlantic Treaty, that we do not expect to stand firm short of the North Atlantic area – which under the Treaty includes Berlin – and the Americas covered traditionally by the Monroe Doctrine and now by the Rio Pact.

If our conduct seems to confirm that conclusion, then we can expect an accelerated deterioration of our influence in the Mediterranean, Near East, Asia and the Pacific. The situation in Japan may become untenable and possibly that in the Philippines. Indonesia, with its vast natural resources may be lost and the oil of the Middle East will be in jeopardy. None of these places provide good "holding" grounds once the people feel that Communism is the wave of the future and that even we are retreating before it.

This series of disasters can probably be prevented if at some doubtful point we quickly take a dramatic and strong stand that shows our confidence and resolution. Probably this series of disasters cannot be prevented in any other way.

Of the doubtful areas where such a stand might be taken, Formosa has advantages superior to any other. It is not subject to the immediate influence of Soviet land power. It is close to our naval and air power. It is occupied by the remnants of the non-Communists who have traditionally been our friends and allies. Its status internationally is undetermined by any international act and we have at least some moral responsibility for the native inhabitants. It is gravely menaced by a joint Chinese–Russian expedition in formation. The eyes of the world are focused upon it.

If the United States were to announce that it would neutralize Formosa, not permitting it either to be taken by Communists or to be used as a base of military operations against the mainland, that is a decision which we could certainly maintain, short of open war by the Soviet Union. Everyone knows that this is the case. If we do not act, it will be everywhere interpreted that we are making another retreat because we do not dare risk war. If it is inferred that we do not dare take a stand that risks war unless our own citadel of the North Atlantic and American areas is directly attacked, then the disasters referred to above will almost surely happen.

We are not so situated that time is working for us so that it can be argued that we have to buy time. The further losses possible in Indonesia and the Near East would greatly increase the war-making power of the Soviet Union. Quite apart from that, the Soviet Union is increasing its force-in-being, its atomic stockpile and its basic military potential at a rate so rapid that the relative position will be worse two years from now than it is today. That would be so, even though we [have] somewhat increased our own efforts. That also is something that is generally known. In consequence, if the rest of the world feels that we are today afraid to take a stand which would involve a possible risk of war then they would judge that almost certainly we will not take that risk tomorrow unless it is forced upon us by actual attack upon either the North Atlantic or American area.

Admittedly the determination to withhold Formosa from Communists would involve complications with the Nationalist Government and with their elements on Formosa. It would involve spreading of our own military force, and possibly some actual losses. However, these aspects are of a secondary order. It is within our power to solve the political complications if we have the resolute will. Also, these same problems will embarrass us if we allow Formosa to fall. The efforts at evacuation, particularly attempts to evacuate to the Philippines large numbers of Nationalists, will pose new problems and difficulties perhaps as embarrassing as those that would be posed by an affirmative policy. It will not leave a good taste if we allow our political problems to be solved by the extermination of our war allies ...

Admittedly, a strong stand at Formosa would involve a slightly increased risk of early war. But sometimes such a risk has to be taken in order to preserve peace in the world and to keep the national prestige required if we are to play our indispensable part in sustaining a free world.

Action to be effective must be prompt.

Source: *Documents Relating to the Foreign Relations of the United States, 1950,* vol. VI, "The China Area" (Washington, DC: US Government Printing Office), pp. 349–51.

Suggested Questions for Discussion:

1. Why did Dean Rusk believe that the communist threat was growing?
2. Why did Rusk worry about perceptions of American weakness?
3. What policies did Rusk advocate?

4 Senator Joseph McCarthy, Speech in Wheeling, West Virginia, 1950

The Soviet detonation of an atomic bomb and the successful Chinese Communist Revolution led many Americans to question why their leaders had not responded more effectively. Senator Joseph McCarthy exploited the fears and uncertainties of the moment. He wildly claimed that communists had infiltrated all of the elite institutions in American society – including nuclear laboratories, the State Department, universities, and Hollywood studios – to undermine American democracy from within. A populist from Wisconsin, McCarthy targeted the privileged and those who did not appear fully "American" – especially political radicals, Jews, and recent immigrants. The hysteria created by McCarthy's demagogic behavior destroyed thousands of careers and damaged American standing around the world. The Soviet Union had, in fact, infiltrated spies into the United States (especially the Manhattan Project), but McCarthy never targeted the actual spies. His actions diverted attention from the real threats and discredited legitimate anti-communism in the eyes of many observers.[4]

Six years ago, at the time of the first conference to map out the peace – Dumbarton Oaks – there was within the Soviet orbit 180,000,000 people. Lined up on the antitotalitarian side there were in the world at that time roughly 1,625,000,000 people. Today, only six years later, there are 800,000,000 people under the absolute domination of Soviet Russia – an increase of over 400 percent. On our side, the figure has shrunk to around

[4] See David M. Oshinsky, *A Conspiracy So Immense: The World of Joe McCarthy*, new edn. (New York: Oxford University Press, 2005); Richard M. Fried, *Nightmare in Red: The McCarthy Era in Perspective* (New York: Oxford University Press, 1990); Ellen Schrecker, *Many Are the Crimes: McCarthyism in America* (New York: Little Brown, 1998).

500,000,000. In other words, in less than six years the odds have changed from nine to one in our favor to eight to five against us. This indicates the swiftness of the tempo of Communist victories and American defeats in the cold war. As one of our outstanding historical figures once said: "When a great democracy is destroyed, it will not be because of enemies from without, but rather because of enemies from within."

The truth of this statement is becoming terrifyingly clear as we see this country each day losing on every front.

At war's end we were physically the strongest nation on earth and, at least potentially, the most powerful intellectually and morally. Ours could have been the honor of being a beacon in the desert of destruction, a shining living proof that civilization was not yet ready to destroy itself. Unfortunately, we have failed miserably and tragically to arise to the opportunity.

The reason why we find ourselves in a position of impotency is not because our only powerful potential enemy has sent men to invade our shores, but rather because of the traitorous actions of those who have been treated so well by this Nation. It has not been the less fortunate or members of minority groups who have been selling this Nation out, but rather those who have had all the benefits that the wealthiest nation on earth has had to offer – the finest homes, the finest college education, and the finest jobs in government we can give.

This is glaringly true in the State Department. There the bright young who are born with silver spoons in their mouths are the ones who have the worst. . . .

I have in my hand fifty-seven cases of individuals who would appear to be either card carrying members or certainly loyal to the Communist Party, but who nevertheless are still helping to shape our foreign policy.

One thing to remember in discussing the Communists in our Government is that we are not dealing with spies who get thirty pieces of silver to steal the blueprints of a new weapon. We are dealing with a far more sinister type of activity because it permits the enemy to guide and shape our policy.

Source: Ellen Schrecker, *Age of McCarthyism* (Boston, MA: Bedford, 1994), pp. 211–14.

Suggested Questions for Discussion:

1. How did Joseph McCarthy define the enemy?
2. Who did McCarthy blame?
3. Why were McCarthy's words so persuasive to audiences at the time?

5 NSC 68, 1950

Shaken by the Soviet atomic bomb test, the Chinese Communist Revolution, and domestic anti-communist recriminations, in early 1950 the State Department Policy Planning Staff wrote a new top secret national strategy document for the United States. Labeled NSC 68, this document sought to revise George Kennan's policy guidance and the Truman Doctrine for new threats. NSC 68 called for a more aggressive American foreign policy, including more spending and more deployments of force across the globe to counteract communist advances. President Truman was initially skeptical about the expansive agenda outlined in NSC 68, especially the calls for increased government spending on military forces and foreign aid. NSC 68 did not drive American policy in mid-1950, but it gained influence over policy in the aftermath of the North Korean invasion of South Korea.[5]

United States Objectives and Programs for National Security (April 14, 1950)

A Report to the President

Pursuant to the President's Directive of January 31, 1950

TOP SECRET

... It is quite clear from Soviet theory and practice that the Kremlin seeks to bring the free world under its dominion by the methods of the cold war. The preferred technique is to subvert by infiltration and intimidation. Every institution of our society is an instrument which it is sought to stultify and turn against our purposes. Those that touch most closely our material and moral strength are obviously the prime targets, labor unions, civic enterprises, schools, churches, and all media for influencing opinion. The effort is not so much to make them serve obvious Soviet ends as to prevent them from serving our ends, and thus to make them sources of confusion in our economy, our culture, and our body politic. The doubts and diversities that in terms of our values are part of the merit of a free system, the weaknesses

---

[5]   John Lewis Gaddis, *Strategies of Containment: A Critical Appraisal of American National Security Policy during the Cold War*, new edn. (New York: Oxford University Press, 2005); Melvyn P. Leffler, *A Preponderance of Power: National Security, the Truman Administration, and the Cold War* (Stanford, CA: Stanford University Press, 1992); William Stueck, *The Korean War: An International History* (Princeton, NJ: Princeton University Press, 1995).

and the problems that are peculiar to it, the rights and privileges that free men enjoy, and the disorganization and destruction left in the wake of the last attack on our freedoms, all are but opportunities for the Kremlin to do its evil work. Every advantage is taken of the fact that our means of prevention and retaliation are limited by those principles and scruples which are precisely the ones that give our freedom and democracy its meaning for us. None of our scruples deter those whose only code is "morality is that which serves the revolution."

Since everything that gives us or others respect for our institutions is a suitable object for attack, it also fits the Kremlin's design that where, with impunity, we can be insulted and made to suffer indignity the opportunity shall not be missed, particularly in any context which can be used to cast dishonor on our country, our system, our motives, or our methods. Thus the means by which we sought to restore our own economic health in the 30's, and now seek to restore that of the free world, come equally under attack. The military aid by which we sought to help the free world was frantically denounced by the Communists in the early days of the last war, and of course our present efforts to develop adequate military strength for ourselves and our allies are equally denounced.

At the same time the Soviet Union is seeking to create overwhelming military force, in order to back up infiltration with intimidation. In the only terms in which it understands strength, it is seeking to demonstrate to the free world that force and the will to use it are on the side of the Kremlin, that those who lack it are decadent and doomed. In local incidents it threatens and encroaches both for the sake of local gains and to increase anxiety and defeatism in all the free world.

The possession of atomic weapons at each of the opposite poles of power, and the inability (for different reasons) of either side to place any trust in the other, puts a premium on a surprise attack against us. It equally puts a premium on a more violent and ruthless prosecution of its design by cold war, especially if the Kremlin is sufficiently objective to realize the improbability of our prosecuting a preventive war. It also puts a premium on piecemeal aggression against others, counting on our unwillingness to engage in atomic war unless we are directly attacked. We run all these risks and the added risk of being confused and immobilized by our inability to weigh and choose, and pursue a firm course based on a rational assessment of each.

The risk that we may thereby be prevented or too long delayed in taking all needful measures to maintain the integrity and vitality of our system is great. The risk that our allies will lose their determination is greater. And the risk that in this manner a descending spiral of too little and too late, of doubt and recrimination, may present us with ever narrower and more desperate alternatives, is the greatest risk of all. For example, it is clear that our present weakness would prevent us from offering effective resistance at any of several vital pressure points. The only deterrent we can present to the Kremlin is the evidence we give that we may make any of the critical points which we cannot hold the occasion for a global war of annihilation.

The risk of having no better choice than to capitulate or precipitate a global war at any of a number of pressure points is bad enough in itself, but it is multiplied by the weakness it imparts to our position in the cold war. Instead of appearing strong and resolute we are continually at the verge of appearing and being alternately irresolute and desperate; yet it is the cold war which we must win, because both the Kremlin design, and our fundamental purpose give it the first priority. . . .

But there are risks in making ourselves strong. A large measure of sacrifice and discipline will be demanded of the American people. They will be asked to give up some of the benefits which they have come to associate with their freedoms. Nothing could be more important than that they fully understand the reasons for this. The risks of a superficial understanding or of an inadequate appreciation of the issues are obvious and might lead to the adoption of measures which in themselves would jeopardize the integrity of our system. At any point in the process of demonstrating our will to make good our fundamental purpose, the Kremlin may decide to precipitate a general war, or in testing us, may go too far. These are risks we will invite by making ourselves strong, but they are lesser risks than those we seek to avoid. Our fundamental purpose is more likely to be defeated from lack of the will to maintain it, than from any mistakes we may make or assault we may undergo because of asserting that will. No people in history have preserved their freedom who thought that by not being strong enough to protect themselves they might prove inoffensive to their enemies. . . .

A more rapid build-up of political, economic, and military strength and thereby of confidence in the free world than is now contemplated is the only course which is consistent with progress toward achieving our fundamental purpose. The frustration of the Kremlin design requires the free world to develop a successfully functioning political and economic system and a vigorous political offensive against the Soviet Union. These, in turn, require an adequate military shield under which they can develop. It is necessary to have the military power to deter, if possible, Soviet expansion, and to defeat, if necessary, aggressive Soviet or Soviet-directed actions of a limited or total character. The potential strength of the free world is great; its ability to develop these military capabilities and its will to resist Soviet expansion will be determined by the wisdom and will with which it undertakes to meet its political and economic problems.

1.   Military aspects. It has been indicated … that US military capabilities are strategically more defensive in nature than offensive and are more potential than actual. It is evident, from an analysis of the past and of the trend of weapon development, that there is now and will be in the future no absolute defense. The history of war also indicates that a favorable decision can only be achieved through offensive action. Even a defensive strategy, if it is to be successful, calls not only for defensive forces to hold vital positions while mobilizing and preparing for the offensive, but also for offensive forces to attack the enemy and keep him off balance.

The two fundamental requirements which must be met by forces in being or readily available are support of foreign policy and protection against disaster. To meet the second requirement, the forces in being or readily available must be able, at a minimum, to perform certain basic tasks:

a.   To defend the Western Hemisphere and essential allied areas in order that their war-making capabilities can be developed;
b.   To provide and protect a mobilization base while the offensive forces required for victory are being built up;
c.   To conduct offensive operations to destroy vital elements of the Soviet war-making capacity, and to keep the enemy off balance until the full offensive strength of the United States and its allies can be brought to bear;
d.   To defend and maintain the lines of communication and base areas necessary to the execution of the above tasks; and
e.   To provide such aid to allies as is essential to the execution of their role in the above tasks.

In the broadest terms, the ability to perform these tasks requires a build-up of military strength by the United States and its allies to a point at which the combined strength will be superior for at least these tasks, both initially and throughout a war, to the forces that can be brought to bear by the Soviet Union and its satellites. In specific terms, it is not essential to match item for item with the Soviet Union, but to provide an adequate defense against air attack on the United States and Canada and an adequate defense against air and surface attack on the United Kingdom and Western Europe, Alaska, the Western Pacific, Africa, and the Near and Middle East, and on the long lines of communication to these areas. Furthermore, it is mandatory that in building up our strength, we enlarge upon our technical superiority by an accelerated exploitation of the scientific potential of the United States and our allies.

Forces of this size and character are necessary not only for protection against disaster but also to support our foreign policy. In fact, it can be argued that larger forces in being and readily available are necessary to inhibit a would-be aggressor than to provide the nucleus of strength and the mobilization base on which the tremendous forces required for victory can be built. For example, in both World Wars I and II the ultimate victors had the strength, in the end, to win though they had not had the strength in being or readily available to prevent the outbreak of war. In part, at least, this was because they had not had the military strength on which to base a strong foreign policy. At any rate, it is clear that a substantial and rapid building up of strength in the free world is necessary to support a firm policy intended to check and to roll back the Kremlin's drive for world domination.

Moreover, the United States and the other free countries do not now have the forces in being and readily available to defeat local Soviet moves with local action, but must accept reverses or make these local moves the occasion for war – for which we are not prepared. This situation makes for great uneasiness among our allies, particularly in Western Europe, for whom total war means, initially, Soviet occupation. Thus, unless our combined strength is rapidly increased, our allies will tend to become increasingly reluctant to support a firm foreign policy on our part and increasingly anxious to seek other solutions, even though they are aware that appeasement means defeat. An important advantage in adopting the fourth course of action lies in its psychological impact – the revival of confidence and hope in the future. It is recognized, of course, that any announcement of the recommended course of action could be exploited by the Soviet Union in its peace campaign and would have adverse psychological effects in certain parts of the free world until the necessary increase in strength has been achieved. Therefore, in any announcement of policy and in the character of the measures adopted, emphasis should be given to the essentially defensive character and care should be taken to minimize, so far as possible, unfavorable domestic and foreign reactions.

2.   Political and economic aspects. The immediate objectives – to the achievement of which such a build-up of strength is a necessary though not a sufficient condition – are a renewed initiative in the cold war and a situation to which the Kremlin would find it expedient to accommodate itself, first by relaxing tensions and pressures and then by gradual withdrawal. The United States cannot alone provide the resources required for such a build-up of strength. The other free countries must carry their part of the burden, but their ability and determination to do it will depend on the action the United States takes to develop its own strength and on the adequacy of its foreign political and economic policies. Improvement in political and economic conditions in the free world, as has been emphasized above, is necessary as a basis for building up the will and the means to resist and for dynamically affirming the integrity and vitality of our free and democratic way of life on which our ultimate victory depends.

At the same time, we should take dynamic steps to reduce the power and influence of the Kremlin inside the Soviet Union and other areas under its control. The objective would be the establishment of friendly regimes not under Kremlin domination. Such action is essential to engage the Kremlin's attention, keep it off balance, and force an increased expenditure of Soviet resources in counteraction. In other words, it would be the current Soviet cold war technique used against the Soviet Union.

A program for rapidly building up strength and improving political and economic conditions will place heavy demands on our courage and intelligence; it will be costly; it will be dangerous. But half-measures will be more costly and more dangerous, for they will be inadequate to prevent and may actually invite war. Budgetary considerations will need to be subordinated to the stark fact that our very independence as a nation may be at stake.

Source: From http://www.mtholyoke.edu/acad/intrel/nsc-68/nsc68-1.htm (accessed August 20, 2008).

Suggested Questions for Discussion:

1. How did NSC 68 define the threat to the United States?
2. How did NSC 68 seek to transform American foreign policy?
3. How did NSC 68 differ from the Truman Doctrine and Kennan's Long Telegram?

6 President Dwight Eisenhower, the "Falling Domino" Theory in Indochina, 1954

In 1954, as the French military forces in Indochina were facing defeat at the hands of the Vietminh anti-colonial army, President Dwight Eisenhower contemplated an increased American commitment to the region. Eisenhower rejected French calls for direct American military intervention, but he sought to increase US aid to anti-communist forces. Questioned by news reporters about the importance of Indochina, Eisenhower articulated what became known as the "domino theory:" the fall of Indochina to communists would undermine surrounding countries, including Japan, according to Eisenhower.[6]

---

[6]   David L. Anderson, *Trapped By Success: The Eisenhower Administration and Vietnam, 1953–1961* (New York: Columbia University Press, 1991); Richard H. Immerman and Robert R. Bowie, *Waging Peace: How Eisenhower Shaped Enduring Cold War Strategy* (New York: Oxford University Press, 2000); Andrew J. Rotter, *The Path to Vietnam: Origins of the American Commitment to Southeast Asia* (Ithaca, NY: Cornell University Press, 1988).

The President's News Conference of April 7, 1954

Question from Robert Richards, Copley Press:

Mr. President, would you mind commenting on the strategic importance of Indochina to the free world? I think there has been, across the country, some lack of understanding on just what it means to us.

The President's Response:

You have, of course, both the specific and the general when you talk about such things.

First of all, you have the specific value of a locality in its production of materials that the world needs.

Then you have the possibility that many human beings pass under a dictatorship that is inimical to the free world.

Finally, you have broader considerations that might follow what you would call the "falling domino" principle. You have a row of dominoes set up, you knock over the first one, and what will happen to the last one is the certainty that it will go over very quickly. So you could have a beginning of a disintegration that would have the most profound influences.

Now, with respect to the first one, two of the items from this particular area that the world uses are tin and tungsten. They are very important. There are others, of course, the rubber plantations and so on.

Then with respect to more people passing under this domination, Asia, after all, has already lost some 450 million of its peoples to the Communist dictatorship, and we simply can't afford greater losses.

But when we come to the possible sequence of events, the loss of Indochina, of Burma, of Thailand, of the Peninsula, and Indonesia following, now you begin to talk about areas that not only multiply the disadvantages that you would suffer through loss of materials, sources of materials, but now you are talking really about millions and millions and millions of people.

Finally, the geographical position achieved thereby does many things. It turns the so-called island defensive chain of Japan, Formosa, of the Philippines and to the southward; it moves in to threaten Australia and New Zealand.

It takes away, in its economic aspects, that region that Japan must have as a trading area or Japan, in turn, will have only one place in the world to go – that is, toward the Communist areas in order to live.

So, the possible consequences of the loss are just incalculable to the free world.

Source: *Public Papers of the President Dwight D. Eisenhower, 1954* (Washington, DC: US Government Printing Office), pp. 381–90.

Suggested Questions for Discussion:

1. What were the American interests in Indochina, according to Eisenhower?
2. How would communist control of Indochina undermine surrounding countries, according to Eisenhower?
3. Why was the logic of the "domino theory" so compelling for policy-makers and citizens?

Chapter 6   Rebellions Against the Cold War

1 Martin Luther King, Jr., "The Rising Tide of Racial Consciousness," 1960

The American Civil Rights Movement was part of a broader global movement for racial equality and self-determination. As citizens of Africa asserted control of their own destinies in formerly colonized lands, African-Americans claimed full citizenship in the United States. The two movements drew inspiration from one another. They contributed to a perception, held by a growing number of diverse observers, that change was now inevitable. Martin Luther King, Jr., one of the most compelling American Civil Rights leaders, highlighted the global dimensions of his struggle, and he drew actively on tactics, ideas, and pressures emanating from Africa, India, and other distant lands. By the early 1960s civil rights were a key Cold War issue.[1]

This is an abridged version of a speech that Dr King gave at a Conference of the National Urban League.

[1]   See Mary L. Dudziak, *Cold War Civil Rights: Race and the Image of American Democracy* (Princeton, NJ: Princeton University Press, 2000); Thomas Borstelmann, *The Cold War and the Color Line: American Race Relations in the Global Arena* (Cambridge, MA: Harvard University Press, 2001); Penny Von Eschen, *Satchmo Blows Up the World: Jazz Ambassadors Play the Cold War* (Cambridge, MA: 2004); Brenda Gayle Plummer (ed.), *Window on Freedom: Race, Civil Rights, and Foreign Affairs, 1945–1988* (Chapel Hill, NC: University of North Carolina Press, 2007).

What are the factors that have led to this new sense of dignity and self-respect on the part of the Negro? First, we must mention the population shift from rural to urban life. For many years the vast majority of Negroes were isolated on the rural plantation. They had very little contact with the world outside their geographical boundaries. But gradually circumstances made it possible and necessary for them to migrate to new and larger centers – the spread of the automobile, the Great Depression, and the social upheavals of the two world wars. These new contacts led to a broadened outlook. These new levels of communication brought new and different attitudes.

A second factor that has caused the Negroes' new self-consciousness has been rapid educational advance. Over the years there has been a steady decline of crippling illiteracy. At emancipation only five percent of the Negroes were literate; today more than ninety-five percent are literate. Constant streams of Negro students are finishing colleges and universities every year. More than sixteen hundred Negroes have received the highest academic degree bestowed by an American university. These educational advances have naturally broadened his thinking. They have given the Negro not only a larger view of the world, but also a larger view of himself.

A third factor that produced the new sense of pride in the Negro was the gradual improvement of his economic status. While the Negro is still the victim of tragic economic exploitation, significant strides have been made. The annual collective income of the Negro is now approximately eighteen billion dollars, which is more than the national income of Canada and all of the exports of the United States. This augmented purchasing power has been reflected in more adequate housing, improved medical care, and greater educational opportunities. As these changes have taken place they have driven the Negro to change his image of himself.

A fourth factor that brought about the new sense of pride in the Negro was the Supreme Court's decision outlawing segregation in the public schools. For all men of good will May 17, 1954, came as a joyous daybreak to end the long night of enforced segregation. In simple, eloquent, and unequivocal language the court affirmed that "separate but equal" facilities are inherently unequal and that to segregate a child on the basis of his race is to deny that child equal protection of the law. This decision brought hope to millions of disinherited Negroes who had formerly dared only to dream of freedom. Like an exit sign that suddenly appeared to one who had walked through a long and desolate corridor, this decision came as a way out of the darkness of segregation. It served to transform the fatigue of despair into the buoyancy of hope. It further enhanced the Negro's sense of dignity.

A fifth factor that has accounted for the new sense of dignity on the part of the Negro has been the awareness that his struggle for freedom is a part of a worldwide struggle. He has watched developments in Asia and Africa with rapt attention. On these vast prodigious continents dwell two-thirds of the world's people. For years they were exploited economically, dominated politically, segregated and humiliated by foreign powers. Thirty years ago there were only three independent countries in the whole of Africa – Liberia, Ethiopia, and South Africa. By 1962, there may be as many as thirty independent nations in Africa. These rapid changes have naturally influenced the thinking of the American Negro. He knows that his struggle for human dignity is not an isolated event. It is a drama being played on the stage of the world with spectators and supporters from every continent. . . .

THE PRIMARY RESPONSIBILITY

In the final analysis if first class citizenship is to become a reality for the Negro he must assume the primary responsibility for making it so. The Negro must not be victimized with the delusion of thinking that others should be more concerned than himself about his citizenship rights.

In this period of social change the Negro must work on two fronts. On the one hand we must continue to break down the barrier of segregation. We must resist all forms of racial injustice. This resistance must always be on the highest level of dignity and discipline. It must never degenerate to the crippling level of violence. There is another way – a way as old as the insights of Jesus of Nazareth and as modern as the methods of Mahatma Gandhi. It is a way not for the weak and cowardly but for the strong and courageous. It has been variously called passive resistance, nonviolent resistance, or simply Christian love. It is my great hope that, as the Negro plunges deeper into the quest for freedom, he will plunge deeper into the philosophy of nonviolence. As a race we must work passionately and unrelentingly for first-class citizenship, but we must never use second-class methods to gain it. Our aim must be not to defeat or humiliate the white man, but to win his friendship and understanding. We must never become bitter nor should we succumb to the temptation of using violence in the struggle, for if this happens, unborn generations will be the recipients of a long and desolate night of bitterness and our chief legacy to the future will be an endless reign of meaningless chaos.

I feel that this way of nonviolence is vital because it is the only way to reestablish the broken community. It is the method which seeks to implement the just law by appealing to the conscience of the great decent majority who through blindness, fear, pride lowed their consciences to sleep.

The nonviolent resisters can summarize their message in the following simple terms: we will take direct action against injustice without waiting for other agencies to act. We will not obey unjust laws or submit to unjust practices. We will do this peacefully, openly, and cheerfully because our aim is to persuade. We adopt the means of nonviolence because our end is a community at peace with itself. We will try to persuade with our words, but, if our words fail, we will try to persuade with our acts. We will always be willing to talk and seek fair compromise, but we are ready to suffer when necessary and even risk our lives to become witnesses to the truth as we see it.

I realize that this approach will mean suffering and sacrifice. It may mean going to jail. If such is the case the resister must be willing to fill the jail houses of the South. It may even mean physical death. But if physical death is the price that a man must pay to free his children and his white brethren from a permanent death of the spirit, then nothing could be more redemptive. This is the type of soul force that I am convinced will triumph over the physical force of the oppressor.

This approach to the problem of oppression is not without successful precedent. We have the magnificent example of Gandhi who challenged the might of the British Empire and won independence for his people by using only the weapons of truth, noninjury, courage, and soul force. Today we have the example of thousands of Negro students in the South who have courageously challenged the principalities of segregation. These young students have taken the deep groans and the passionate yearnings of the Negro people and filtered them in their own souls and fashioned them in a creative protest which is an epic known all over our nation. For the last few months they have moved in a uniquely meaningful orbit imparting light and heat to distant satellites. Through their nonviolent direct action they have been able to open hundreds of formerly segregated lunch counters in almost eighty cities. It is no overstatement to characterize these events as historic. Never before in the United States has so large a body of students spread a struggle over so great an area in pursuit of a goal of human dignity and freedom. I am convinced that future historians will have to record this student movement as one of the greatest epics of our heritage.

Let me mention another front on which we must work that is equally significant. The Negro must make a vigorous effort to improve his personal standards. The only answer that we can give to those who through blindness and fear would question our readiness and capability is that our lagging standards exist because of the legacy of slavery and segregation, inferior schools, slums, and second-class citizenship, and not because of an inherent inferiority. The fact that so many Negroes have made lasting and significant contributions to the cultural life of America in spite of these crippling restrictions is sufficient to refute all of the myths and half-truths disseminated by the segregationist.

Yet we cannot ignore the fact that our standards do often fall short. One of the sure signs of maturity is the ability to rise to the point of self-criticism. We have been affected by our years of economic deprivation and social isolation. Some Negroes have become cynical and disillusioned. Some have so conditioned themselves to the system of segregation that they have lost that creative something called initiative. So many have used their oppression as an excuse for mediocrity. Many of us live above our means, spend money on nonessentials and frivolities, and fail to give to serious causes, organizations, and educational institutions that so desperately need funds. Our crime rate is far too high. . . .

We must work assiduously and with determined boldness to remove from the body politic this cancerous disease of discrimination which is preventing our democratic and Christian health from being realized. Then and only then will we be able to bring dream of our American democracy – a dream yet unfulfilled. A dream of equality of opportunity, of privilege and property widely distributed; a dream of a land where men will not take necessities from the many to give luxuries to the few; a dream of a land where men do not argue that the color of a man's skin determines the content of his character; a dream of a place where all our gifts and resources are held not for ourselves alone but as instruments of service for the rest of humanity; the dream of a country where every man will respect the dignity and worth of all human personality, and men will dare to live together as brothers – that is the dream. Whenever it is fulfilled we will emerge from the bleak and desolate midnight of man's inhumanity to man into the bright and glowing daybreak of freedom and justice for all of God's children.

Source: James Melvin (ed.), *A Testament of Hope: The Essential Writings and Speeches of Martin Luther King Jr.* (Washington, DC: HarperCollins, 1986), pp. 145–51.

Suggested Questions for Discussion:

1. How did Martin Luther King, Jr. describe the "rising tide of racial consciousness?"
2. What was its significance for politics and society?
3. Who was King's intended audience for this speech?

2 "Spy vs. Spy," 1961

The "Spy vs. Spy" cartoon first appeared in Mad Magazine *in 1961. Drawn by a Cuban émigré to the United States, the cartoon depicted the futility of Cold War conflict. It also satirized the pretensions to superiority that colored the rhetoric of both superpowers. According to the cartoon, the representatives of both countries had become mirror images of one another, mimicking and promoting the same devious behavior. "Spy vs. Spy" and* Mad Magazine *reached thousands of young readers in the United States, challenging the dominant Cold War consensus with humor and wit.[2]*

Figure 6.1 *"Spy vs. Spy," 1961. SPY vs. SPY*™ *& © E.C. Publications, Inc. All rights reserved. Used with permission.*

Source: http://www.cs.virginia.edu/~horton/cs453/slides/Spy_vs_Spy.jpg (accessed June 1, 2009).

[2] See the "Spy vs. Spy" "unofficial fan site," available at: http://www.spyvsspyhq.com (accessed June 1, 2009). See also the *Mad Magazine* website, available at: http://www.dccomics.com/mad (accessed June 1, 2009).

Suggested Questions for Discussion:

1. Why was "Spy vs. Spy" so appealing for young readers in the 1960s and 1970s?
2. How does the cartoon challenge basic elements of Cold War rhetoric and policy?
3. Why is a cartoon of this kind so difficult for political opponents to refute?

3 SANE, Public Petition, 1961

During the second half of the 1950s research by scientists in numerous countries revealed the long-term health and ecological dangers of above-ground nuclear weapons testing. The growth in the explosive and radioactive power of thermonuclear bombs, the rapid expansion of American and Soviet arsenals, and the continuation of above-ground nuclear tests raised alarm among public activists. A formerly small collection of anti-nuclear intellectuals in the early 1950s became a powerful international movement by the end of the decade. The Committee for a SANE Nuclear Policy, founded in 1957, attracted support from prominent celebrities, politicians, and academics. SANE founded local branches across the country, many of which remained active through the 1980s.[3]

Public Petition to American and Soviet Leaders, 1961

Mr. Eisenhower, Mr. Khrushchev,

WE CALL FOR A PERMANENT END TO ATOMIC BOMB TESTING

Dear Mr. President: Dear Mr. Premier:

There is one tangible act you can perform that will be a clear and unmistakable sign to all humanity that your meetings have been fruitful.

You can remove the few remaining obstacles to a permanent end to nuclear weapons test under inspection and control. On behalf of the human commonwealth, will you place this question high on your agenda?

We, and people the world over, welcome your exchange of visits. We hope this direct approach will bring durable peace within the orbit of possibility.

---

[3] See Lawrence Wittner, *The Struggle Against the Bomb: A History of the World Nuclear Disarmament Movement, 1954–1970* (Stanford, CA: Stanford University Press, 1997); Robert A. Divine, *Blowing on the Wind: The Nuclear Test Ban Debate, 1954–1960* (New York: Oxford University Press, 1978).

A durable peace demands a permanent end to nuclear tests, comprehensive arms control, negotiated political settlements, and establishment of the rule of world law in international affairs.

Your Historic Meeting can be the turning point that will guarantee human survival. We welcome your initiative. We wish you well.

National Signers (partial list)

Steve Allen	Brig. Gen. Hugh B. Hester	Dr. Linus Pauling
Norman Cousins	(US Army, Retired)	Elmo Roper
Rev. Harry Emerson	Dr. Martin Luther King	Mrs. Franklin
Fosdick		D. Roosevelt
Dr. Erich Fromm	Dr. William Menninger	Louis Untermeyer
Oscar Hammerstein II	Lewis Mumford	

Madison Signers

Rev. Robert Adams	Aaron Ihde	Mr. and Mrs. William
Mr. and Mrs. Thomas	Father Alvin Kutchera	Gorham Rice
Amile		
Howard K. Beale	Henry A. Lardy	John R. Roebuck
Mr. and Mrs. Eugene	Mr. and Mrs. H. H.	Morris Rubin
Boardman	Lettau	
Charles Bunn	Mr. and Mrs. Karl	Robert Schumpert
	Paul Link	
Walter Engelke	Rev. James R. Love	William Skaar
Rev. Max D. Gaebler	Camilla M. Low	Rev. Carl W. Stromberg
Mr. and Mrs. Chester	John McGrath	Rev. Alfred W. Swan
Graham		
Dr. Frances Graham	George L. Mosse	Rabbi Manfred
		Swarsensky
Rev. Robert H. Hamill	Bishop H. Clifford	Rabbi Max Ticktin
	Northcutt	
Mr. and Mrs. Francis	George Parzen	Jackson Tiffany
D. Hole		
Rev. Robert W. Towner	May S. Reynolds	Rev. Robert W. Towner
Emory Via	G. I. Wallace	Mr. and Mrs. Paul Wiley
William Appleman		
Williams		

Source: Committee for a Sane Nuclear Policy, Pamphlet Collection 68–758, Wisconsin Historical Society Library, Madison, WI.

Suggested Questions for Discussion:

1. How did SANE define the dangers to the United States, and human society in general?
2. How did SANE claim political authority to influence foreign policy?
3. What did SANE advocate?

4 Students for a Democratic Society, Port Huron Statement, 1962

In June 1962 a small group of college students, joined by a few veteran activists, met in Port Huron, Michigan – the site of a United Auto Workers retreat facility – to craft a public testament for their new organization, "Students for a Democratic Society" (SDS). The eloquent "Agenda for a Generation" that they wrote and distributed widely articulated a thoughtful model of "participatory democracy" for social change and foreign policy reform. In sections on "values," "deterrence policy," "the colonial revolution," and "discrimination," the Port Huron statement linked progressive reforms at home to a turn away from Cold War policies abroad. SDS mobilized young citizens to challenge basic assumptions about America's place in the world, years before the Vietnam War became a symbol of the nation's Cold War failings. SDS encouraged civil rights activists to think in global terms. It demanded that foreign policy experts reexamine their home communities.[4]

Introduction: Agenda for a Generation

We are people of this generation, bred in at least modest comfort, housed now in universities, looking uncomfortably to the world we inherit.

When we were kids the United States was the wealthiest and strongest country in the world: the only one with the atom bomb, the least scarred by modern war, an initiator of the United Nations that we thought would distribute Western influence throughout the world. Freedom and equality for each individual, government of, by, and for the people – these American

---

[4] See Tom Hayden and Dick Flacks, "The Port Huron Statement at 40," *The Nation* (August 5, 2002); Maurice Isserman and Michael Kazin, *America Divided: The Civil War of the 1960s* (New York: Oxford University Press, 1999); James Miller, *Democracy is in the Streets: From Port Huron to the Siege of Chicago* (Cambridge, MA: Harvard University Press, 1994); Jeremi Suri, *Power and Protest: Global Revolution and the Rise of Détente* (Cambridge, MA: Harvard University Press, 2003).

values we found good, principles by which we could live as men. Many of us began maturing in complacency.

As we grew, however, our comfort was penetrated by events too troubling to dismiss. First, the permeating and victimizing fact of human degradation, symbolized by the Southern struggle against racial bigotry, compelled most of us from silence to activism. Second, the enclosing fact of the Cold War, symbolized by the presence of the Bomb, brought awareness that we ourselves, and our friends, and millions of abstract "others" we knew more directly because of our common peril, might die at any time. We might deliberately ignore, or avoid, or fail to feel all other human problems, but not these two, for these were too immediate and crushing in their impact, too challenging in the demand that we as individuals take the responsibility for encounter and resolution.

While these and other problems either directly oppressed us or rankled our consciences and became our own subjective concerns, we began to see complicated and disturbing paradoxes in our surrounding America. The declaration "all men are created equal ... " rang hollow before the facts of Negro life in the South and the big cities of the North. The proclaimed peaceful intentions of the United States contradicted its economic and military investments in the Cold War status quo.

We witnessed, and continue to witness, other paradoxes. With nuclear energy whole cities can easily be powered, yet the dominant nation-states seem more likely to unleash destruction greater than that incurred in all wars of human history. Although our own technology is destroying old and creating new forms of social organization, men still tolerate meaningless work and idleness. While two-thirds of mankind suffers undernourishment, our own upper classes revel amidst superfluous abundance. Although world population is expected to double in forty years, the nations still tolerate anarchy as a major principle of international conduct and uncontrolled exploitation governs the sapping of the earth's physical resources. Although mankind desperately needs revolutionary leadership, America rests in national stalemate, its goals ambiguous and tradition-bound instead of informed and clear, its democratic system apathetic and manipulated rather than "of, by, and for the people." ...

Deterrence Policy

The accumulation of nuclear arsenals, the threat of accidental war, the possibility of limited war becoming illimitable holocaust, the impossibility of achieving final arms superiority or invulnerability, the approaching nativity of a cluster of infant atomic powers; all of these events are tending to undermine traditional concepts of power relations among nations. War can no longer be considered as an effective instrument of foreign policy, a means of strengthening alliances, adjusting the balance of power, maintaining national sovereignty, or preserving human values. War is no longer simply a forceful extension of foreign policy; it can obtain no constructive ends in the modern world. Soviet or American "megatonnage" is sufficient to destroy all existing social structures as well as value systems. Missiles have (figuratively) thumbed their nosecones at national boundaries. But America, like other countries, still operates by means of national defense and deterrence systems. These are seen to be useful so long as they are never fully used: unless we as a national entity can convince Russia that we are willing to commit the most heinous action in human history, we will be forced to commit it.

Deterrence advocates, all of them prepared at least to threaten mass extermination, advance arguments of several kinds. At one pole are the minority of open partisans of preventive war – who falsely assume the inevitability of violent conflict and assert the lunatic efficacy of striking the first blow, assuming that it will be easier to "recover" after thermonuclear war than to recover now from the grip of the Cold War. Somewhat more reluctant to advocate initiating a war, but perhaps more disturbing for their numbers within the Kennedy Administration, are the many advocates of the "counterforce" theory of aiming strategic nuclear weapons at military installations – though this might "save" more lives than a preventive war, it would require drastic, provocative and perhaps impossible social change to separate many cities from weapons sites, it would be impossible to ensure the immunity of cities after one or two counterforce nuclear "exchanges," it would generate a perpetual arms race for less vulnerability and greater weapons power and mobility, it would make outer space a region subject to militarization, and accelerate the suspicions and arms build-ups which are incentives to precipitate nuclear action. Others would support fighting "limited wars" which use conventional (all but atomic) weapons, backed by deterrents so mighty that both sides would fear to use them – although underestimating the implications of numerous new atomic powers on the world stage, the extreme difficulty of anchoring international order with weapons of only transient invulnerability, the potential tendency for a "losing side" to push limited protracted fighting on the soil of underdeveloped countries. Still other deterrence artists propose limited, clearly defensive and retaliatory, nuclear capacity, always potent enough to deter an opponent's aggressive designs – the best of deterrence stratagems, but inadequate when it rests on the equation of an arms "stalemate" with international stability.

All the deterrence theories suffer in several common ways. They allow insufficient attention to preserving, extending, and enriching democratic values, such matters being subordinate rather than governing in the process of conducting foreign policy. Second, they inadequately realize the inherent instabilities of the continuing arms race and balance of fear. Third, they operationally tend to eclipse interest and action towards disarmament by solidifying economic, political and even moral investments in continuation of tensions. Fourth, they offer a disinterested and even patriotic rationale for the boondoggling, belligerence, and privilege of military and economic elites. Finally, deterrence stratagems invariably understate or dismiss the relatedness of various dangers; they inevitably lend tolerability to the idea of war by neglecting the dynamic interaction of problems – such as the menace of accidental war, the probable future tensions surrounding the emergence of ex-colonial nations, the imminence of several new nations joining the "Nuclear Club," the destabilizing potential of technological breakthrough by either arms race contestant, the threat of Chinese atomic might, the fact that "recovery" after World War III would involve not only human survivors but, as well, a huge and fragile social structure and culture which would be decimated perhaps irreparably by total war.

Such a harsh critique of what we are doing as a nation by no means implies that sole blame for the Cold War rests on the United States. Both sides have behaved irresponsibly – the Russians by an exaggerated lack of trust, and by much dependence on aggressive military strategists rather than on proponents of nonviolent conflict and coexistence. But we do contend, as Americans concerned with the conduct of our representative institutions, that our government has blamed the Cold War stalemate on nearly every thing but its own hesitations, its own anachronistic dependence on weapons. To be sure, there is more to disarmament than wishing for it. There are inadequacies in international rule-making institutions – which could be corrected. There are faulty inspection mechanisms – which could be perfected by disinterested scientists. There is Russian intransigency and evasiveness – which do not erase the fact that the Soviet Union, because of a strained economy, an expectant population, fears of Chinese potential, and interest in the colonial revolution, is increasingly disposed to real disarmament with real controls. But there is, too, our own reluctance to face the uncertain world beyond the Cold War, our own shocking assumption that the risks of the present are fewer than the risks of a policy re-orientation to disarmament, our own unwillingness to face the implementation of our rhetorical commitments to peace and freedom.

Today the world alternatively drifts and plunges towards a terrible war when vision and change are required, our government pursues a policy of macabre dead-end dimensions – conditioned, but not justified, by actions of the Soviet bloc. Ironically, the war which seems to close will not be fought between the United States and Russia, not externally between two national entities, but as an international civil war throughout the unrespected and unprotected human civitas which spans the world.

The Colonial Revolution

While weapons have accelerated man's opportunity for self-destruction, the counter-impulse to life and creation are superbly manifest in the revolutionary feelings of many Asian, African and Latin American peoples. Against the individual initiative and aspiration, and social sense of organism characteristic of these upsurges, the American apathy and stalemate stand in embarrassing contrast.

It is difficult today to give human meaning to the welter of facts that surrounds us. That is why it is especially hard to understand the facts of "underdevelopment": in India, man and beast together produced 65 percent of the nation's economic energy in a recent year, and of the remaining 35 percent of inanimately produced power almost three-fourths was obtained by burning dung. But in the United States, human and animal power together account for only one percent of the national economic energy – that is what stands humanly behind the vague term "industrialization." Even to maintain the misery of Asia today at a constant level will require a rate of growth tripling the national income and the aggregate production in Asian countries by the end of the century. For Asians to have the (unacceptable) 1950 standard of Europeans, less than $2,000 per year for a family, national production must increase 21-fold by the end the century, and that monstrous feat only to reach a level that Europeans find intolerable.

What has America done? During the years 1955–57 our total expenditures in economic aid were equal to one-tenth of one percent of our total Gross National Product. Prior to that time it was less; since then it has been a fraction higher. Immediate social and economic development is needed – we have helped little, seeming to prefer to create a growing gap between "have" and "have not" rather than to usher in social revolutions which would threaten our investors and out military alliances. The new nations want to avoid power entanglements that will open their countries to foreign domination – and we have often demanded loyalty oaths. They do not see the relevance of uncontrolled free enterprise in societies without accumulated capital and a significant middle class – and we have looked calumniously on those who would not try "our way." They seek empathy – and we have sided with the old colonialists, who now are trying to take credit for "giving" all the freedom that has been wrested from them, or we "empathize" when pressure absolutely demands it.

With rare variation, American foreign policy in the Fifties was guided by a concern for foreign investment and a negative anti-communist political stance linked to a series of military alliances, both undergirded by military threat. We participated unilaterally – usually through the Central Intelligence Agency – in revolutions against governments in Laos, Guatemala, Cuba, Egypt, Iran. We permitted economic investment to decisively affect our foreign policy: fruit in Cuba, oil in the Middle East, diamonds and gold in South Africa (with whom we trade more than with any African nation). More exactly: America's "foreign market" in the late Fifties, including exports of goods and services plus overseas sales by American firms, averaged about $60 billion annually. This represented twice the investment of 1950, and it is predicted that the same rates of increase will continue. The reason is obvious: *Fortune* said in 1958, "foreign earnings will be more than double in four years, more than twice the probable gain in domestic profits." These investments are concentrated primarily in the Middle East and Latin America, neither region being an impressive candidate for the long-run stability, political caution, and lower-class tolerance that American investors typically demand.

Our pugnacious anti-communism and protection of interests has led us to an alliance inappropriately called the "Free World." It included four major parliamentary democracies: ourselves, Canada, Great Britain, and India. It also has included through the years Batista, Franco, Verwoerd, Salazar, De Gaulle, Boun Oum, Ngo Diem, Chiang Kai Shek, Trujillo, the Somozas, Saud, Ydigoras – all of these non-democrats separating us deeply from the colonial revolutions.

Since the Kennedy Administration began, the American government seems to have initiated policy changes in the colonial and underdeveloped areas. It accepted "neutralism" as a tolerable principle; it sided more than once with the Angolans in the United Nations; it invited Souvanna Phouma to return to Laos after having overthrown his neutralist government there; it implemented the Alliance for Progress that President Eisenhower proposed when Latin America appeared on the verge of socialist revolutions; it made derogatory statements about the Trujillos; it cautiously suggested that a democratic socialist government in British Guiana might be necessary to support; in inaugural oratory, it suggested that a moral imperative was involved in sharing the world's resources with those who have been previously dominated. These were hardly sufficient to heal the scars of past activity and present associations, but nevertheless they were motions away from the Fifties. But quite unexpectedly, the President ordered the Cuban invasions, and while the

American press railed about how we had been "shamed" and defied by that "monster Castro," the colonial peoples of the world wondered whether our foreign policy had really changed from its old imperialist ways (we had never supported Castro, even on the eve of his taking power, and had announced early that "the conduct of the Castro government toward foreign private enterprise in Cuba" would be a main State Department concern). Any heralded changes in our foreign policy are now further suspect in the wake of the Punta Del Este foreign minister's conference where the five countries representing most of Latin America refused to cooperate in our plans to further "isolate" the Castro government.

Ever since the colonial revolution began, American policy makers have reacted to new problems with old "gunboat" remedies, often thinly disguised. The feeble but desirable efforts of the Kennedy Administration to be more flexible are coming perhaps too late, and are of too little significance to really change the historical thrust of our policies. The hunger problem is increasing rapidly mostly as a result of the worldwide population explosion that cancels out the meager triumphs gained so far over starvation. The threat of population to economic growth is simply documented: in 1960–70 population in Africa south of the Sahara will increase 14 percent; in South Asia and the Far East by 22 percent; in North Africa 26 percent; in the Middle East by 27 percent; in Latin America 29 percent. Population explosion, no matter how devastating, is neutral. But how long will it take to create a relation of thrust between America and the newly-developing societies? How long to change our policies? And what length of time do we have?

The world is in transformation. But America is not. It can race to industrialize the world, tolerating occasional authoritarianisms, socialisms, neutralisms along the way – or it can slow the pace of the inevitable and default to the eager and self-interested Soviets and, much more importantly, to mankind itself. Only mystics would guess we have opted thoroughly for the first. Consider what our people think of this, the most urgent issue on the human agenda. Fed by a bellicose press, manipulated by economic and political opponents of change, drifting in their own history, they grumble about "the foreign aid waste," or about "that beatnik down in Cuba," or how "things will get us by" ... thinking confidently, albeit in the usual bewilderment, that Americans can go right on like always, five percent of mankind producing forty percent of its goods.

Anti-Communism

An unreasoning anti-communism has become a major social problem for those who want to construct a more democratic America. McCarthyism and other forms of exaggerated and conservative anti-communism seriously weaken democratic institutions and spawn movements contrary to the interests of basic freedoms and peace. In such an atmosphere even the most intelligent of Americans fear to join political organizations, sign petitions, speak out on serious issues. Militaristic policies are easily "sold" to a public fearful of a democratic enemy. Political debate is restricted, thought is standardized, action is inhibited by the demands of "unity" and "oneness" in the face of the declared danger. Even many liberals and socialists share static and repetitious participation in the anti-communist crusade and often discourage tentative, inquiring discussion about "the Russian question" within their ranks – often by employing "stalinist," "stalinoid," "trotskyite" and other epithets in an oversimplifying way to discredit opposition.

Thus much of the American anti-communism takes on the characteristics of paranoia. Not only does it lead to the perversion of democracy and to the political stagnation of a warfare society, but it also has the unintended consequence of preventing an honest and effective approach to the issues. Such an approach would require public analysis and debate of world politics. But almost nowhere in politics is such a rational analysis possible to make.

It would seem reasonable to expect that in America the basic issues of the Cold War should be rationally and fully debated, between persons of every opinion – on television, on platforms and through other media. It would seem, too, that there should be a way for the person or an organization to oppose communism without contributing to the common fear of associations and public actions. But these things do not happen; instead, there is finger-pointing and comical debate about the most serious of issues. This trend of events on the domestic scene, towards greater irrationality on major questions, moves us to greater concern than does the "internal threat" of domestic communism. Democracy, we are convinced, requires every effort to set in peaceful opposition the basic viewpoints of the day; only by conscious, determined, though difficult, efforts in this direction will the issue of communism be met appropriately.

Source: http://www.campusactivism.org/server-new/uploads/porthuron.htm (accessed December 3, 2009).

Suggested Questions for Discussion:

1. Why did the writers of the Port Huron Statement view the Cold War as an impediment to democracy?
2. How did they propose to change American foreign policy?
3. What made this document, written by students, so powerful?

5 Women Strike for Peace, "What Every Woman Knows," 1962

Women played a vital role in anti-nuclear and civil rights activism during the 1950s, but they were generally relegated to secondary positions by male leaders. In 1961 a group of female activists formed Women Strike for Peace, one of the first and most prominent women's peace groups. Through publications, protests, and a proliferation of local chapters Women Strike for Peace drew attention to the harmful effects of nuclear testing and the Cold War in general. Articulating both a feminist critique of traditional masculine military politics and a maternal demand for a safer and more nurturing society, Women Strike for Peace called for a redefinition of citizenship. They looked to the United Nations and other international organizations to control the aggressiveness of nation-states. They hoped to build a new "world community" that transcended the Cold War.[5]

"What Every Woman Knows," May 1962

In mid-April I got a long letter from a gentleman in the Middle West who felt that "if women" would take over all the seats in Congress we would have no more war. In a return postcard thanking him for his interest I indicated that I didn't think matters were quite that simple. His heated and immediate response: "Do you believe that if mothers and grandmothers around the world were in charge, we would be facing a world genocide as we do now? If you do, you better let someone else edit your bulletin." Well, while I was debating with myself about my fitness to edit the bulletin according to such a criterion, along came the start of testing, and an editorial in the *New York Times* which suddenly cleared my mind of all doubt: "As the miracle that might have averted nuclear tests has failed to materialize, President Kennedy has now issued the fateful order. ..." Why these grown-up male children really do pin their ultimate hopes on miracles! They continue in their wildly unrealistic, but comfortingly familiar rituals of military preparations while they hope against hope for a miracle which will prevent their preparations from coming to fruition.

I am not now and never have been a feminist, but one thing I will say for women, they know there are no miracles except the one ultimate miracle of

---

[5]   See Amy Swerdlow, *Women Strike for Peace: Traditional Motherhood and Radical Politics in the 1960s* (Chicago, IL: University of Chicago Press, 1993); Ruth Rosen, *The World Split Open: How the Modern Women's Movement Changed America*, rev. edn. (New York: Penguin, 2006); Lawrence Wittner, *The Struggle Against the Bomb: A History of the World Nuclear Disarmament Movement, 1954–1970* (Stanford, CA: Stanford University Press, 1997).

the seed of life. Babies aren't born without labor, children don't grow without nurture, families aren't clothed and fed without housework, peace won't come unless we <u>work</u> for it. I may still have my qualms about an all-woman Congress, but it couldn't possibly be worse than a Congress full of naive men voting arms increases and waiting for miracles! So may I remind you, ladies, that while it takes only 9 months to produce a baby, it may take longer to produce an effective candidacy. Some of you have plunged in early and may succeed in the fall elections (see especially New York report), but for those who got to thinking about it later, plan now for a 17-month political pregnancy and see what we can do in the fall of 1963. Learning the political ropes takes time, but it is fun, absorbing, stimulating – and IMPORTANT. (Secretary of the Interior Udall may not know it, but he is with us. The same issue of the *N.Y. Times* which carried the "miracles" editorial also carried this quote from Udall: "I was out in a farm state a few days ago and I found that the women generally had a firmer grip than the men in a handshake. I think that is a commentary on conditions today.")

Many of us felt that the height of unreality had been reached with the announcement of the proposed high-altitude tests which would bend or possibly break up sections of the Van Allen Belt. We assumed scientists would rise up en masse about this, and all we got was a faint squeak of protest from radio astronomers, whose observations will be interfered with. A University of Michigan meteorologist pointed out that the spaces involved in these outer reaches are so vast, and man-made disturbances so tiny compared to every-day atmospheric turbulences, that this is hard to get excited about. On the other hand he was perfectly willing to be eloquent about the appalling misdirection of valuable research resources. Out of all this, here are two suggestions for changes in our approach to the scientist and his role:

(1) our relationship with scientists may be more fruitful if we help to mobilize public opinion for a redirection of research energies toward what they themselves would like to be doing, rather than spending all our energy protesting what they are doing, often reluctantly; (2) Congress has to be sold on the need for new research directions. It hears only what it wants to hear, and one word from Teller sounds louder on Capitol Hill than a carefully prepared testimony from the most distinguished scientists of our country. Let's not put the burden on scientists to change this situation.

Let us put pressure on Congress directly ourselves. We have addressed too many communications to the President, too few to Congress. In the vital pre-testing weeks, Congressional mail, unlike the President's mail, was largely in favor of testing. Congressmen are in a listening mood now. Why not snow them under with letters at the layman's level, along the line of Art

Hoppe's "Chicken Little vs. the Men of Science" in the May 2 *San Francisco Chronicle*. They may be immune to distinguished scientists, but they are not immune to popular feeling. (If we are writing our Congressmen on this subject, let's indicate our approval of the National Aeronautics and Space Administration's steps toward cooperation with the Soviet Union, and our displeasure with the Pentagon's attempts to spike this. Protest trigger-happy SAC Commander Power too! See page 7, May War/Peace Report.)

It may well be that our greatest task right now lies in familiarizing our Congressmen with the best current thinking on disarmament. Congressmen read thoughtful letters written in between legislation-crisis periods with care. Let us take I. F. Stone's April 23 quote from Senator Clark to heart: "The Senate, even today, is badly informed on the President's disarmament policy. An incident during last week's debate on the UN bond issue illustrates the point. A press story indicated that our delegation in Geneva would submit a plan that called 'for the elimination of national armies within nine years.' The statement differed little from those of the President I have quoted. Yet a Senator drew attention to this article in obvious surprise and alarm. ... May we not be heading for another Versailles? Is the Congress being prepared to 'advise and consent' to a meaningful disarmament treaty? I fear not, and, more important perhaps, does the country understand what the Administration is up to? Again I fear the answer must be negative. Is not the conclusion that if disarmament should become diplomatically possible, it would nonetheless fail for want of Congressional approval? As of today, I fear the answer is yes. ... In the end, much depends on the American people themselves. The incentive ... must come from the grass roots of public opinion."

Source: *Woman's Peace Movement Bulletin*, vol. 1, No. 5, May 19, 1962.

Suggested Questions for Discussion:

1. What were the main critiques voiced by Women Strike for Peace?
2. What kinds of changes in society and politics did Women Strike for Peace demand?
3. What made Women Strike for Peace different from SANE and SDS?

6 "Dr. Strangelove," 1964

Stanley Kubrick's dark comedy, "Dr. Strangelove," offered a devastating and enduring criticism of Cold War nuclear strategy, and the men who made foreign policy. In depicting an unauthorized American nuclear strike against the Soviet Union, and the bungling response of American and Soviet leaders, Kubrick captured the irrational – perhaps insane – consequences of reasoned plans to deploy enormously destructive weapons as protections of peace. Kubrick also depicted the insular, narcissistic, and sexist atmosphere of policy deliberations.[6]

The President's chair rises up into position at a huge Conference Table. Twenty-nine top ranking civilian and military officials rise.

PRESIDENT MUFFLEY: (*blowing his nose*) Good morning, gentleman. Please sit down.

All Sit.

PRESIDENT MUFFLEY: Is everyone here?

There is a general stirring and clearing of throats.

TURGIDSON: Mr. President, the Secretary of State is in Vietnam, the Secretary of Defense is in Laos and the Vice President is in Mexico City. We can establish contact with them at any time if it is necessary.

PRESIDENT MUFFLEY: (*wretched with his cold*) Fine fine. (*Looking to Four-Star General "Buck" O'Connor, the Air Force Chief of the Joint Chiefs of Staff*) Now, Buck, what the hell's going on here?

General "Buck" O'Connor rises and assumes his maximum dignity. He is a man who conceals hostility with sickening sincerity and a crinkly smile.

---

[6]   See Margot Henriksen, *Dr. Strangelove's America: Society and Culture in the Atomic Age* (Berkeley, CA: University of California Press, 1997); Paul Boyer, *By the Bomb's Early Light: American Thought and Culture at the Dawn of the Atomic Age* (Chapel Hill, NC: University of North Carolina Press, 1994); Stephen J. Whitfield, *The Culture of the Cold War* (Baltimore, MD: Johns Hopkins University Press, 1996).

GENERAL "BUCK" O'CONNOR: Mr. President, about thirty-five minutes ago General Jack Ripper, the Commanding General at Burpelson Air Force Base, issued orders to the thirty-four 3.53's of his Wing which were airborne at the time as part of a special exercise we called "Operation Dropkick". It appears as if the order called for the planes to attack their targets inside Russia. The planes are fully loaded with nuclear weapons with an average load of forty megatons each. (Pointing to wall) The central display of Russia will indicate the planes positions – the squares are their primary targets, the triangles are their secondary targets. The aircraft will begin penetrating Russian radar cover within twenty-five minutes.

PRESIDENT MUFFLEY: I find this very difficult to understand General O'Connor. I am the only one who has the authority to order the use of nuclear weapons.

GENERAL "BUCK" O'CONNOR: That's right, sir. You are the only person authorized to do so, and, though I hate to judge before all the facts are in, it's beginning to look like General Ripper exceeded his authority.

PRESIDENT MUFFLEY: But that's *impossible*!

GENERAL "BUCK" O'CONNOR: Perhaps you are forgetting the provisions of Plan-R, sir?

PRESIDENT MUFFLEY: Plan-R???

GENERAL "BUCK" O'CONNOR: That's right, sir. Plan-R. Surely you must recall – Plan-R is an emergency war plan in which a lower echelon commander can order nuclear retaliation after a sneak attack, if the normal chain of command has been disrupted. You approved it, sir. You must remember.

The President sits in a kind of stunned silence

GENERAL "BUCK" O'CONNOR: Surely you must remember, sir, when Senator Duff made that big hassle about our deterent [sic] lacking credibility. The idea was for Plan-R to be a sort of retaliatory safeguard.

PRESIDENT MUFFLEY: A safeguard?

GENERAL "BUCK" O'CONNOR: Well, sir, I have to admit the human element seems to have failed us here, but the idea was to discourage the Ruskies from any hope that they could knock out Washington and – yourself – as part of a general sneak attack and escape retaliation because of lack of proper command and control.

PRESIDENT MUFFLEY: Has there been any indication whatsoever of Russian hostile interactions in the last twenty-four hours?

GENERAL "BUCK" O'CONNOR: No, sir, there hasn't, and the more I think about it this is really beginning to look like a very unfortunate misuse of Plan-R.

PRESIDENT MUFFLEY: Well, I assume though that the planes will return automatically as soon as they reach their Fail-Safe points.

GENERAL "BUCK" O'CONNOR: No, sir, I'm afraid not. The planes were holding at their Fail-Safe point when the Go-code was issued. Once they fly beyond Fail-Safe they do not require a second order to proceed. They will continue until they reach their targets.

PRESIDENT MUFFLEY: Well, why haven't you radioed the planes counter-manding the Go-code???

GENERAL "BUCK" O'CONNOR: I'm afraid we are unable to communicate with any of the aircraft.

PRESIDENT MUFFLEY: Well, that's absurd!

GENERAL "BUCK" O'CONNOR: As you may recall, Mr. President, one of the provisions of Plan-R provides that once the Go-code is received the normal SSB radios in the aircraft are switched into a special coded device, which I believe is designated as CRM-114. To prevent the enemy from issuing fake or confusing orders the CRM-114 is designed not to receive at all unless the message is preceded by the correct three letter code group prefix.

PRESIDENT MUFFLEY: Well, surely this is part of the SAC Master Code.

GENERAL "BUCK" O'CONNOR: No, sir, it is not. Since this is an emergency war plan and has to be activated at a lower echelon, the lower echelon commander designates the code, and in this case, it is known only to General Ripper since he changed it just before take-off and gave it person-ally to the crews at their pre-flight briefing.

PRESIDENT MUFFLEY: Then do you mean to say you will be unable to recall the aircraft????

GENERAL "BUCK" O'CONNOR: I'm afraid that's about the size of it, sir. We are plowing through every possible three-letter combination of the code, but there are apparently seventeen thousand permutations, and it will take us two and a half days to transmit them all.

PRESIDENT MUFFLEY: How soon did you say the planes would penetrate Russian radar cover?

GENERAL "BUCK" O'CONNOR: About eighteen minutes from now, sir.

PRESIDENT MUFFLEY: Are you in contact with General Ripper?

GENERAL "BUCK" O'CONNOR: No, sir. General Ripper has sealed off the base and cut off all communications.

PRESIDENT MUFFLEY: Where did you get all this information?

GENERAL "BUCK" O'CONNOR: General Ripper called Strategic Air Command Headquarters shortly after he issued the Go-code. I have a portion of the conversation here, if you'd like me to read it.

PRESIDENT MUFFLEY: Go ahead.

GENERAL "BUCK" O'CONNOR: The duty officer asked General Ripper to confirm the fact that he had issued the Go-code and he said, (*clears throat*) "Yes, gentlemen, they are on their way in and no one can bring them back. For the sake of our country and our way of life I suggest you get the rest of SAC in after them, otherwise will be totally destroyed by Red retaliation. My boys will give you the best kind of start – 1400 megatons worth – and you sure as hell won't stop them now. So let's get going, there's no other choice. God willing we will prevail, in peace and freedom from fear and in true health through the purity and essence of our natural fluids. God bless you all." Then he hung up.

PRESIDENT MUFFLEY: Did he say something about *fluids*???

GENERAL "BUCK" O'CONNOR: Yes, sir – um – "We shall prevail in peace and freedom from fear and in true health through the purity and essence of our natural fluids." We are still trying to figure out the meaning of that last phrase, sir.

PRESIDENT MUFFLEY: There's nothing to figure out, General O'Connor, the man's obviously a psychotic.

GENERAL "BUCK" O'CONNOR: Well, Mr. President, I'd like to hold off judgment on a thing like that until all the facts are in.

PRESIDENT MUFFLEY: General O'Connor, when you instituted the Human Reliability tests you assured me there was no possibility of such a thing ever occurring.

GENERAL "BUCK" O'CONNOR: I don't think it's fair to condemn a whole program for a single slip-up, sir.

PRESIDENT MUFFLEY: Never mind, we're wasting time. I want to speak to General Ripper on the telephone personally.

GENERAL "BUCK" O'CONNOR: I'm afraid that will be impossible, sir.

PRESIDENT MUFFLEY: (*blowing up*) General O'Connor, I am beginning to have less and less interest on your estimates of what is possible and impossible!!!

Source: "*Dr. Strangelove," Or: How I Learned to Stop Worrying and Love the Bomb* (Screenplay), Hawk Films Ltd, Shepperton Studios, Shepperton, Middlesex, Revised January 27, 1963. Scene 30 (30–1 to 30–7).

Suggested Questions for Discussion:

1. According to the film, how did American leaders lose control of the nation's nuclear weapons?
2. How did the logic of nuclear deterrence encourage the creation of something like "Plan-R?"
3. What kinds of policy changes is the film advocating?

7 President Lyndon Johnson, "Peace Without Conquest," 1965

President Lyndon Johnson and many of his closest advisors came of age during the New Deal. They idolized Franklin Roosevelt. They believed that a powerful and wealthy American federal government could improve the lives of citizens around the world. Contributing to economic development in impoverished domestic and foreign areas – places largely untouched by the benefits of modern technology and science – they believed the United States could win the "hearts and minds" of people across the globe. Johnson thought of civil rights, education, and domestic anti-poverty programs in similar terms, and he accomplished more than any other Cold War president in each of these areas. Johnson also believed that the Vietnam War was fundamentally about a struggle for development and modernization. In one of the most important speeches of his presidency, Johnson laid out a vision for how the United States would support the creation of a Mekong River development project, modeled on the Tennessee Valley Authority. This project would provide citizens of Vietnam with access to a better way of life through modern electricity and technology – a way of life that communists could not offer on the same scale.[7]

President Lyndon B. Johnson's Address at Johns Hopkins University,
April 7, 1965

Mr. Garland, Senator Brewster, Senator Tydings, Members of the congressional delegation, members of the faculty of Johns Hopkins, student body, my fellow Americans:

Last week 17 nations sent their views to some two dozen countries having an interest in southeast Asia. We are joining those 17 countries and stating our American policy tonight which we believe will contribute toward peace in this area of the world.

I have come here to review once again with my own people the views of the American Government.

Tonight Americans and Asians are dying for a world where each people may choose its own path to change.

[7] Lloyd Gardner, *Pay Any Price: Lyndon Johnson and the Wars for Vietnam* (Chicago, IL: Ivan Dee, 1995); Michael E. Latham, *Modernization as Ideology: American Social Science and "Nation-Building" in the Kennedy Era* (Chapel Hill, NC: University of North Carolina Press, 2000); Randall Woods, *LBJ: Architect of American Ambition* (New York: Free Press, 2006).

This is the principle for which our ancestors fought in the valleys of Pennsylvania. It is the principle for which our sons fight tonight in the jungles of Viet-Nam.

Viet-Nam is far away from this quiet campus. We have no territory there, nor do we seek any. The war is dirty and brutal and difficult. And some 400 young men, born into an America that is bursting with opportunity and promise, have ended their lives on Viet-Nam's steaming soil.

Why must we take this painful road?

Why must this Nation hazard its ease, and its interest, and its power for the sake of a people so far away?

We fight because we must fight if we are to live in a world where every country can shape its own destiny. And only in such a world will our own freedom be finally secure.

This kind of world will never be built by bombs or bullets. Yet the infirmities of man are such that force must often precede reason, and the waste of war, the works of peace.

We wish that this were not so. But we must deal with the world as it is, if it is ever to be as we wish.

THE NATURE OF THE CONFLICT

The world as it is in Asia is not a serene or peaceful place.

The first reality is that North Viet-Nam has attacked the independent nation of South Viet-Nam. Its object is total conquest.

Of course, some of the people of South Viet-Nam are participating in attack on their own government. But trained men and supplies, orders and arms, flow in a constant stream from north to south.

This support is the heartbeat of the war.

And it is a war of unparalleled brutality. Simple farmers are the targets of assassination and kidnapping. Women and children are strangled in the night because their men are loyal to their government. And helpless villages are ravaged by sneak attacks. Large-scale raids are conducted on towns, and terror strikes in the heart of cities.

The confused nature of this conflict cannot mask the fact that it is the new face of an old enemy.

Over this war – and all Asia – is another reality: the deepening shadow of Communist China. The rulers in Hanoi are urged on by Peking. This is a regime which has destroyed freedom in Tibet, which has attacked India, and has been condemned by the United Nations for aggression in Korea. It is a nation which is helping the forces of violence in almost every continent. The contest in Viet-Nam is part of a wider pattern of aggressive purposes.

WHY ARE WE IN VIET-NAM?

Why are these realities our concern? Why are we in South Viet-Nam?

We are there because we have a promise to keep. Since 1954 every American President has offered support to the people of South Viet-Nam. We have helped to build, and we have helped to defend. Thus, over many years, we have made a national pledge to help South Viet-Nam defend its independence.

And I intend to keep that promise.

To dishonor that pledge, to abandon this small and brave nation to its enemies, and to the terror that must follow, would be an unforgivable wrong.

We are also there to strengthen world order. Around the globe, from Berlin to Thailand, are people whose well-being rests, in part, on the belief that they can count on us if they are attacked. To leave Viet-Nam to its fate would shake the confidence of all these people in the value of an American commitment and in the value of America's word. The result would be increased unrest and instability, and even wider war.

We are also there because there are great stakes in the balance. Let no one think for a moment that retreat from Viet-Nam would bring an end to conflict. The battle would be renewed in one country and then another. The central lesson of our time is that the appetite of aggression is never satisfied. To withdraw from one battlefield means only to prepare for the next. We must say in southeast Asia – as we did in Europe – in the words of the Bible: "Hitherto shalt thou come, but no further."

There are those who say that all our effort there will be futile – that China's power is such that it is bound to dominate all southeast Asia. But there is no end to that argument until all of the nations of Asia are swallowed up.

There are those who wonder why we have a responsibility there. Well, we have it there for the same reason that we have a responsibility for the defense of Europe. World War II was fought in both Europe and Asia, and when it ended we found ourselves with continued responsibility for the defense of freedom.

OUR OBJECTIVE IN VIET-NAM

Our objective is the independence of South Viet-Nam, and its freedom from attack. We want nothing for ourselves – only that the people of South Viet-Nam be allowed to guide their own country in their own way.

We will do everything necessary to reach that objective. And we will do only what is absolutely necessary.

In recent months attacks on South Viet-Nam were stepped up. Thus, it became necessary for us to increase our response and to make attacks by air. This is not a change of purpose. It is a change in what we believe that purpose requires.

We do this in order to slow down aggression.

We do this to increase the confidence of the brave people of South Viet-Nam who have bravely borne this brutal battle for so many years with so many casualties.

And we do this to convince the leaders of North Viet-Nam – and all who seek to share their conquest – of a very simple fact: We will not be defeated. We will not grow tired.

We will not withdraw, either openly or under the cloak of a meaningless agreement.

We know that air attacks alone will not accomplish all of these purposes. But it is our best and prayerful judgment that they are a necessary part of the surest road to peace.

We hope that peace will come swiftly. But that is in the hands of others besides ourselves. And we must be prepared for a long continued conflict. It will require patience as well as bravery, the will to endure as well as the will to resist.

I wish it were possible to convince others with words of what we now find it necessary to say with guns and planes: Armed hostility is futile. Our resources are equal to any challenge. Because we fight for values and we fight for principles, rather than territory or colonies, our patience and our determination are unending.

Once this is clear, then it should also be clear that the only path for reasonable men is the path of peaceful settlement.

Such peace demands an independent South Viet-Nam – securely guaranteed and able to shape its own relationships to all others – free from outside interference – tied to no alliance – a military base for no other country.

These are the essentials of any final settlement.

We will never be second in the search for such a peaceful settlement in Viet-Nam.

There may be many ways to this kind of peace: in discussion or negotiation with the governments concerned; in large groups or in small ones; in the reaffirmation of old agreements or their strengthening with new ones.

We have stated this position over and over again, fifty times and more, to friend and foe alike. And we remain ready, with this purpose, for unconditional discussions.

And until that bright and necessary day of peace we will try to keep conflict from spreading. We have no desire to see thousands die in battle – Asians or Americans. We have no desire to devastate that which the people of North Viet-Nam have built with toil and sacrifice. We will use our power with restraint and with all the wisdom that we can command.

But we will use it.

This war, like most wars, is filled with terrible irony. For what do the people of North Viet-Nam want? They want what their neighbors also desire: food for their hunger; health for their bodies; a chance to learn; progress for their country; and an end to the bondage of material misery. And they would find all these things far more readily in peaceful association with others than in the endless course of battle.

A COOPERATIVE EFFORT FOR DEVELOPMENT

These countries of southeast Asia are homes for millions of impoverished people. Each day these people rise at dawn and struggle through until the night to wrestle existence from the soil. They are often wracked by disease, plagued by hunger, and death comes at the early age of 40.

Stability and peace do not come easily in such a land. Neither independence nor human dignity will ever be won, though, by arms alone. It also requires the work of peace. The American people have helped generously in times past in these works. Now there must be a much more massive effort to improve the life of man in that conflict-torn corner of our world.

The first step is for the countries of southeast Asia to associate themselves in a greatly expanded cooperative effort for development. We would hope that North Viet-Nam would take its place in the common effort just as soon as peaceful cooperation is possible.

The United Nations is already actively engaged in development in this area. As far back as 1961 I conferred with our authorities in Viet-Nam in connection with their work there. And I would hope tonight that the Secretary General of the United Nations could use the prestige of his great office, and his deep knowledge of Asia, to initiate, as soon as possible, with the countries of that area, a plan for cooperation in increased development.

For our part I will ask the Congress to join in a billion dollar American investment in this effort as soon as it is underway.

And I would hope that all other industrialized countries, including the Soviet Union, will join in this effort to replace despair with hope, and terror with progress.

The task is nothing less than to enrich the hopes and the existence of more than a hundred million people. And there is much to be done.

The vast Mekong River can provide food and water and power on a scale to dwarf even our own TVA.

The wonders of modern medicine can be spread through villages where thousands die every year from lack of care.

Schools can be established to train people in the skills that are needed to manage the process of development.

And these objectives, and more, are within the reach of a cooperative and determined effort.

I also intend to expand and speed up a program to make available our farm surpluses to assist in feeding and clothing the needy in Asia. We should not allow people to go hungry and wear rags while our own warehouses overflow with an abundance of wheat and corn, rice and cotton.

So I will very shortly name a special team of outstanding, patriotic, distinguished Americans to inaugurate our participation in these programs. This team will be headed by Mr. Eugene Black, the very able former President of the World Bank.

In areas that are still ripped by conflict, of course development will not be easy. Peace will be necessary for final success. But we cannot and must not wait for peace to begin this job.

Source: *Public Papers of the Presidents of the United States: Lyndon B. Johnson, 1965*, vol. 1 (Washington, DC: US Government Printing Office, 1966), pp. 394–9.

Suggested Questions for Discussion:

1. What was President Lyndon Johnson's vision for the future of Vietnam?
2. How did he think the United States could make this vision a reality?
3. Why was Johnson's vision compelling to many Americans, particularly the most educated figures in government?

8 Phil Ochs, "I ain't marchin' anymore," 1965

The conscription of young Americans for the Vietnam War in 1965 sparked resistance among educated men and women. Many draft-age college students questioned not only the war in Vietnam, but the purposes of war in general in American history. Phil Ochs – a popular young musician – captured the emerging anti-war protest culture. He was part of a larger anti-war sensibility in American folk and rock music at the time.[8]

Oh I marched to the battle of New Orleans
At the end of the early British war
The young land started growing
The young blood started flowing
But I ain't marchin' anymore

For I've killed my share of Indians
In a thousand different fights
I was there at the Little Big Horn
I heard many men lying I saw many more dying
But I ain't marchin' anymore

(chorus:)

It's always the old to lead us to the war
It's always the young to fall
Now look at all we've won with the saber and the gun
Tell me is it worth it all

For I stole California from the Mexican land
Fought in the bloody Civil War
Yes I even killed my brothers
And so many others But I ain't marchin' anymore

[8]   See Michael Schumacher, *There but for Fortune: The Life of Phil Ochs* (New York: Hyperion Books, 1996); Howard Sounes, *Down the Highway: The Life of Bob Dylan* (New York: Grove Press, 2001); David Hajdu, *Positively Fourth Street: The Lives and Times of Joan Baez, Bob Dylan, Mimi Baez Farina, and Richard Farina* (New York: Farrar, Straus, and Giroux, 2001).

For I marched to the battles of the German trench
In a war that was bound to end all wars
Oh I must have killed a million men
And now they want me back again
But I ain't marchin' anymore

(chorus)

For I flew the final mission in the Japanese sky
Set off the mighty mushroom roar
When I saw the cities burning I knew that I was learning
That I ain't marchin' anymore

Now the labor leader's screamin'
when they close the missile plants,
United Fruit screams at the Cuban shore,
Call it "Peace" or call it "Treason,"
Call it "Love" or call it "Reason,"
But I ain't marchin' any more,
No I ain't marchin' any more

Suggested Questions for Discussion:

1. How did Ochs define the role of war in American society?
2. What did Ochs advocate?
3. Why were Ochs' lyrics popular among young listeners?

9 Christian Appy, Oral Histories from the Vietnam War

The Vietnam War is a subject that continues to elicit strong and polarized opinions. Some observers argue that the United States fought a brutal war of aggression with horrific consequences. Others contend that American leaders believed they were defending humane ideals against communist repression. According to the latter view, the United States did not succeed because of its determined enemies, its corrupt allies, and its weak citizens at home. These differences of perspective have played out in every American military engagement since Vietnam. The oral histories reprinted here capture three voices that challenge and complicate both of the standard interpretations of the war. The speakers illustrate the complexity of personal experiences, the mix of patriotism and self-interest, and the lingering emotional residue of the war in the United States and Vietnam. These oral histories describe the Vietnam War as an uneasy combination of personal tragedy and triumph, rather than consistent grand policy.[9]

ROGER DONLON

"We were babes in arms in every way."

He was the first American in the Vietnam War to receive the Medal of Honor, the highest military decoration the United States can confer. A Green Beret captain, he commanded the Nam Dong Special Forces camp in the mountains of northern South Vietnam near the Laotian Border. It was that time in the war just before the full-scale build-up of US forces, when small teams of Americans worked with much larger South Vietnamese military units.

Our mission was to advise, assist, and train the Vietnamese. The central government was trying to do some things to give the impression that it was in control of all the country, including the countryside. They had set up "strategic hamlets" to give the people a sense of belonging to a program that came from the central government. Our job was to make sure these people could defend these outposts of freedom scattered throughout the whole country.

We trained a Vietnamese Strike Force of about three hundred men – a Civilian Irregular Defense Group. Some of them were coastal folks. Their families had been fishermen for generations and they were relocated as part of the strategic hamlet program and told to make their new homes there in the mountains. But when you start to move populations, the enemy knows what's going on and will put in infiltrators. Whenever you have population relocation it's bound to happen. Of the three hundred members of our Strike Force it turned out that about a hundred sympathized with the enemy. We never had a sense of the magnitude of the problem because we never had

---

[9]   The literature on the Vietnam War is enormous, and ever growing. For books that discuss both policy deliberations and personal experiences in the United States and Vietnam, readers may begin with Neil Sheehan, *A Bright Shining Lie: John Paul Vann and America in Vietnam* (New York: Random House, 1988); George Herring, *America's Longest War: The United States and Vietnam, 1950–1975*, 4th edn. (New York: McGraw-Hill, 2001); Marilyn Young, *Vietnam Wars, 1945–1990* (New York: Harper, 1991).

any real outside intelligence from higher headquarters. We were babes in arms in every way. We were working with and against cultures that were two thousand years old. They could manipulate us.

On the inner perimeter of the camp we had a Special Forces team of twelve Americans. That was our nucleus. We also had six Vietnamese Special Forces. They had airborne training but were political appointees and so they lacked the same commitment we found among ourselves. Then I had my sixty Nung mercenaries. We inherited them from the CIA who had used them for years. We hoped we could trust the Vietnamese, but we knew we could trust our Nungs. They were a Chinese ethnic minority that came out of mainland China after World War II and had stayed one step ahead of Communism when Mao took over. When North Vietnam fell in '54, the Nungs came south. They were very, very dedicated anti-Communists. We were being placed in isolated situations and we needed dependable security. We paid them more than the Vietnamese.

On the outer perimeter of the camp we had our Vietnamese Strike Force. The day before we were attacked, there was a fight between some of the Vietnamese and the Nungs. The Vietnamese were milling around the inner perimeter fence and started pummeling the Nungs with rocks. That sent the Nungs running toward their mortars and machine guns. The Vietnamese peppered the inner perimeter with their carbines. Sergeant Alamo got up between the two sides and the firing stopped. We estimated that about five hundred rounds were fired, but somehow no one was killed.

About two-thirty in the morning I had just finished making my rounds of the inner perimeter and gotten back to the mess hall when it was hit by a white phosphorous mortar shell. I was knocked back through the door. My first thought was that the Vietnamese Strike Force was back in action against the Nungs, but we were under heavy attack by the Viet Congo. My communications sergeant got on the transmitter. There was no time for code so he said in plain English: "Hello Danang ... Nam Dong calling ... We are under heavy mortar fire ... Request flare ship and air strike." He fled the communications room just before it went up in a fireball. So with the first mortar rounds all our communications were eliminated. The enemy knew us so well, they knew exactly what to hit and where it was. And all our buildings were thatch and rattan, so the white phosphorous not only set everything on fire, but silhouetted us when we tried to move.

Higher headquarters knew we were under attack but it was Fourth of July weekend and everybody was celebrating. When they went to scramble a plane, the hangar was locked and the plane wasn't fueled. So what could have been a twenty-minute response took several hours.

As commander, my job was not only to lead but to communicate, and the only way to do it was to move from point A to B to C. I just had to take my time and pray I could survive. I'd say a third of our Vietnamese forces on the outer perimeter fought for the other side. The first thing each of the traitors did when the attack started – and they knew it was coming – was to slit the throat or break the neck of the person next to them. So right off the bat our Strike Force went from three hundred down to two hundred, and possibly closer to a hundred. And the people we thought would be shooting outward were now shooting inward. It got pretty spicy very rapidly. We didn't have much help on the outer perimeter so we just had to hang on.

The VC used the veil of darkness to their advantage. Our job was to strip that veil as best we could. Just a few days before, we had received a high-tech, handheld flare. You just took off the top, slapped it on something hard, and it'd shoot. You'd get about twenty or thirty seconds of illumination. It was just pure luck that we had fifty or sixty of them in each of our five mortar pits.

The enemy came over the wire. They were gallant and brave and they thought by being numerically superior they could easily overrun us. We found out after the fact that a similar force had attacked another Special Forces camp the night before and overrun it. We didn't even get word of it. That shows you how bad our communications were with higher headquarters.

Early in the attack George Tuan, one of our Vietnamese interpreters, was running like mad to his assigned mortar pit. Partway there a 57-millimeter round caught him right at the knees and took his legs off. He just kept running on the stumps. Within about thirty seconds he was dead. That's one of the things you'd like to forget.

Primarily my job was to make sure we got our mortars firing in the key areas. Our guys were pretty good – they practically had the mortars vertical. It was pretty dangerous. Some of our mortars were going up a thousand feet and coming down within twenty-five yards of us.

You try to keep a cool head, but emotions would get in there. When John Houston died I knew he had just received a letter from his wife, Alice, informing him that they were going to be the proud parents of twins. Alice later gave premature birth to those twins. One of them died and is interred with his father in Arlington. The casualties of war go far beyond the immediate battlefield.

What I remember most was my effort to rescue Pop Alamo, a forty-six-year-old veteran of World War II and Korea who was our senior non-commissioned officer. He was pretty severely wounded and I tried to get him out of a mortar pit. As I carried him out we were blasted back into the pit. I thought that was the end. I don't know how long I was unconscious but when I came to, I found that Pop had died in my arms. What keeps you going at times like that is the love you feel for your fellow teammates. At the time you called it respect, but as the years go on you realize it was really a deep, deep love.

I just kind of ran out of fuel about eight o'clock in the morning. I got it in the shoulder and the arm and the gut and the leg and a few other places. Even breathing was excruciating and by the time they evacuated me I was unconscious. As they unloaded the chopper I regained consciousness. They were putting the dead in body bags and I heard somebody say, "Put that guy in a bag." He thought I was gone.

When I got out of the hospital I took some visits to the beach where I saw a navy ship that had Old Glory flying. It was beautiful and healing in a lot of ways. Since we were in Vietnam as guests just to advise and assist, the only place the American flag flew in-country was at the US Embassy. We had to do what we could to help the Vietnamese develop a sense of pride in their own flag, so we used to have a flag ceremony every morning in the center of the camp. We always wished we could put our flag up at the camp too, but that wasn't permitted. Not seeing it made us all a little more lonely.

NGUYEN THI KIM CHUY

"We came home hairless with ghostly white eyes."

She worked in the jungles of the Truong Son as a Youth Volunteer for four years. Today, she lives on the outskirts of Hanoi where she grows and sells flowers.

I was sent to the Truong Son to help make three new trails – Number Fifteen, Number Twenty-One, and Number Twenty-Two. That was my contribution 1 to the war against the Americans. We worked in Quang Binh Province, the gateway to the Truong Son, where the United States dropped so many bombs I that we called it the "bombing capital." We could distinguish every kind of I bomb by its sound. For example, a cluster bomb lands with a thud. That's because it's a "mother bomb" and doesn't itself cause the destruction. It just opens and out fly the "baby bombs." Those small baby bombs are lethal.

One day we had to withstand seven bombing attacks, while working day and night to fill the craters: At one point my commander asked me to go check on a group of girls about a hundred meters away. As I was walking in their direction, I saw with my own eyes a bomb drop into a shelter hole. Everyone stopped working and rushed there, screaming and crying. We were on our hands and knees clawing at the dirt. Our arms were smeared with blood. There were five people in that shelter. Four of them just turned to porridge. We couldn't tell them apart. We just divided the parts arbitrarily into four small mounds, gave each one a name, and buried them. Only one body was recognizable – a local woman who was visiting us. An official of the Communist Party, I think. She had her two-year-old child with her. That woman was holding her child so tightly we couldn't separate them. We buried them together. After that terrible experience we still had two craters to fill. So we went on with our work as if it hadn't happened.

If we had to travel from one part of the Truong Son to another we always moved in the middle of the night to reduce the risk of being bombed. When I was a young child I never had a sleepless night. I couldn't get used to losing so much sleep. Sometimes, I actually slept a little as I walked. One night I sleepwalked right off the trail into a thicket and they had to pull me out. From then on we tied ourselves together with a long rope looped around each of our waists. So a few nights later I took the lead on a small footpath. Once again I fell asleep, only this time I pulled everybody into the woods. [Laughs.]

We saw many soldiers traveling down the Truong Son. They loved us because we were courageous girls and worked so hard. When the Americans came to bomb us our boyfriends were very eager to protect us, but it was just innocent romance. No babies were born. Even if we wanted to do more, how could we? We lived apart from the boy volunteers and most of the soldiers moved so quickly to the South. We didn't have much time together.

Almost everyone got malaria and quite a few died from it. When I had it, I was told that eating a worm was a good folk remedy. They gave me a worm that was dirty, disgusting, and black, but I felt so sick I was willing to do anything to get better and I ate it without hesitation. I don't think it helped. Many of us temporarily lost our hair from malaria and living in the jungle for so many years made us look terrible. After the war we came home hairless with ghost white eyes, pale skin, and purple lips. Some girls lost their ability to have children. I developed terrible arthritis. When my old boyfriend came back from the war, I didn't think my health was good enough to have a family so I said good-bye to him. It was a very painful parting since his house was just around the corner in our village. Even after my family nourished me and gave me medicine, I weighed only thirty-seven kilos [eighty-two pounds]. Though I never married, I did adopt my older sister's daughter.

CLARK DOUGAN

"He Was Only 19 – Did You Know Him?"

In the 1980s, he co-authored seven books for The Vietnam Experience, *a twenty-volume series published by* Time-Life Books. *Now an editor for a university press, we meet at a conference of the Organization of American Historians.*

I went to Valley Forge High School in Parma Heights, Ohio – a big, working class, white, ethnic neighborhood just outside Cleveland. We were the Valley Forge "Patriots." Something like thirty-five kids from Parma died in the war. The principal would come on the intercom periodically and say, "We've just received the very sad news that Terry Kilbane, a marine lance corporal, has been killed in Vietnam. Let's please observe a moment of silence."

I think we sensed that we were all pawns of forces much larger than we were all pawns of forces much later than we were, and over which we had no control. It all seemed somehow like a roll of the dice. Some would go, some wouldn't, and it depended on accident, on how well we did in school, on what our parents' expectations were for us, lots of factors – but none of us were really that different from one another.

There was this one guy who sat next to me in homeroom named Greg Fischer. I played basketball, he played hockey. We didn't know each other very well, but because my last name began with D and his with F, we were in the same homeroom for three years. Toward the end of our senior year I remember talking with him about our plans for the future.

I said, "Well, actually I'm going to college next year. I just went down to visit this place called Kenyon and it seemed kind of cool. What are you going to do?"

He said, "Ah, I don't think I'm going to go to college. I'm thinking about going into the marines."

"The marines? Really?"

"Yeah, I mean, I'm going to get drafted anyhow, so if I'm going to get drafted, why not the best, you know?"

When we heard those obituaries over the school intercom it was a reminder that the war was there, and it was real. But one of the ways we coped with it was through a sort of black humor. It was almost as if the humor was an ort to make it go away, to make it unreal. For example, a few months after talk with Greg Fischer, all eight hundred and thirty-five of us marched into Cleveland Public Auditorium for commencement – the class of 1967. Suddenly some kid starts whistling the theme song to *The Bridge on the River Kwai* – the movie about British prisoners of war. And we all joined in! Believe me, it's not easy to whistle when you're laughing. This was followed by a very low, teenage, guttural version of "The Caissons Go Rolling Along." I'm not kidding. Meanwhile, in the background, the high school band is wailing away on "Pomp and Circumstance." You can just imagine all these guys in bright blue caps and gowns with the gold tassels, laughing away. It was fantastic.

So I go off to my first year in college and I'm really kind of oblivious of the war. The Tet Offensive is raging across South Vietnam and I'm trying to figure out what the hell *Paradise Lost* is all about. But I came home from college in late May.

On Memorial Day 1968, I opened up the *Cleveland Press* and there was an editorial on the front page with the title "He Was Only 19 – Did You Know Him?" It turns out to be about Greg Fischer and how he died at Dong Ha up near the DMZ. It just hit me like a hammer. I remembered that conversation in homeroom and it suddenly had this profound significance, I had gone off to this cloistered college while he was going off to die in Vietnam.

Unlike some, I've never had any guilt for not going to Vietnam. But I understand how easily it could have been me. Like any kid who had grown up in the fifties there was a certain allure to the military. And especially the marines. But my parents hadn't been able to go to college and they were determined that I would.

The *Cleveland Press* article concluded by quoting a letter Greg had left in the drawer of his desk. On the envelope he had written, "Open this if I don't come back from Vietnam." The letter was about what to do with the ten thousand bucks his family would get from his military life insurance – the standard death benefit for an American KIA. Primarily he wanted the money to go to his sister so she could go to college. The letter ended with a P.S., "Don't forget to give Joey my hockey skates."

The editorial was really asking, how many more people like Greg willing to waste? This is just an ordinary kid we're talking about. He wasn't an Eagle Scout, or a class president, or an all-American athlete. He was a kid who had worked in the local pharmacy. We all know the high school kid who works in the pharmacy, even if we don't know his name.

I think that was the moment when "Middle America" really turned against the war. The *Cleveland Press* was part of the Scripps-Howard chain, a conservative syndicate that had strongly supported the war. So it was remarkable this newspaper would run such an angry editorial about an American casualty. It reflected a feeling that was spreading all over working-class communities like Parma. I think a lot of World War II vets who had been sitting around kitchen tables saying, "You've got to fight for your country," were starting say, "Fuck this. It's not worth Greg Fischer's life or his buddy's life." Or they weren't saying it, but they were starting to feel it.

In 1982, I went to Greg Fischer's grave. What struck me more than thing else was the simplicity of Greg's marker. There's just one small plaque the ground surrounded by hundreds of marble headstones. It has his name, dates of his life, and one word: "Vietnam." That's the only epitaph.

I felt good about having gone. And stood there. And remembered. The only tribute you could really pay, and I can still pay, is to remember. What else is there?

Source: Christian Appy, *Patriots: The Vietnam War Remembered from All Sides* (New York: Penguin Books, 2003), pp. 12–15, 105–6, 304–6.

Suggested Questions for Discussion:

1. What are the similarities and differences in the accounts offered by the three individuals?
2. How did the Vietnam War change their lives?
3. How have their memories of the Vietnam War become part of their contemporary experiences?

10 My Lai Massacre, 1968

On the morning of March 16, 1968 soldiers from the US Army 11th Brigade, under the command of Lieutenant William Calley, entered the South Vietnamese village of My Lai. The American servicemen had been engaged in heavy fighting with National Liberation Front (NLF or "Vietcong") forces, and they had suffered serious casualties. My Lai had long served as a base for NLF forces, but by the time the American soldiers entered the village, the enemy units had already retreated from the area. Only old men, women, and children remained. Frustrated by the unwillingness of these frightened residents to cooperate in locating the armed NLF fighters, American soldiers proceeded, in a few short hours, to murder more than two hundred civilians. Many of the villagers died when American servicemen herded them into a ditch, firing upon the population en masse. Although the US military leadership initially hid the evidence of this illegal massacre, the story became a public scandal in late 1969 when journalist, Seymour Hersh, published a detailed account. Photographs, reports, and subsequent investigations forced

Americans to confront the murder of South Vietnamese civilians by young, unprepared, poorly led, and overwhelmed American soldiers. Photographs like this one undermined the ideals that Americans hoped they were fighting for in Vietnam, and the Cold War in general.[10]

Figure 6.2 *My Lai Massacre, 1968. Photograph by Ronald S. Haeberle/Time Life Pictures/Getty Images*

Source: http://www.learnnc.org/lp/multimedia/3290 (accessed June 4, 2009).

Suggested Questions for Discussion:

1. Why is this photograph so disturbing?
2. What message does the photo send about the Vietnam War?
3. How do you think this picture affected viewers in the United States?

---

[10]   See Seymour M. Hersh, *My Lai 4: A Report on the Massacre and Its Aftermath* (New York: Random House, 1970); Ronald H. Spector, *After Tet: The Bloodiest Year in Vietnam* (New York: Free Press, 1993); David L. Anderson (ed.), *Facing My Lai: Moving Beyond the Massacre* (Lawrence, KA: University Press of Kansas, 1998).

Chapter 7 Détente, Human Rights, and the Continuation of the Cold War

1 President Richard Nixon, "Opening" to China, 1972

For more than twenty years the United States refused to open diplomatic relations with the Communist regime that governed the People's Republic of China after 1949. In 1972 President Richard Nixon and his closest foreign policy advisor, Henry Kissinger, changed that. In dramatic fashion, they traveled to China and held meetings with Mao Zedong and Zhou Enlai, the two leading figures in China and the men whom Nixon had spent much of his career condemning for their communism. Meeting with Mao, Nixon and Kissinger now identified with the Chinese leaders as fellow statesmen, seeking to bring stability to a world torn apart by foreign wars and domestic turmoil. Nixon and Kissinger were more comfortable negotiating with Mao and Zhou than with their own citizens. They built a new American relationship with China based on personal connections among leaders, and hopes for mutual benefits through trade and cooperation.[1]

---

[1] See Margaret Macmillan, *Nixon and Mao: The Week that Changed the World* (New York: Random House, 2007); Jussi Hanhimäki, *The Flawed Architect: Henry Kissinger and American Foreign Policy* (New York: Oxford University Press, 2004); Warren I. Cohen, *America's Response to China*, 4th edn. (New York: Columbia University Press, 2000); Jeremi Suri, *Power and Protest: Global Revolution and the Rise of Détente* (Cambridge, MA: Harvard University Press, 2003).

Excerpts from Richard Nixon and Henry Kissinger's meeting with Mao Zedong, February 21, 1972

Participants: Chairman Mao Zedong
                Prime Minister Zhou Enlai
                Wang Hai-jung
                   Deputy Chief of Protocol of the Foreign Ministry
                [Nancy] Tang Wen-sheng
                   Interpreter

                President Nixon
                Henry A. Kissinger
                   Assistant to the President for National Security Affairs
                Winston Lord
                   National Security Council Staff (Notetaker)

Date and Time: Monday, February 21, 1972 – 2:50–3:55 p.m.

Place: Chairman Mao's Residence, Peking

(*There were opening greetings during which the Chairman welcomed President Nixon, and the President expressed his great pleasure at meeting the Chairman.*)

PRESIDENT NIXON: You read a good deal. The Prime Minister said that you read more than he does.

CHAIRMAN MAO: Yesterday in the airplane you put forward a very difficult problem for us. You said that what it is required to talk about are philosophic problems.

PRESIDENT NIXON: I said that because I have read the Chairman's poems and speeches, and I knew he was a professional philosopher. (*Chinese laugh*)

CHAIRMAN MAO: (*looking at Dr. Kissinger*) He is a doctor of philosophy?

PRESIDENT NIXON: He is a doctor of brains.

CHAIRMAN MAO: What about asking him to be the main speaker today?

PRESIDENT NIXON: He is an expert in philosophy.

DR. KISSINGER: I used to assign the Chairman's collective writings to my classes at Harvard.

CHAIRMAN MAO: Those writings of mine aren't anything. There is nothing instructive that I wrote.

(*Looking toward photographers*) Now they are trying to interrupt our meeting, our order here.

PRESIDENT NIXON: The Chairman's writings moved a nation and have changed the world.

CHAIRMAN MAO: I haven't been able to change it. I've only been able to change a few places in the vicinity of Peking.

Our common old friend, Generalissimo Chiang Kai-shek, doesn't approve of this. He called us communist bandits. He recently issued a speech. Have you seen it?

PRESIDENT NIXON: Chiang Kai-shek calls the Chairman a bandit. What does the Chairman call Chiang Kai-shek?

PRIME MINISTER ZHOU: Generally speaking we call them Chiang Kai-shek's clique. In the newspapers sometimes we call him a bandit: we are also called bandits in turn. Anyway, we abuse each other.

CHAIRMAN MAO: Actually, the history of our friendship with him is much longer than the history of your friendship with him.

PRESIDENT NIXON: Yes, I know.

CHAIRMAN MAO: We two must not monopolize the whole show. It won't do if we don't let Dr. Kissinger have a say. You have been famous about your trips to China.

DR. KISSINGER: It was the President who set the direction and worked out the plan.

PRESIDENT NIXON: He is a very wise assistant to say it that way. (*Mao and Zhou laugh*)

CHAIRMAN MAO: He is praising you, saying you are clever in doing so.

PRESIDENT NIXON: He doesn't look like a secret agent. He is the only man in captivity who could go to Paris 12 times and Peking once and no one knew it, except possibly a couple of pretty girls. (*Zhou laughs*)

DR. KISSINGER: They didn't know it; I used it as a cover.

CHAIRMAN MAO: In Paris?

PRESIDENT NIXON: Anyone who uses pretty girls as a cover must be the greatest diplomat of all time.

CHAIRMAN MAO: So your girls are very often made use of?

PRESIDENT NIXON: His girls, not mine. It would get me into great trouble if I used girls as a cover.

PRIME MINISTER ZHOU: (*laughs*) Especially during elections. (*Kissinger laughs*) Dr. Kissinger doesn't run for President because he wasn't born a citizen of the United States.

DR. KISSINGER: Miss Tang is eligible to be President of the United States.

PRESIDENT NIXON: She would be the first woman President. There's our candidate.

CHAIRMAN MAO: It would be very dangerous if you have such a candidate. But let us speak the truth. As for the Democratic Party, if they come into office again, we cannot avoid contacting them.

PRESIDENT NIXON: We understand. We will hope that we don't give you that problem.

CHAIRMAN MAO: Those questions are not questions to be discussed in my place. They should be discussed with the Premier. I discuss the philosophical questions. That is to say, I voted for you during your election. There is an American here called Mr. Frank Coe, and he wrote an article precisely at the time when your country was in havoc, during your last electoral campaign. He said you were going to be elected President. I appreciate that article very much. But now he is against the visit.

PRESIDENT NIXON: When the Chairman says he voted for me, he voted for the lesser of evils.

CHAIRMAN MAO: I like rightists. People say you are rightists, that the Republican Party is to the right, that Prime Minister Heath is also to the right.

PRESIDENT NIXON: And General De Gaulle.

CHAIRMAN MAO: De Gaulle is a different question. They also say the Christian Democratic Party of West Germany is also to the right. I am comparatively happy when these people on the right come into power.

PRESIDENT NIXON: I think the important thing to note is that in America, at least at this time, those on the right can do what those on the left talk about.

DR. KISSINGER: There is another point, Mr. President. Those on the left are pro-Soviet and would not encourage a move toward the People's Republic, and in fact criticize you on those grounds.

CHAIRMAN MAO: Exactly that. Some are opposing you. In our country there is also a reactionary group which is opposed to our contact with you. The result was that they got on an airplane and fled abroad. [*This is a reference to Lin Biao, and his attempted coup against Mao Zedong in 1971.*]

PRIME MINISTER ZHOU: Maybe you know this.

CHAIRMAN MAO: Throughout the whole world, the US intelligence reports are comparatively accurate. The next was Japan. As for the Soviet Union, they finally went to dig out the corpses, but they didn't say anything about it.

PRIME MINISTER ZHOU: In Outer Mongolia.

PRESIDENT NIXON: We had similar problems recently in the crisis on India–Pakistan. The American left criticized me very heavily for failing to side with India. This was for two reasons: they were pro-India and they were pro-Soviet.

I thought it was important to look at the bigger issue. We could not let a country, no matter how big, gobble up its neighbor. It cost me – I don't say this with sorrow because it was right – it cost me politically, but I think history will record that it was the right thing to do.

CHAIRMAN MAO: As a suggestion, may I suggest that you do a little less briefing? (*The President points at Dr. Kissinger and Zhou laughs*) Do you think it is good if you brief others on what we talk about our philosophic discussions here?

PRESIDENT NIXON: The Chairman can be sure that whatever we discuss or whatever I and the Prime Minister discuss, nothing goes beyond the room. That is the only way to have conversations at the highest level.

CHAIRMAN MAO: That is good.

PRESIDENT NIXON: For example, I hope to talk with the Prime Minister and later with the Chairman about issues like Taiwan, Vietnam and Korea. I also want to talk about – and this is very sensitive – the future of Japan, the future of the subcontinent, and what India's role will be; and on the broader world scene, the future of US–Soviet relations. Because only if we see the whole picture of the world and the great forces that move the world will we be able to make the right decisions about the immediate and urgent problems that always completely dominate our vision.

CHAIRMAN MAO: All those troublesome problems I don't want to get into much. I think your topic is better – philosophic questions.

PRESIDENT NIXON: For example, Mr. Chairman, it is interesting to note that most nations would approve of this meeting, but the Soviets disapprove, the Japanese have doubts which they express, and the Indians disapprove. So we must examine why, and determine how our policies should develop to deal with the whole world, as well as the immediate problems such as Korea, Vietnam, and of course, Taiwan.

CHAIRMAN MAO: Yes, I agree.

PRESIDENT NIXON: We, for example, must ask ourselves – again in the confines of this room – why the Soviets have more forces on the border facing you than on the border facing Western Europe. We must ask ourselves, what is the future of Japan? Is it better – here I know we have disagreements – is it better for Japan to be neutral, totally defenseless, or it is better for a time for Japan to have some relations with the United States? The point being – I am talking now in the realm of philosophy – in international relations there are no good choices. One thing is sure – we can leave no vacuums, because they can be filled. The Prime Minister, for example, has pointed out that the United States reaches out its hands and that the Soviet Union reaches out its hands. The question is which danger the People's Republic faces, whether it is the danger of American aggression or Soviet aggression. These are hard questions, but we have to discuss them.

CHAIRMAN MAO: At the present time, the question of aggression from the United States or aggression from China is relatively small; that is, it could be said that this is not a major issue, because the present situation is one in which a state of war does not exist between our two countries. You want to withdraw some of your troops back on your soil; ours do not go abroad.

Therefore, the situation between our two countries is strange because during the past 22 years our ideas have never met in talks. Now the time is less than 10 months since we began playing table tennis; if one counts the time since you put forward your suggestion at Warsaw it is less than two years. Our side also is bureaucratic in dealing with matters. For example, you wanted some exchange of persons on a personal level, things like that; also trade. But rather than deciding that we stuck with our stand that without settling major issues there is nothing to do with smaller issues. I myself persisted in that position. Later on I saw you were right, and we played table tennis. The Prime Minister said this was also after President Nixon came to office.

The former President of Pakistan introduced President Nixon to us. At that time, our Ambassador in Pakistan refused to agree on our having contact with you. He said it should be compared whether President Johnson or President Nixon would be better. But President Yahya said the two men cannot be compared, that these two men are incomparable. He said that one was like a gangster – he meant President Johnson. I don't know how he got that impression. We on our side were not very happy with that President either. We were not very happy with your former Presidents, beginning from Truman through Johnson. We were not happy with these Presidents, Truman and Johnson.

In between there were eight years of a Republican President. During that period probably you hadn't thought things out either.

PRIME MINISTER ZHOU: The main thing was John Foster Dulles' policy.

CHAIRMAN MAO: He (*Zhou*) also discussed this with Dr. Kissinger before.

PRESIDENT NIXON: But they (*gesturing towards Prime Minister Zhou and Dr. Kissinger*) shook hands. (*Zhou laughs*)

DR. KISSINGER: Mr. Chairman, the world situation has also changed dramatically during that period. We've had to learn a great deal. We thought all socialist/communist states were the same phenomenon. We didn't understand until the President came into office the different nature of revolution in China and the way revolution had developed in other socialist states.

PRESIDENT NIXON: Mr. Chairman, I am aware of the fact that over a period of years my position with regard to the People's Republic was one that the Chairman and Prime Minister totally disagreed with. What brings us together is a recognition of a new situation in the world and a recognition on our part that what is important is not a nation's internal political philosophy. What is important is its policy toward the rest of the world and towards us. That is why – this point I think I can be said to be honest – we have differences. The Prime Minister and Dr. Kissinger discussed these differences.

It also should be said – looking at the two great powers, the United States and China – we know China doesn't threaten the territory designs on China. We know China doesn't want to dominate the United States. We believe you too realize the United Sates doesn't want to dominate the world. Also – maybe you don't believe this, but I do – neither China nor the United States, both great nations, want to dominate the world. Because our attitudes are the same on these two issues, we don't threaten each others' territories.

Therefore, we can find common ground, despite our differences, to build a world structure in which both can be safe to develop in our own ways on our own roads. That cannot be said about some other nations in the world.

CHAIRMAN MAO: Neither do we threaten Japan or South Korea.

PRESIDENT NIXON: Nor any country. Nor do we.

CHAIRMAN MAO: (*Checking the time with Zhou*) Do you think we have covered enough today?

PRESIDENT NIXON: Yes. I would like to say as we finish, Mr. Chairman, we know you and the Prime Minister have taken great risks in inviting us here. For us also it was a difficult decision. But having read some of the Chairman's statements, I know he is one who sees when an opportunity comes, that you must seize the hour and seize the day.

I would also like to say in a personal sense – and this to you Mr. Prime Minister – you do not know me. Since you do not know me, you shouldn't trust me. You will find I never say something I cannot do. And I always will do more than I can say. On this basis I want to have frank talks with the Chairman and, of course, with the Prime Minister.

CHAIRMAN MAO: (*Pointing to Dr. Kissinger*) "Seize the hour and seize the day." I think that, generally speaking, people like me sound a lot of big cannons. (*Zhou laughs*) That is, things like "the whole world should unite and defeat imperialism, revisionism, and all reactionaries, and establish socialism."

PRESIDENT NIXON: Like me. And bandits.

CHAIRMAN MAO: But perhaps you as an individual may not be among those to be overthrown. They say that he (*Dr. Kissinger*) is also among those not to be overthrown personally. And if all of you are overthrown we wouldn't have any more friends left.

PRESIDENT NIXON: Mr. Chairman, the Chairman's life is well known to all of us. He came from a very poor family to the top of the most populous nation in the world, a great nation.

My background is not so well known. I also came from a very poor family, and to the top of a very great nation. History has brought us together. The question is whether we, with different philosophies, but both with feet on the ground, and having come from the people, can make a breakthrough that will serve not just China and America, but the whole world in the years ahead. And that is why we are here.

CHAIRMAN MAO: Your book, "The Six Crises," is not a bad book.

PRESIDENT NIXON: He (*Mao*) reads too much.

CHAIRMAN MAO: Too little. I don't know much about the United States. I must ask you to send some teachers here, mainly teachers of history and geography

PRESIDENT NIXON: That's good, the best.

CHAIRMAN MAO: That's what I said to Mr. Edgar Snow, the correspondent who passed away a few days ago.

PRESIDENT NIXON: That was very sad.

CHAIRMAN MAO: Yes, indeed.

It is alright to talk well and also alright if there are no agreements, because what use is there if we stand in deadlock? Why is it that we must be able to reach results? People will say ... if we fail the first time, then people will talk why are we not able to succeed the first time? The only reason would be that we have taken the wrong road. What will they say if we succeed the second time?

(There were then some closing pleasantries. The Chairman said he was not well. President Nixon responded that he looked good. The Chairman said that appearances were deceiving. After handshakes and more pictures, Prime Minister Chou then escorted the President out of the residence.)

Source: Jeremi Suri, *The Global Revolutions of 1968* (New York: W. W. Norton, 2007), pp. 259–68.

Suggested Questions for Discussion:

1. How did Richard Nixon and Henry Kissinger build common ground with their Chinese counterparts?
2. What did Nixon and Kissinger accomplish through their meetings with Mao Zedong and Zhou Enlai?
3. Why was this trip to China so transformative for American foreign policy and international relations in general?

2 Agreement on Basic Principles between the United States and the Soviet Union, 1972

Richard Nixon was the first US president to visit the Soviet Union since World War II. His May 1972 trip announced a new era of "détente" between the superpowers, codified in their agreement on "Basic Principles." In this document, the two governments pledged themselves to conflict avoidance, arms control, mutual consultation, increased economic and cultural cooperation, and "non-interference in internal affairs." Henry Kissinger played an instrumental role in writing the document, applying his long-held desire for agreed "rules" to manage the international system. The Basic Principles did not include any language about human rights or social justice. They reaffirmed the dominance of the two superpowers across a broad range of international issues.[2]

---

[2]   See Jeremi Suri, *Henry Kissinger and the American Century* (Cambridge, MA: Belknap Press of Harvard University Press, 2007); Raymond Garthoff, *Détente and Confrontation: American–Soviet Relations from Nixon to Reagan*, rev. edn. (Washington DC: Brookings Institution Press, 1994); Vladislav Zubok, *A Failed Empire: The Soviet Union in the Cold War from Stalin to Gorbachev* (Chapel Hill, NC: University of North Carolina Press, 2007).

Text of the "Basic Principles of Relations Between the United States of America and the Union of Soviet Socialist Republics"

The United States of America and the Union of Soviet Socialist Republics

Guided by their obligations under the Charter of the United Nations and by a desire to strengthen peaceful relations with each other and to place these relations on the firmest possible basis,

Aware of the need to make every effort to remove the threat of war and to create conditions which promote the reduction of tensions in the world and the strengthening of universal security and international cooperation,

Believing that the improvement of US–Soviet relations and their mutually advantageous development in such areas as economics, science and culture, will meet these objectives and contribute to better mutual understanding and business-like cooperation, without in any way prejudicing the interests of third countries,

Conscious that these objectives reflect the interests of the peoples of both countries,

Have agreed as follows:

First. They will proceed from the common determination that in the nuclear age there is no alternative to conducting their mutual relations on the basis of peaceful coexistence. Differences in ideology and in the social systems of the USA and the USSR are not obstacles to the bilateral development of normal relations based on the principles of sovereignty, equality, non-interference in internal affairs and mutual advantage.

Second. The USA and the USSR attach major importance to preventing the development of situations capable of causing a dangerous exacerbation of their relations. Therefore, they will do their utmost to avoid military confrontations and to prevent the outbreak of nuclear war. They will always exercise restraint in their mutual relations, and will be prepared to negotiate and settle differences by peaceful means. Discussions and negotiations on outstanding issues will be conducted in a spirit of reciprocity, mutual accommodation and mutual benefit.

Both sides recognize that efforts to obtain unilateral advantage at the expense of the other, directly or indirectly, are inconsistent with these objectives. The prerequisites for maintaining and strengthening peaceful relations between the USA and the USSR are the recognition of the security interests of the Parties based on the principle of equality and the renunciation of the use or threat of force.

Third. The USA and the USSR have a special responsibility, as do other countries which are permanent members of the United Nations Security Council, to do everything in their power so that conflicts or situations will not arise which would serve to increase international tensions. Accordingly, they will seek to promote conditions in which all countries will live in peace and security and will not be subject to outside interference in their internal affairs.

Fourth. The USA and the USSR intend to widen the juridical basis of their mutual relations and to exert the necessary efforts so that bilateral agreements which they have concluded and multilateral treaties and agreements to which they are jointly parties are faithfully implemented.

Fifth. The USA and the USSR reaffirm their readiness to continue the practice of exchanging views on problems of mutual interest and, when necessary, to conduct such exchanges at the highest level, including meetings between leaders of the two countries.

The two governments welcome and will facilitate an increase in productive contacts between representatives of the legislative bodies of the two countries.

Sixth. The Parties will continue their efforts to limit armaments on a bilateral as well as on a multilateral basis. They will continue to make special efforts to limit strategic armaments. Whenever possible, they will conclude concrete agreements aimed at achieving these purposes.

The USA and the USSR regard as the ultimate objective of their efforts the achievement of general and complete disarmament and the establishment of an effective system of international security in accordance with the purposes and principles of the United Nations.

Seventh. The USA and the USSR regard commercial and economic ties as an important and necessary element in the strengthening of their bilateral relations and thus will actively promote the growth of such ties. They will facilitate cooperation between the relevant organizations and enterprises of the two countries and the conclusion of appropriate agreements and contracts, including long-term ones.

The two countries will contribute to the improvement of maritime and air communications between them.

Eighth. The two sides consider it timely and useful to develop mutual contacts and cooperation in the fields of science and technology. Where suitable, the USA and the USSR will conclude appropriate agreements dealing with concrete cooperation in these fields.

Ninth. The two sides reaffirm their intention to deepen cultural ties with one another and to encourage fuller familiarization with each other's cultural values. They will promote improved conditions for cultural exchanges and tourism.

Tenth. The USA and the USSR will seek to ensure that their ties and cooperation in all the above-mentioned fields and in any others in their mutual interest are built on a firm and long-term basis. To give a permanent character to these efforts, they will establish in all fields where this is feasible joint commissions or other joint bodies.

Eleventh. The USA and the USSR make no claim for themselves and would not recognize the claims of anyone else to any special rights or advantages in world affairs. They recognize the sovereign equality of all states.

The development of US–Soviet relations is not directed against third countries and their interests.

Twelfth. The basic principles set forth in this document do not affect any obligations with respect to other countries earlier assumed by the USA and the USSR.

Moscow, May 29, 1972

FOR THE UNITED STATES OF AMERICA

RICHARD NIXON
President of the United States of America

FOR THE UNION OF SOVIET SOCIALIST REPUBLICS
LEONID I. BREZHNEV
General Secretary of the Central Committee, CPSU

Source: www.presidency.ucsb.edu/ws/index.php?pid=3438 (accessed August 20, 2008).

Suggested Questions for Discussion:

1. How did the Basic Principles change the Cold War?
2. How did the Basic Principles contribute to international and domestic stability?
3. Why did American and Soviet leaders attach so much importance to these Basic Principles?

3 American Complicity in Chilean Repression, 1973

On September 4, 1970 the Popular Action Front Party in Chile received 36.3 percent of the vote in national elections. This was more than any other party. According to custom, the party's leader, Salvador Allende Gossens, became the Chilean president. The United States had long provided aid to Allende's opponents, fearful that he would allow communist influence to grow in Chile.

American policy-makers were especially anxious about Allende's personal ties to Cuban leader, Fidel Castro. The Nixon administration initially attempted to prevent Allende from becoming president, and then sought to force him from power. American policy included a multifaceted strategy of economic pressures, propaganda, and covert funding for a coup. On September 11, 1973 General Augusto Pinochet, operating with financial support from the US government, overthrew Allende. Pinochet established dictatorial rule, and began a brutal campaign to murder his opponents in Chile and across the region. As this November 1973 report indicates, Secretary of State Henry Kissinger was well informed about the atrocities committed by the Chilean military after the American-supported coup. The United States government did little to alleviate the suffering or curtail the Pinochet regime's brutality.[3]

Department of State
Briefing Memorandum for Secretary of State Henry Kissinger
November 27, 1973

SECRET

To: Secretary of State Henry Kissinger
From: Jack B. Kubisch, State Department

Chilean Executions

You requested by cable from Tokyo a report on this subject.

On October 24 the Junta announced that summary, on-the-spot executions would no longer be carried out and that persons caught in the act of resisting the government would henceforth be held for military courts. Since that date 17 executions following military trials have been announced. Publicly acknowledged executions, both summary and in compliance with court martial sentences, now total approximately 100, with an additional 40 prisoners shot while "trying to escape." An internal, confidential report prepared for the Junta puts the number of executions for the period

---

[3]   See Steve J. Stern, *Battling for Hearts and Minds: Memory Struggles in Pinochet's Chile, 1973–1988* (Durham, NC: Duke University Press, 2006); Jonathan Haslam, *The Nixon Administration and the Death of Allende's Chile: A Case of Assisted Suicide* (London: Verso, 2005); John Dinges, *The Condor Years: How Pinochet and His Allies Brought Terrorism to Three Continents* (New York: New Press, 2004); Jussi Hanhimäki, *The Flawed Architect: Henry Kissinger and American Foreign Policy* (New York: Oxford University Press, 2004); Jeremi Suri, *Henry Kissinger and the American Century* (Cambridge, MA: Harvard University Press, 2007).

September 11–30 at 320. The latter figure is probably a more accurate indication of the extent of this practice.

Our best estimate is that the military and police units in the field are generally complying with the order to desist from summary executions. At least the rather frequent use of random violence that marked the operations of these units in the early post-coup days has clearly abated for the time being. However, there are no indications as yet of a disposition to forego executions <u>after</u> military trial.

The Chilean leaders justify these executions as entirely legal in the application of martial law under what they have declared to be a "state of siege in time of war." Their code of military justice permits death by firing squad for a range of offenses, including treason, armed resistance, illegal possession of arms and auto theft. Sentences handed down by military tribunals during a state of siege are not reviewable by civilian courts.

The purpose of the executions is in part to discourage by example those who see to organize armed opposition to the Junta. The Chilean military, persuaded to some degree by years of Communist Party propaganda, expected to be confronted by heavy resistance when they overthrew Allende. Fear of civil war was an important factor in their decision to employ a heavy hand from the outset. Also present is a puritanical, crusading spirit – a determination to cleanse and rejuvenate Chile. (A number of those executed seem to have been petty criminals.)

The Junta now has more confidence in the security situation and more awareness of the pressure of international opinion. It may be a hopeful sign that the Junta continues to stall on bringing to trial former cabinet ministers and other prominent Marxists – people the military initially had every intention of standing up before firing squads. How the military leaders proceed in this area from now on will be influenced to some degree by outside opinion and particularly by ours, but the major consideration will continue to be their assessment of the security situation. ...

FACT SHEET – HUMAN RIGHTS IN CHILE
(Prepared November 15, 1973)

Figures without asterisk are from public sources.

Total arrested in Chile since September 11	13,500*
Arrested originally and held in National Stadium in Santiago	7–8,000
Released from Stadium	6,500
Presently held in Stadium	0

Detained in Santiago jails	550
Detained outside Santiago	2,000
Estimated number serving sentence or pending trial	1,500*
Executions acknowledged	100 (approx)
Executions according to intelligence source	320*
Number killed attempting to escape military custody	40
American citizens detained (27 detainees had been released by October 17)	0
Americans dead since coup	2
Safeconducts issued to asylees in Embassies	1,791
Safeconducts issued to others	3,100
Safeconduct requests not yet acted upon	408
Departed from Chile (Chileans and foreigners)	2,000 (approx)
Foreigners registered with UNHCR for permanent resettlement	
In safe havens (refugee camps, etc.)	820
At home (possibly some under house arrest)	824
In diplomatic missions	172
In GOC detention centers	203
Total number still in foreign Embassies	N.A. (368 as of mid-Oct)
Total dead:	600 (approx)
According to Chilean authorities	
According to Barnes article in October 8 Newsweek	2,796
According to Oct 21 Washington Post article on CIA Director Colby's statement to Congressional Committee	2–3,000
Recent SRF source estimate	1,500 +

Source: Peter Kornbluh, *The Pinochet File: A Declassified Dossier on Atrocity and Accountability* (New York: The New Press, 2003), pp. 174–6.

Suggested Questions for Discussion:

1. What were the conditions in Chile after the September 11, 1973 coup?
2. What were American options?
3. Why didn't this account of the atrocities in Chile change American policy?

4 The Helsinki Final Act, 1975

The November 1972 opening of the Conference on Security and Cooperation in Europe (CSCE) marked a major turning point in the Cold War. For the first time, all the nations of Europe (East and West), as well as the Soviet Union, the United States, and Canada engaged in an extended series of negotiations about the future stability and prosperity of the continent. Pushed by many of the smaller the European powers, the CSCE was an effort to overcome Cold War divisions. The concluding "Final Act" of nearly three years of negotiations set out three main provisions (known as "baskets"). These included the inviolability of established territorial boundaries, increased trade and cultural exchange, and protections for basic human rights. The first of these provisions provided legitimacy for imposed Soviet control on Eastern Europe, but the third challenged the repressive use of force by Moscow and its allies. This contradiction between territorial sovereignty and transnational human rights remained unresolved. It provided inspiration for dissident groups within the Soviet bloc, and human rights activists elsewhere, who could now point to the Final Act as an affirmation of their claims.[4]

Declaration on Principles Guiding Relations between Participating States

. . .

I. Sovereign equality, respect for the rights inherent in sovereignty

The participating States will respect each other's sovereign equality and individuality as well as all the rights inherent in and encompassed by its sovereignty, including in particular the right of every State to juridical equality, to territorial integrity and to freedom and political independence. They will also respect each other's right freely to choose and develop its political, social, economic and cultural systems as well as its right to determine its laws and regulations.

Within the framework of international law, all the participating States have equal rights and duties. They will respect each other's right to define and conduct as it wishes its relations with other States in accordance with

[4] Andreas Wenger, Vojtech Mastny, and Christian Nuenlist (eds.), *Origins of the European Security System: The Helsinki Process Revisited, 1965–1975* (London: Routledge, 2008); Daniel C. Thomas, *The Helsinki Effect: International Norms, Human Rights, and the Demise of Communism* (Princeton, NJ: Princeton University Press, 2001).

international law and in the spirit of the present Declaration. They consider that their frontiers can be changed, in accordance with international law, by peaceful means and by agreement. They also have the right to belong or not to belong to international organizations, to be or not to be a party to bilateral or multilateral treaties including the right to be or not to be a party to treaties of alliance; they also have the right to neutrality.

II. Refraining from the threat or use of force

The participating States will refrain in their mutual relations, as well as in their international relations in general, from the threat or use of force against the territorial integrity or political independence of any State, or in any other manner inconsistent with the purposes of the United Nations and with the present Declaration. No consideration may be invoked to serve to warrant resort to the threat or use of force in contravention of this principle.

Accordingly, the participating States will refrain from any acts constituting a threat of force or direct or indirect use of force against another participating State.

Likewise they will refrain from any manifestation of force for the purpose of inducing another participating State to renounce the full exercise of its sovereign rights. Likewise they will also refrain in their mutual relations from any act of reprisal by force.

No such threat or use of force will be employed as a means of settling disputes, or questions likely to give rise to disputes, between them.

III. Inviolability of frontiers

The participating States regard as inviolable all one another's frontiers as well as the frontiers of all States in Europe and therefore they will refrain now and in the future from assaulting these frontiers.

Accordingly, they will also refrain from any demand for, or act of, seizure and usurpation of part or all of the territory of any participating State.

IV. Territorial integrity of States

The participating States will respect the territorial integrity of each of the participating States. Accordingly, they will refrain from any action inconsistent with the purposes and principles of the Charter of the United Nations against the territorial integrity, political independence or the unity of any participating State, and in particular from any such action constituting a threat or use of force.

The participating States will likewise refrain from making each other's territory the object of military occupation or other direct or indirect measures of force in contravention of international law, or the object of acquisition by means of such measures or the threat of them. No such occupation or acquisition will be recognized as legal.

V. Peaceful settlement of disputes

The participating States will settle disputes among them by peaceful means in such a manner as not to endanger international peace and security, and justice.

They will endeavour in good faith and a spirit of cooperation to reach a rapid and equitable solution on the basis of international law.

For this purpose they will use such means as negotiation, enquiry, mediation, conciliation, arbitration, judicial settlement or other peaceful means of their own choice including any settlement procedure agreed to in advance of disputes to which they are parties.

In the event of failure to reach a solution by any of the above peaceful means, the parties to a dispute will continue to seek a mutually agreed way to settle the dispute peacefully.

Participating States, parties to a dispute among them, as well as other participating States, will refrain from any action which might aggravate the situation to such a degree as to endanger the maintenance of international peace and security and thereby make a peaceful settlement of the dispute more difficult.

VI. Non-intervention in internal affairs

The participating States will refrain from any intervention, direct or indirect, individual or collective, in the internal or external affairs falling within the domestic jurisdiction of another participating State, regardless of their mutual relations.

They will accordingly refrain from any form of armed intervention or threat of such intervention against another participating State.

They will likewise in all circumstances refrain from any other act of military, or of political, economic or other coercion designed to subordinate to their own interest the exercise by another participating State of the rights inherent in its sovereignty and thus to secure advantages of any kind.

Accordingly, they will, *inter alia*, refrain from direct or indirect assistance to terrorist activities, or to subversive or other activities directed towards the violent overthrow of the regime of another participating State.

VII.   Respect for human rights and fundamental freedoms, including the freedom of thought, conscience, religion or belief

The participating States will respect human rights and fundamental freedoms, including the freedom of thought, conscience, religion or belief, for all without distinction as to race, sex, language or religion.

They will promote and encourage the effective exercise of civil, political, economic, social, cultural and other rights and freedoms all of which derive from the inherent dignity of the human person and are essential for his free and full development.

Within this framework the participating States will recognize and respect the freedom of the individual to profess and practice, alone or in community with others, religion or belief acting in accordance with the dictates of his own conscience.

The participating States on whose territory national minorities exist will respect the right of persons belonging to such minorities to equality before the law, will afford them the full opportunity for the actual enjoyment of human rights and fundamental freedoms and will, in this manner, protect their legitimate interests in this sphere.

The participating States recognize the universal significance of human rights and fundamental freedoms, respect for which is an essential factor for the peace, justice and well-being necessary to ensure the development of friendly relations and co-operation among themselves as among all States.

They will constantly respect these rights and freedoms in their mutual relations and will endeavour jointly and separately, including in co-operation with the United Nations, to promote universal and effective respect for them.

They confirm the right of the individual to know and act upon his rights and duties in this field.

In the field of human rights and fundamental freedoms, the participating States will act in conformity with the purposes and principles of the Charter of the United Nations and with the Universal Declaration of Human Rights. They will also fulfil their obligations as set forth in the international declarations and agreements in this field, including *inter alia* the International Covenants on Human Rights, by which they may be bound.

VIII.   Equal rights and self-determination of peoples

The participating States will respect the equal rights of peoples and their right to self-determination, acting at all times in conformity with the purposes and principles of the Charter of the United Nations and with the relevant norms of international law, including those relating to territorial integrity of States.

By virtue of the principle of equal rights and self-determination of peoples, all peoples always have the right, in full freedom, to determine, when and as they wish, their internal and external political status, without external interference, and to pursue as they wish their political, economic, social and cultural development.

The participating States reaffirm the universal significance of respect for and effective exercise of equal rights and self-determination of peoples for the development of friendly relations among themselves as among all States; they also recall the importance of the elimination of any form of violation of this principle.

IX.   Cooperation among States

The participating States will develop their co-operation with one another and with all States in all fields in accordance with the purposes and principles of the Charter of the United Nations. In developing their co-operation the participating States will place special emphasis on the fields as set forth within the framework of the Conference on Security and Co-operation in Europe, with each of them making its contribution in conditions of full equality.

They will endeavour, in developing their co-operation as equals, to promote mutual understanding and confidence, friendly and good-neighbourly relations among themselves, international peace, security and justice. They will equally endeavour, in developing their co-operation, to improve the well-being of peoples and contribute to the fulfilment of their aspirations through, *inter alia*, the benefits resulting from increased mutual knowledge and from progress and achievement in the economic, scientific, technological, social, cultural and humanitarian fields. They will take steps to promote conditions favourable to making these benefits available to all; they will take into account the interest of all in the narrowing of differences in the levels of economic development, and in particular the interest of developing countries throughout the world.

They confirm that governments, institutions, organizations and persons have a relevant and positive role to play in contributing toward the achievement of these aims of their cooperation.

They will strive, in increasing their cooperation as set forth above, to develop closer relations among themselves on an improved and more enduring basis for the benefit of peoples.

X.   *Fulfilment in good faith of obligations under international law*

The participating States will fulfil in good faith their obligations under international law, both those obligations arising from the generally recognized principles and rules of international law and those obligations arising from treaties or other agreements, in conformity with international law, to which they are parties.

In exercising their sovereign rights, including the right to determine their laws and regulations, they will conform with their legal obligations under international law; they will furthermore pay due regard to and implement the provisions in the Final Act of the Conference on Security and Cooperation in Europe.

The participating States confirm that in the event of a conflict between the obligations of the members of the United Nations under the Charter of the United Nations and their obligations under any treaty or other international agreement, their obligations under the Charter will prevail, in accordance with Article 103 of the Charter of the United Nations.

All the principles set forth above are of primary significance and, accordingly, they will be equally and unreservedly applied, each of them being interpreted taking into account the others.

The participating States express their determination fully to respect and apply these principles, as set forth in the present Declaration, in all aspects, to their mutual relations and cooperation in order to ensure to each participating State the benefits resulting from the respect and application of these principles by all.

The participating States, paying due regard to the principles above and, in particular, to the first sentence of the tenth principle, "Fulfilment in good faith of obligations under international law", note that the present Declaration does not affect their rights and obligations, nor the corresponding treaties and other agreements and arrangements.

The participating States express the conviction that respect for these principles will encourage the development of normal and friendly relations and the progress of co-operation among them in all fields. They also express the conviction that respect for these principles will encourage the development of political contacts among them which in time would contribute to better mutual understanding of their positions and views.

Source: http://www1.umn.edu/humanrts/osce/basics/finact75.htm (accessed August, 20 2008).

Suggested Questions for Discussion:

1. What made the Helsinki Final Act such an unprecedented Cold War agreement?
2. What were the contradictions and limitations of the Helsinki Final Act?
3. Why did the Helsinki Final Act become so inspirational for dissidents and human rights activists?

5 President Jimmy Carter, Address at the University of Notre Dame, 1977

President Jimmy Carter entered the White House in 1977, determined to set a new course for American foreign policy. He rejected the secretiveness, the alliances with dictators, and the brutality tolerated by Richard Nixon and Henry Kissinger. Instead, Carter committed the United States to a foreign policy that emphasized human rights, arms control, economic development, and negotiated compromise. Carter remained firm in his criticisms of communism aggression, but he believed that a more democratic approach to foreign policy would produce better results.[5]

... I want to speak to you today about the strands that connect our actions overseas with our essential character as a nation. I believe we can have a foreign policy that is democratic, that is based on fundamental values, and that uses power and influence, which we have, for humane purposes. We can also have a foreign policy that the American people both support and, for a change, know about and understand.

I have a quiet confidence in our own political system. Because we know that democracy works, we can reject the arguments of those rulers who deny human rights to their people.

We are confident that democracy's example will be compelling, and so we seek to bring that example closer to those from whom in the past few years we have been separated and who are not yet convinced about the advantages of our kind of life.

We are confident that the democratic methods are the most effective, and so we are not tempted to employ improper tactics here at home or abroad.

[5] See Melvyn P. Leffler, *For the Soul of Mankind: The United States, the Soviet Union, and the Cold War* (New York: Hill and Wang, 2007); Odd Arne Westad, *The Global Cold War: Third World Interventions and the Making of Our Times* (Cambridge: Cambridge University Press, 2005); Gaddis Smith, *Morality, Reason, and Power: American Diplomacy in the Carter Years* (New York: Hill and Wang, 1986).

We are confident of our own strength, so we can seek substantial mutual reductions in the nuclear arms race.

And we are confident of the good sense of American people, and so we let them share in the process of making foreign policy decisions. We can thus speak with the voices of 215 million, and not just of an isolated handful.

Democracy's great recent successes – in India, Portugal, Spain, Greece – show that our confidence in this system is not misplaced. Being confident of our own future, we are now free of that inordinate fear of communism which once led us to embrace any dictator who joined us in that fear. I'm glad that that's being changed.

For too many years, we've been willing to adopt the flawed and erroneous principles and tactics of our adversaries, sometimes abandoning our own values for theirs. We've fought fire with fire, never thinking that fire is better quenched with water. This approach failed, with Vietnam the best example of its intellectual and moral poverty. But through failure we have now found our way back to our own principles and values, and we have regained our lost confidence.

By the measure of history, our Nation's 200 years are very brief, and our rise to world eminence is briefer still. It dates from 1945, when Europe and the old international order lay in ruins. Before then, America was largely on the periphery of world affairs. But since then, we have inescapably been at the center of world affairs.

Our policy during this period was guided by two principles: a belief that Soviet expansion was almost inevitable but that it must be contained, and the corresponding belief in the importance of an almost exclusive alliance among non-Communist nations on both sides of the Atlantic. That system could not last forever unchanged. Historical trends have weakened its foundation. The unifying threat of conflict with the Soviet Union has become less intensive, even though the competition has become more extensive.

The Vietnamese war produced a profound moral crisis, sapping worldwide faith in our own policy and our system of life, a crisis of confidence made even more grave by the covert pessimism of some of our leaders.

In less than a generation, we've seen the world change dramatically. The daily lives and aspirations of most human beings have been transformed. Colonialism is nearly gone. A new sense of national identity now exists in almost 100 new countries that have been formed in the last generation. Knowledge has become more widespread. Aspirations are higher. As more people have been freed from traditional constraints, more have been determined to achieve, for the first time in their lives, social justice.

The world is still divided by ideological disputes, dominated by regional conflicts, and threatened by danger that we will not resolve the differences of race and wealth without violence or without drawing into combat the major military powers. We can no longer separate the traditional issues of war and peace from the new global questions of justice, equity, and human rights.

It is a new world, but America should not fear it. It is a new world, and we should help to shape it. It is a new world that calls for a new American foreign policy – a policy based on constant decency in its values and on optimism in our historical vision.

We can no longer have a policy solely for the industrial nations as the foundation of global stability, but we must respond to the new reality of a politically awakening world.

We can no longer expect that the other 150 nations will follow the dictates of the powerful, but we must continue – confidently – our efforts to inspire, to persuade, and to lead.

Our policy must reflect our belief that the world can hope for more than simple survival and our belief that dignity and freedom are fundamental spiritual requirements. Our policy must shape an international system that will last longer than secret deals.

We cannot make this kind of policy by manipulation. Our policy must be open; it must be candid; it must be one of constructive global involvement, resting on five cardinal principles.

I've tried to make these premises clear to the American people since last January. Let me review what we have been doing and discuss what we intend to do.

First, we have reaffirmed America's commitment to human rights as a fundamental tenet of our foreign policy. In ancestry, religion, color, place of origin, and cultural background, we Americans are as diverse a nation as the world has ever seen. No common mystique of blood or soil unites us. What draws us together, perhaps more than anything else, is a belief in human freedom. We want the world to know that our Nation stands for more than financial prosperity.

This does not mean that we can conduct our foreign policy by rigid moral maxims. We live in a world that is imperfect and which will always be imperfect – a world that is complex and confused and which will always be complex and confused.

I understand fully the limits of moral suasion. We have no illusion that changes will come easily or soon. But I also believe that it is a mistake to undervalue the power of words and of the ideas that words embody. In our own history, that power has ranged from Thomas Paine's "Common Sense" to Martin Luther King, Jr's "I Have a Dream."

In the life of the human spirit, words are action, much more so than many of us may realize who live in countries where freedom of expression is taken for granted. The leaders of totalitarian nations understand this very well. The proof is that words are precisely the action for which dissidents in those countries are being persecuted.

Nonetheless, we can already see dramatic, worldwide advances in the protection of the individual from the arbitrary power of the state. For us to ignore this trend would be to lose influence and moral authority in the world. To lead it will be to regain the moral stature that we once had.

The great democracies are not free because we are strong and prosperous. I believe we are strong and influential and prosperous because we are free.

Throughout the world today, in free nations and in totalitarian countries as well, there is a preoccupation with the subject of human freedom, human rights. And I believe it is incumbent on us in this country to keep that discussion, that debate, that contention alive. No other country is as well-qualified as we to set an example. We have our own shortcomings and faults, and we should strive constantly and with courage to make sure that we are legitimately proud of what we have.

Second, we've moved deliberately to reinforce the bonds among our democracies. In our recent meetings in London, we agreed to widen our economic cooperation, to promote free trade, to strengthen the world's monetary system, to seek ways of avoiding nuclear proliferation. We prepared constructive proposals for the forthcoming meetings on North–South problems of poverty, development, and global well-being. And we agreed on joint efforts to reinforce and to modernize our common defense.

You may be interested in knowing that at this NATO meeting, for the first time in more than 25 years, all members are democracies. Even more important, all of us reaffirmed our basic optimism in the future of the democratic system. Our spirit of confidence is spreading. Together, our democracies can help to shape the wider architecture of global cooperation.

Third, we've moved to engage the Soviet Union in a joint effort to halt the strategic arms race. This race is not only dangerous, it's morally deplorable. We must put an end to it. I know it will not be easy to reach agreements. Our goal is to be fair to both sides, to produce reciprocal stability, parity, and security. We desire a freeze on further modernization and production of weapons and a continuing, substantial reduction of strategic nuclear weapons as well. We want a comprehensive ban on all nuclear testing, a prohibition against all chemical warfare, no attack capability against space satellites, and arms limitations in the Indian Ocean.

We hope that we can take joint steps with all nations toward a final agreement eliminating nuclear weapons completely from our arsenals of death. We will persist in this effort.

Now, I believe in detente with the Soviet Union. To me it means progress toward peace. But the effects of detente should not be limited to our own two countries alone. We hope to persuade the Soviet Union that one country cannot impose its system of society upon another, either through direct military intervention or through the use of a client state's military force, as was the case with Cuban intervention in Angola.

Cooperation also implies obligation. We hope that the Soviet Union will join with us and other nations in playing a larger role in aiding the developing world, for common aid efforts will help us build a bridge of mutual confidence in one another.

Fourth, we are taking deliberate steps to improve the chances of lasting peace in the Middle East. Through wide-ranging consultation with leaders of the countries involved – Israel, Syria, Jordan, and Egypt – we have found some areas of agreement and some movement toward consensus. The negotiations must continue.

Through my own public comments, I've also tried to suggest a more flexible framework for the discussion of the three key issues which have so far been so intractable: the nature of a comprehensive peace – what is peace; what does it mean to the Israelis; what does it mean to their Arab neighbors; secondly, the relationship between security and borders – how can the dispute over border delineations be established and settled with a feeling of security on both sides; and the issue of the Palestinian homeland.

The historic friendship that the United States has with Israel is not dependent on domestic politics in either nation; it's derived from our common respect for human freedom and from a common search for permanent peace.

We will continue to promote a settlement which all of us need. Our own policy will not be affected by changes in leadership in any of the countries in the Middle East. Therefore, we expect Israel and her neighbors to continue to be bound by United Nations Resolutions 242 and 338, which they have previously accepted.

This may be the most propitious time for a genuine settlement since the beginning of the Arab–Israeli conflict almost 30 years ago. To let this opportunity pass could mean disaster not only for the Middle East but, perhaps, for the international political and economic order as well.

And fifth, we are attempting, even at the risk of some friction with our friends, to reduce the danger of nuclear proliferation and the worldwide spread of conventional weapons.

At the recent summit, we set in motion an international effort to determine the best ways of harnessing nuclear energy for peaceful use while reducing the risks that its products will be diverted to the making of explosives.

We've already completed a comprehensive review of our own policy on arms transfers. Competition in arms sales is inimical to peace and destructive of the economic development of the poorer countries.

We will, as a matter of national policy now in our country, seek to reduce the annual dollar volume of arms sales, to restrict the transfer of advanced weapons, and to reduce the extent of our coproduction arrangements about weapons with foreign states. And just as important, we are trying to get other nations, both free and otherwise, to join us in this effort.

But all of this that I've described is just the beginning. It's a beginning aimed towards a clear goal: to create a wider framework of international cooperation suited to the new and rapidly changing historical circumstances.

We will cooperate more closely with the newly influential countries in Latin America, Africa, and Asia. We need their friendship and cooperation in a common effort as the structure of world power changes.

Source: http://www.presidency.ucsb.edu/ws/index.php?pid=7552 (accessed August 20, 2008).

Suggested Questions for Discussion:

1. Why did President Jimmy Carter believe that the United States needed to adopt a new kind of foreign policy?
2. What were the key elements of Carter's foreign policy?
3. Was Carter's vision practical?

6 President Ronald Reagan, "Evil Empire" Speech, 1983

In his first term as president, Ronald Reagan rejected Jimmy Carter's alleged "softness" on the communist threat. Reagan made a forceful argument for American strength and righteousness. He famously condemned the Soviet Union as an "evil empire" that would respond only to American force and determination. Reagan did not call for war against the Soviet Union, but he rejected hopes for a peaceful end to the Cold War without intensive American military, economic, and cultural pressure. The United States could negotiate, but only from overwhelming strength, according to Reagan.[6]

---

[6] See Paul Lettow, *Ronald Reagan and His Quest to Abolish Nuclear Weapons* (New York: Random House, 2005); John Lewis Gaddis, *The Cold War: A New History* (New York: Penguin, 2005); Sean Wilentz, *The Age of Reagan: A History, 1974–2008* (New York: HarperCollins, 2008).

Remarks at the Annual Convention of the National Association of
Evangelicals in Orlando, Florida, March 8, 1983

I'm pleased to be here today with you who are keeping America great by keeping her good. Only through your work and prayers and those of millions of others can we hope to survive this perilous century and keep alive this experiment in liberty, this last, best hope of man.

I want you to know that this administration is motivated by a political philosophy that sees the greatness of America in you, her people, and in your families, churches, neighborhoods, communities – the institutions that foster and nourish values like concern for others and respect for the rule of law under God.

Now, I don't have to tell you that this puts us in opposition to, or at least out of step with, a prevailing attitude of many who have turned to a modern-day secularism, discarding the tried and time-tested values upon which our very civilization is based. No matter how well intentioned, their value system is radically different from that of most Americans. And while they proclaim that they're freeing us from superstitions of the past, they've taken upon themselves the job of superintending us by government rule and regulation. Sometimes their voices are louder than ours, but they are not yet a majority. . . .

There is sin and evil in the world, and we're enjoined by Scripture and the Lord Jesus to oppose it with all our might. Our nation, too, has a legacy of evil with which it must deal. The glory of this land has been its capacity for transcending the moral evils of our past. For example, the long struggle of minority citizens for equal rights, once a source of disunity and civil war, is now a point of pride for all Americans. We must never go back. There is no room for racism, anti-Semitism, or other forms of ethnic and racial hatred in this country.

I know that you've been horrified, as have I, by the resurgence of some hate groups preaching bigotry and prejudice. Use the mighty voice of your pulpits and the powerful standing of your churches to denounce and isolate these hate groups in our midst. The commandment given us is clear and simple: "Thou shalt love thy neighbor as thyself."

But whatever sad episodes exist in our past, any objective observer must hold a positive view of American history, a history that has been the story of hopes fulfilled and dreams made into reality. Especially in this century, America has kept alight the torch of freedom, but not just for ourselves but for millions of others around the world.

And this brings me to my final point today. During my first press conference as President, in answer to a direct question, I pointed out that, as good

Marxist–Leninists, the Soviet leaders have openly and publicly declared that the only morality they recognize is that which will further their cause, which is world revolution. I think I should point out I was only quoting Lenin, their guiding spirit, who said in 1920 that they repudiate all morality that proceeds from supernatural ideas – that's their name for religion – or ideas that are outside class conceptions. Morality is entirely subordinate to the interests of class war. And everything is moral that is necessary for the annihilation of the old, exploiting social order and for uniting the proletariat.

Well, I think the refusal of many influential people to accept this elementary fact of Soviet doctrine illustrates an historical reluctance to see totalitarian powers for what they are. We saw this phenomenon in the 1930s. We see it too often today.

This doesn't mean we should isolate ourselves and refuse to seek an understanding with them. I intend to do everything I can to persuade them of our peaceful intent, to remind them that it was the West that refused to use its nuclear monopoly in the forties and fifties for territorial gain and which now proposes 50-percent cut in strategic ballistic missiles and the elimination of an entire class of land-based, intermediate-range missiles.

At the same time, however, they must be made to understand we will never compromise our principles and standards. We will never give away our freedom. We will never abandon our belief in God. And we will never stop searching for a genuine peace. But we can assure none of these things America stands for through the so-called nuclear freeze solutions proposed by some.

The truth is that a freeze now would be a very dangerous fraud, for that is merely the illusion of peace. The reality is that we must find peace through strength.

I would agree to a freeze if only we could freeze the Soviets' global desires. A freeze at current levels of weapons would remove any incentive for the Soviets to negotiate seriously in Geneva and virtually end our chances to achieve the major arms reductions which we have proposed. Instead, they would achieve their objectives through the freeze.

A freeze would reward the Soviet Union for its enormous and unparalleled military buildup. It would prevent the essential and long overdue modernization of United States and allied defenses and would leave our aging forces increasingly vulnerable. And an honest freeze would require extensive prior negotiations on the systems and numbers to be limited and on the measures to ensure effective verification and compliance. And the kind of a freeze that has been suggested would be virtually impossible to verify. Such a major effort would divert us completely from our current negotiations on achieving substantial reductions.

A number of years ago, I heard a young father, a very prominent young man in the entertainment world, addressing a tremendous gathering in California. It was during the time of the cold war, and communism and our own way of life were very much on people's minds. And he was speaking to that subject. And suddenly, though, I heard him saying, "I love my little girls more than anything – " And I said to myself, "Oh, no, don't. You can't – don't say that." But I had underestimated him. He went on: "I would rather see my little girls die now, still believing in God, than have them grow up under communism and one day die no longer believing in God."

There were thousands of young people in that audience. They came to their feet with shouts of joy. They had instantly recognized the profound truth in what he had said, with regard to the physical and the soul and what was truly important.

Yes, let us pray for the salvation of all of those who live in that totalitarian darkness – pray they will discover the joy of knowing God. But until they do, let us be aware that while they preach the supremacy of the state, declare its omnipotence over individual man, and predict its eventual domination of all peoples on the Earth, they are the focus of evil in the modern world.

It was C. S. Lewis who, in his unforgettable "Screwtape Letters," wrote: "The greatest evil is not done now in those sordid 'dens of crime' that Dickens loved to paint. It is not even done in concentration camps and labor camps. In those we see its final result. But it is conceived and ordered (moved, seconded, carried and minuted) in clear, carpeted, warmed, and well-lighted offices, by quiet men with white collars and cut fingernails and smooth-shaven cheeks who do not need to raise their voice."

Well, because these "quiet men" do not "raise their voices," because they sometimes speak in soothing tones of brotherhood and peace, because, like other dictators before them, they're always making "their final territorial demand," some would have us accept them at their word and accommodate ourselves to their aggressive impulses. But if history teaches anything, it teaches that simple-minded appeasement or wishful thinking about our adversaries is folly. It means the betrayal of our past, the squandering of our freedom.

So, I urge you to speak out against those who would place the United States in a position of military and moral inferiority. You know, I've always believed that old Screwtape reserved his best efforts for those of you in the church. So, in your discussions of the nuclear freeze proposals, I urge you to beware the temptation of pride – the temptation of blithely declaring yourselves above it all and label both sides equally at fault, to ignore the facts of history and the aggressive impulses of an evil empire, to simply call the arms race a giant misunderstanding and thereby remove yourself from the struggle between right and wrong and good and evil.

I ask you to resist the attempts of those who would have you withhold your support for our efforts, this administration's efforts, to keep America strong and free, while we negotiate real and verifiable reductions in the world's nuclear arsenals and one day, with God's help, their total elimination.

While America's military strength is important, let me add here that I've always maintained that the struggle now going on for the world will never be decided by bombs or rockets, but armies or military might. The real crisis we face today is a spiritual one; at root, it is a test of moral will and faith.

Source: *Public Papers of Ronald Reagan, 1983*, vol. 1 (Washington DC: US Government Printing Office, 1984), pp. 359–64.

Suggested Questions for Discussion:

1. What made the Soviet Union an "evil empire," according to Reagan?
2. What policies did Reagan advocate in response to "evil?"
3. Why were Reagan's words so powerful for listeners at the time?

Chapter 8   The End of the Cold War

1 President Ronald Reagan, Speech and Question-and-Answer Session at Moscow State University, 1988

Ronald Reagan's visit to Moscow in 1988 would have been unthinkable just a few years earlier. This was the president who had, in 1983, condemned the Soviet Union, as an "evil empire." Five years later, superpower relations had warmed and the president could speak sincerely of "growing friendship and closeness between our two peoples." His speech to Soviet students, and his answers to their questions, revealed both his uncanny ability to charm a skeptical audience and his deep belief in a global American mission. He praised the Soviet people as he simultaneously criticized the continued restrictions on freedom in their society, and their larger empire. Many observers have either dismissed or exaggerated Reagan's role in bringing the Cold War to an end. This text points not only to the power of his personality, but also to his change during the course of his presidency. Although Reagan was not responsible for the end of the Cold War, he made important contributions to this outcome.[1]

---

[1]   See John Lewis Gaddis, *The Cold War: A New History* (New York: Penguin Press, 2005); Lou Cannon, *President Reagan: The Role of a Lifetime* (New York: Public Affairs, 2000); Richard Reeves, *President Reagan: The Triumph of Imagination* (New York: Simon & Schuster, 2006); Don Oberdorfer, *From the Cold War to a New Era: The United States and the Soviet Union, 1983–1991* (Baltimore, MD: The Johns Hopkins University Press, 1998); Jeremi Suri, "Explaining the End of the Cold War: A New Historical Consensus?," *Journal of Cold War Studies* 4 (Fall 2002), pp. 60–92.

Standing here before a mural of your revolution, I want to talk about a very different revolution that is taking place right now, quietly sweeping the globe without bloodshed or conflict. Its effects are peaceful, but they will fundamentally alter our world, shatter old assumptions, and reshape our lives. It's easy to underestimate because it's not accompanied by banners or fanfare. It's been called the technological or information revolution, and as its emblem, one might take the tiny silicon chip, no bigger than a fingerprint. One of these chips has more computing power than a roomful of old-style computers.

As part of an exchange program, we now have an exhibition touring your country that shows how information technology is transforming our lives – replacing manual labor with robots, forecasting weather for farmers, or mapping the genetic code of DNA for medical researchers. These microcomputers today aid the design of everything from houses to cars to spacecraft; they even design better and faster computers. They can translate English into Russian or enable the blind to read or help Michael Jackson produce on one synthesizer the sounds of a whole orchestra. Linked by a network of satellites and fiber-optic cables, one individual with a desktop computer and a telephone commands resources unavailable to the largest governments just a few years ago.

Like a chrysalis, we're emerging from the economy of the Industrial Revolution – an economy confined to and limited by the Earth's physical resources – into, as one economist titled his book, "The Economy in Mind," in which there are no bounds on human imagination and the freedom to create is the most precious natural resource. Think of that little computer chip. Its value isn't in the sand from which it is made but in the microscopic architecture designed into it by ingenious human minds. Or take the example of the satellite relaying this broadcast around the world, which replaces thousands of tons of copper mined from the Earth and molded into wire. In the new economy, human invention increasingly makes physical resources obsolete. We're breaking through the material conditions of existence to a world where man creates his own destiny. Even as we explore the most advanced reaches of science, we're returning to the age-old wisdom of our culture, a wisdom contained in the book of Genesis in the Bible: In the beginning was the spirit and it was from this spirit that the material abundance of creation issued forth.

But progress is not foreordained. The key is freedom – freedom of thought, freedom of information, freedom of communication. The renowned scientist, scholar, and founding father of this university, Mikhail Lomonosov, knew that. "It is common knowledge" he said, "that the achievements of science are considerable and rapid, particularly once the yoke of slavery is cast off and replaced by the freedom of philosophy." You know, one of the first contacts between your country and mine took place between Russian and American explorers. The Americans were members of Cook's last voyage on an expedition searching for an Arctic passage; on the island of Unalaska, they came upon the Russians, who took them in, and together with the native inhabitants, held a prayer service on the ice.

The explorers of the modern era are the entrepreneurs, men with vision, with the courage to take risks and faith enough to brave the unknown. These entrepreneurs and their small enterprises are responsible for almost all the economic growth in the United States. They are the prime movers of the technological revolution. In fact, one of the largest personal computer firms in the United States was started by two college students, no older than you, in the garage behind their home. Some people, even in my own country, look at the riot of experiment that is the free market and see only waste. What of all the entrepreneurs that fail? Well, many do, particularly the successful ones; often several times. And if you ask them the secret of their success they'll tell you it's all that they learned in their struggles along the way; yes, it's what they learned from failing. Like an athlete in competition or a scholar in pursuit of the truth, experience is the greatest teacher....

We Americans make no secret of our belief in freedom. In fact, it's something of a national pastime. Every 4 years the American people choose a new President, and 1988 is one of those years. At one point there were 13 major candidates running in the two major parties, not to mention all the others, including the Socialist and Libertarian candidates – all trying to get my job. About 1,000 local television stations, 8,500 radio stations, and 1,700 daily newspapers – each one an independent, private enterprise, fiercely independent of the Government – report on the candidates, grill them in interviews, and bring them together for debates. In the end, the people vote; they decide who will be the next President. But freedom doesn't begin or end with elections.

Go to any American town, to take just an example, and you'll see dozens of churches, representing many different beliefs – in many places, synagogues and mosques – and you'll see families of every conceivable nationality worshiping together. Go into any schoolroom, and there you will see children being taught the Declaration of Independence, that they are endowed by their Creator with certain unalienable rights – among them life, liberty, and the pursuit of happiness – that no government can justly deny; the guarantees in their Constitution for freedom of speech, freedom of assembly, and freedom of religion. Go into any courtroom, and there will preside an independent judge, beholden to no government power. There every defendant has the right to a trial by a jury of his peers, usually 12 men and women – common citizens;

they are the ones, the only ones, who weigh the evidence and decide on guilt or innocence. In that court, the accused is innocent until proven guilty, and the word of a policeman or any official has no greater legal standing than the word of the accused. Go to any university campus, and there you'll find an open, sometimes heated discussion of the problems in American society and what can be done to correct them. Turn on the television, and you'll see the legislature conducting the business of government right there before the camera, debating and voting on the legislation that will become the law of the land. March in any demonstration, and there are many of them; the people's right of assembly is guaranteed in the Constitution and protected by the police. Go into any union hall, where the members know their right to strike is protected by law. As a matter of fact, one of the many jobs I had before this one was being president of a union, the Screen Actors Guild. I led my union out on strike, and I'm proud to say we won.

But freedom is more even than this. Freedom is the right to question and change the established way of doing things. It is the continuing revolution of the marketplace. It is the understanding that allows us to recognize short-comings and seek solutions. It is the right to put forth an idea, scoffed at by the experts, and watch it catch fire among the people. It is the right to dream – to follow your dream or stick to your conscience, even if you're the only one in a sea of doubters. Freedom is the recognition that no single person, no single authority or government has a monopoly on the truth, but that every individual life is infinitely precious, that every one of us put on this world has been put there for a reason and has something to offer.

America is a nation made up of hundreds of nationalities. Our ties to you are more than ones of good feeling; they're ties of kinship. In America, you'll find Russians, Armenians, Ukrainians, peoples from Eastern Europe and Central Asia. They come from every part of this vast continent, from every continent, to live in harmony, seeking a place where each cultural heritage is respected, each is valued for its diverse strengths and beauties and the richness it brings to our lives. Recently, a few individuals and families have been allowed to visit relatives in the West. We can only hope that it won't be long before all are allowed to do so and Ukrainian-Americans, Baltic-Americans, Armenian-Americans can freely visit their homelands, just as this Irish-American visits his.

Freedom, it has been said, makes people selfish and materialistic, but Americans are one of the most religious peoples on Earth. Because they know that liberty, just as life itself, is not earned but a gift from God, they seek to share that gift with the world. "Reason and experience," said George Washington in his Farewell Address, "both forbid us to expect that national morality can prevail in exclusion of religious principle. And it is substantially true, that virtue or morality is a necessary spring of popular government." Democracy is less a system of government than it is a system to keep government limited, unintrusive; a system of constraints on power to keep politics and government secondary to the important things in life, the true sources of value found only in family and faith.

But I hope you know I go on about these things not simply to extol the virtues of my own country but to speak to the true greatness of the heart and soul of your land. Who, after all, needs to tell the land of Dostoyevski about the quest for truth, the home of Kandinski and Scriabin about imagination, the rich and noble culture of the Uzbek man of letters Alisher Navoi about beauty and heart? The great culture of your diverse land speaks with a glowing passion to all humanity. Let me cite one of the most eloquent contemporary passages on human freedom. It comes, not from the literature of America, but from this country, from one of the greatest writers of the 20th century, Boris Pasternak, in the novel "Dr. Zhivago." He writes: "I think that if the beast who sleeps in man could be held down by threats – any kind of threat, whether of jail or of retribution after death then the highest emblem of humanity would be the lion tamer in the circus with his whip, not the prophet who sacrificed himself. But this is just the point – what has for centuries raised man above the beast is not the cudgel, but an inward music – the irresistible power of unarmed truth."

The irresistible power of unarmed truth. Today the world looks expectantly to signs of change, steps toward greater freedom in the Soviet Union. We watch and we hope as we see positive changes taking place. There are some, I know, in your society who fear that change will bring only disruption and discontinuity, who fear to embrace the hope of the future – sometimes it takes faith. It's like that scene in the cowboy movie "Butch Cassidy and the Sundance Kid," which some here in Moscow recently had a chance to see. The posse is closing in on the two outlaws, Butch and Sundance, who find themselves trapped on the edge of a cliff, with a sheer drop of hundreds of feet to the raging rapids below. Butch turns to Sundance and says their only hope is to jump into the river below, but Sundance refuses. He says he'd rather fight it out with the posse, even though they're hopelessly outnumbered. Butch says that's suicide and urges him to jump, but Sundance still refuses and finally admits, "I can't swim." Butch breaks up laughing and says, "You crazy fool, the fall will probably kill you." And, by the way, both Butch and Sundance made it, in case you didn't see the movie. I think what I've just been talking about is *perestroika* and what its goals are.

But change would not mean rejection of the past. Like a tree growing strong through the seasons, rooted in the Earth and drawing life from the Sun, so, too, positive change must be rooted in traditional values – in the land, in culture, in family and community – and it must take its life from the eternal things, from the source of all life, which is faith. Such change will lead to new understandings, new opportunities to a broader future in which the tradition is not supplanted but finds its full flowering. That is the future beckoning to your generation.

At the same time, we should remember that reform that is not institutionalized will always be insecure. Such freedom will always be looking over its shoulder. A bird on a tether, no matter how long the rope can always be pulled back. And that is why in my conversation with General Secretary Gorbachev, I have spoken of how important it is to institutionalize change – to put guarantees on reform. And we've been talking together about one sad reminder of a divided world: the Berlin Wall. It's time to remove the barriers that keep people apart....

Your generation is living in one of the most exciting, hopeful times in Soviet history. It is a time when the first breath of freedom stirs the air and the heart beats to the accelerated rhythm of hope, when the accumulated spiritual energies of a long silence yearn to break free. I am reminded of the famous passage near the end of Gogol's "Dead Souls." Comparing his nation to a speeding troika, Gogol asks what will be its destination. But he writes, "There was no answer save the bell pouring forth marvelous sound."

We do not know what the conclusion will be of this journey, but we're hopeful that the promise of reform will be fulfilled. In this Moscow spring, this May 1988, we may be allowed that hope: that freedom, like the fresh green sapling planted over Tolstoy's grave, will blossom forth at last in the rich fertile soil of your people and culture. We may be allowed to hope that the marvelous sound of a new openness will keep rising through, ringing through, leading to a new world of reconciliation, friendship, and peace. Thank you all very much, and *da blagoslovit vas gospod* – God bless you.

MR. LOGUNOV. Dear friends, Mr. President has kindly agreed to answer your questions. But since he doesn't have too much time, only 15 minutes – so, those who have questions, please ask them.

Strategic Arms Reductions

Q: And this is a student from the history faculty, and he says that he's happy to welcome you on behalf of the students of the university. And the first question is that the improvement in the relations between the two countries has come about during your tenure as President, and in this regard he would like to ask the following question. It is very important to get a handle on the question of arms control and, specifically, the limitation of strategic arms. Do you think that it will be possible for you and the General Secretary to get a treaty on the limitation of strategic arms during the time that you are still President?

THE PRESIDENT: Well, the arms treaty that is being negotiated now is the so-called START treaty, and it is based on taking the intercontinental ballistic missiles and reducing them by half, down to parity between our two countries. Now, this is a much more complicated treaty than the INF treaty, the intermediate-range treaty, which we have signed and which our two governments have ratified and is now in effect. So, there are many things still to be settled. You and we have had negotiators in Geneva for months working on various points of this treaty. Once we had hoped that maybe, like the INF treaty, we would have been able to sign it here at this summit meeting. It is not completed; there are still some points that are being debated. We are both hopeful that it can be finished before I leave office which is in the coming January, but I assure you that if it isn't – I assure you that I will have impressed on my successor that we must carry on until it is signed. My dream has always been that once we've started down this road, we can look forward to a day – you can look forward to a day – when there will be no more nuclear weapons in the world at all....

Regional Conflicts

Q: Mr. President, you have just mentioned that you welcome the efforts – settlement of the Afghanistan question and the difference of other regional conflicts. What conflicts do you mean? Central America conflicts, Southeast Asian, or South African?

THE PRESIDENT: Well, for example, in South Africa, where Namibia has been promised its independence as a nation – another new African nation. But it is impossible because of a civil war going on in another country there, and that civil war is being fought on one side by some 30,000 to 40,000 Cuban troops who have gone from the Americas over there and are fighting on one side with one kind of authoritative government. When that country was freed from being a colony and given its independence, one faction seized power and made itself the government of that nation. And leaders of another – seeming the majority of the people had wanted, simply, the people to have the right to choose the government that they wanted, and that is the civil war that is going on. But what we believe is that those foreign soldiers should get out and let them settle it, let the citizens of that nation settle their problems.

And the same is true in Nicaragua. Nicaragua has been – Nicaragua made a promise. They had a dictator. There was a revolution, there was an organization that – and was aided by others in the revolution, and they appealed to the Organization of American States for help in getting the dictator to step down and stop the killing. And he did. But the Organization of American States had asked, what are the goals of the revolution? And they were given in writing, and they were the goals of pluralistic society, of the right of unions and freedom of speech and press and so forth and free elections – a pluralistic society. And then the one group that was the best organized among the revolutionaries seized power, exiled many of the other leaders, and has its own government, which violated every one of the promises that had been made. And here again, we want – we're trying to encourage the getting back those – or making those promises come true and letting the people of that particular country decide their fate . . . .

US Constitution

Q: The reservation of the inalienable rights of citizens guaranteed by the Constitution faces certain problems; for example, the right of people to have arms, or for example, the problem appears, an evil appears whether spread of pornography or narcotics is compatible with these rights. Do you believe that these problems are just unavoidable problems connected with democracy, or they could be avoided?

THE PRESIDENT: Well, if I understand you correctly, this is a question about the inalienable rights of the people – does that include the right to do criminal acts – for example, in the use of drugs and so forth? No. No, we have a set of laws. I think what is significant and different about our system is that every country has a constitution, and most constitutions or practically all of the constitutions in the world are documents in which the government tells the people what the people can do. Our Constitution is different, and the difference is in three words; it almost escapes everyone. The three words are, "We the people." Our Constitution is a document in which we the people tell the Government what its powers are. And it can have no powers other than those listed in that document. But very carefully, at the same time, the people give the government the power with regard to those things which they think would be destructive to society, to the family, to the individual and so forth – infringements on their rights. And thus, the government can enforce the laws. But that has all been dictated by the people . . . .

American Indians

Q: Mr. President, I've heard that a group of American Indians have come here because they couldn't meet you in the United States of America. If you fail to meet them here, will you be able to correct it and to meet them back in the United States?

THE PRESIDENT: I didn't know that they had asked to see me. If they've come here or whether to see them there [*laughter*] – I'd be very happy to see them.

Let me tell you just a little something about the American Indian in our land. We have provided millions of acres of land for what are called preservations – or reservations, I should say. They, from the beginning, announced that they wanted to maintain their way of life, as they had always lived there in the desert and the plains and so forth. And we set up these reservations so they could, and have a Bureau of Indian Affairs to help take care of them. At the same time, we provide education for them – schools on the reservations. And they're free also to leave the reservations and be American citizens among the rest of us, and many do. Some still prefer, however, that way – that early way of life. And we've done everything we can to meet their demands as to how they want to live. Maybe we made a mistake. Maybe we should not have humored them in that wanting to stay in that kind of primitive lifestyle. Maybe we should have said, no, come join us; be citizens along with the rest of us. As I say, many have; many have been very successful.

And I'm very pleased to meet with them, talk with them at any time and see what their grievances are or what they feel they might be. And you'd be surprised: Some of them became very wealthy because some of those reservations were overlaying great pools of oil, and you can get very rich pumping oil. And so, I don't know what their complaint might be.

Soviet Dissidents

Q: Mr. President, I'm very much tantalized since yesterday evening by the question, why did you receive yesterday – did you receive and when you invite yesterday – refuseniks or dissidents? And for the second part of the question is, just what are your impressions from Soviet people? And among these dissidents, you have invited a former collaborator with a Fascist, who was a policeman serving for Fascist.

THE PRESIDENT: Well, that's one I don't know about, or maybe the information hasn't been all given out on that. But you have to understand that Americans come from every corner of the world. I received a letter from a man that called something to my attention recently. He said, you can go to live in France, but you cannot become a Frenchman; you can go to live in Germany, you cannot become a German – or a Turk, or a Greek, or whatever. But he said anyone, from any corner of the world, can come to live in America and become an American.

You have to realize that we are a people that are made up of every strain, nationality, and race of the world. And the result is that when people in our country think someone is being mistreated or treated unjustly in another country, these are people who still feel that kinship to that country because that is their heritage. In America, whenever you meet someone new and become friends, one of the first things you tell each other is what your bloodline is. For example, when I'm asked, I have to say Irish, English, and Scotch—English and Scotch on my mother's side, Irish on my father's side. But all of them have that.

Well, when you take on to yourself a wife, you do not stop loving your mother. So, Americans all feel a kind of a kinship to that country that their parents or their grandparents or even some great-grandparents came from; you don't lose that contact. So, what I have come and what I have brought to the General Secretary – and I must say he has been very cooperative about it – I have brought lists of names that have been brought to me from people that are relatives or friends that know that – or that believe that this individual is being mistreated here in this country, and they want him to be allowed to emigrate to our country – some are separated families.

One that I met in this, the other day, was born the same time I was. He was born of Russian parents who had moved to America, oh, way back in the early 1900s, and he was born in 1911. And then sometime later, the family moved back to Russia. Now he's grown, has a son. He's an American citizen. But they wanted to go back to America and being denied on the grounds that, well, they can go back to America, but his son married a Russian young lady, and they want to keep her from going back. Well, the whole family said, no, we're not going to leave her alone here. She's a member of the family now. Well, that kind of a case is brought to me personally, so I bring it to the General Secretary. And as I say, I must say, he has been most helpful and most agreeable about correcting these things.

Now, I'm not blaming you; I'm blaming bureaucracy. We have the same type of thing happen in our own country. And every once in a while, somebody has to get the bureaucracy by the neck and shake it loose and say, Stop doing what you're doing! And this is the type of thing and the names that we have brought. And it is a list of names, all of which have been brought to me personally by either relatives or close friends and associates. [*Applause*] …

Source: *Public Papers of President Ronald Reagan, 1988*, vol. 1 (Washington DC: US Government Printing Office, 1990), pp. 683–92.

Suggested Questions for Discussion:

1. How did Reagan describe his vision of peace and freedom in this speech?
2. Why did Reagan believe the Soviet Union was no longer an "evil empire"?
3. What made Reagan's words so powerful for Soviet listeners?

2 *The New York Times*, Mikhail Gorbachev's Heroic Reception in the United States, 1988

> *By the end of 1988 Soviet leader Mikhail Gorbachev had become a larger-than-life figure in the United States. He was a phenomenon. Many Americans perceived him as the enlightened, Westernizing Soviet leader they had only imagined in the past. Gorbachev appeared to promise a world of peace, cooperation, and prosperity on American terms. His energy, his enthusiasm, and his passion were contagious. Gorbachev's December 1988 visit to New York City drew some of the largest adoring crowds on the streets of Manhattan in recent memory.[2]*

"Gambler, Showman, Statesman"

Perhaps not since Woodrow Wilson presented his Fourteen Points in 1918 or since Franklin Roosevelt and Winston Churchill promulgated the Atlantic Charter in 1941 has a world figure demonstrated the vision Mikhail Gorbachev displayed yesterday at the United Nations.

Like the others, the Soviet leader called for the basic restructuring of international politics – for the rule of law, not force; for multilateralism, not unilateralism; and for economic as well as political freedoms. Like them, he used occasion and oratory to command the global stage. Unlike them, he promised to lead the way unilaterally, by reducing Soviet military forces and converting defense industries to peaceful uses.

Breathtaking. Risky. Bold. Naive. Diversionary. Heroic. All fit. So sweeping is his agenda that it will require weeks to sort out. But whatever Mr. Gorbachev's motives, his ideas merit – indeed, compel – the most serious response from President-elect Bush and other leaders.

---

[2] See Jack Matlock, *Reagan and Gorbachev: How the Cold War Ended* (New York: Random House, 2004); Archie Brown, *The Gorbachev Factor* (Oxford: Oxford University Press, 1996); Don Oberdorfer, *From the Cold War to a New Era: The United States and the Soviet Union, 1983–1991*, updated edn. (Baltimore, MD: Johns Hopkins University Press, 1998).

Mr. Gorbachev finds the world now to be radically different from even the recent past. Though he dismisses continuing conflicts too quickly, he's mainly right. New popular movements and revolutions in science, technology and communications are some of the transformations he cited. These, in turn, have magnified threats to human survival from economic deprivation, environmental perils and nuclear weapons. He pleads for new forms of international cooperation.

It's disingenuous for him to say that "the use or threat of force no longer can or must be an instrument of foreign policy." But he could not be more on target when he says that the "one-sided reliance on military power ultimately weakens other components of national security," that economic wellbeing is a critical part of security.

Amazed Americans can only applaud his insistence that the principle of freedom of choice is "absolute." Knowledgeable listeners can only smile when he pledges to forgive poor countries their debts to Moscow, knowing that those are very small compared with the billions owed to the West. And people everywhere will hold him to his promise to solve "human problems, only in a humane way" in his own country.

To prove he's sincere in striving for this kind of international order, Mr. Gorbachev announced he would cut Soviet forces by half a million in the next two years – including 50,000 troops and 5,000 tanks in Eastern Europe. The remaining forces there would be restructured into a defensive posture. These are welcome announcements to Westerners who fear Soviet capacity for surprise attack.

They are perhaps cheered less in Soviet military circles. Soviet officials have just quietly confirmed the "retirement" for health reasons of Marshal Sergei Akhromeyev, the Chief of Staff.

Neither are Soviet conservatives likely to approve Mr. Gorbachev's pledge to begin changing an "economy of armaments to an economy of disarmament" But the Soviet leader is a gambler; he probably calculates that the need for economic reform is so urgent that he must risk displeasing the military.

He risks nothing, however, by taking the global stage during the American Presidential transition. He surely understands that neither George Bush nor Ronald Reagan can respond now. Unchallenged, he shrewdly seizes the world's attention.

While Mr. Bush and others ready their responses, they might contemplate the question with which Mr. Gorbachev crowned his speech. Could his proposals be "a little bit too romantic?" Are we not, he continued, "overestimating the potential and the maturity of the world's social consciousness?" And other leaders would do well to ponder his answer.

"We have entered an era when progress will be shaped by universal human interests," he said. People "ardently wish for an improvement in the situation," and they "want to learn to cooperate."

Source: *The New York Times*, December 8, 1988, p. A34.

Suggested Questions for Discussion:

1. Why was *The New York Times* so effusive about Mikhail Gorbachev?
2. What did *The New York Times* expect Gorbachev to do in the near future?
3. Were American expectations for Gorbachev too high in 1988?

3 *The New York Times*, The Fall of the Berlin Wall, 1989

> *Since its construction in 1961 by East German authorities, the Berlin Wall had served as the most obvious and frustrating symbol of the Cold War. The Wall divided Berlin between a communist East and a capitalist West, marking the larger division of Europe in these terms. The Berlin Wall imprisoned the people of East Germany within their society, forcibly closing what had been the primary escape hatch in the first fifteen years of the Cold War. The opening of the Berlin Wall by East German authorities on November 9, 1989 marked the opening of a post-Cold War world. Citizens from East Germany and other communist East European states could now travel freely to the West. By the end of 1989, communist regimes from East Germany, to Poland, to Hungary, to Czechoslovakia had fallen in peaceful popular revolutions. The building of the Berlin War symbolized the hardening of the Cold War in 1961; the fall of the Berlin Wall marked the end of communism in Eastern Europe and the reemergence of a united Germany.[3]*

Serge Schmemanns, "A Jubilant Horde."

East Berlin, Friday, Nov. 10 – East Germany on Thursday lifted restrictions on emigration or travel to the West, and within hours tens of thousands of East and West Berliners swarmed across the infamous Berlin Wall for a boisterous celebration.

[3] See Timothy Garton Ash, *The Magic Lantern: The Revolution of '89 Witnessed in Warsaw, Budapest, Berlin, and Prague* (New York: Random House, 1990); Gale Stokes, *The Walls Came Tumbling Down: The Collapse of Communism in Eastern Europe* (New York: Oxford University Press, 1993); Padraic Kenney, *A Carnival of Revolution: Central Europe, 1989* (Princeton, NJ: Princeton University Press, 2003); Mary Elise Sarotte, *1989: The Struggle to Create Post-Cold War Europe* (Princeton, NJ: Princeton University Press, 2009).

Border guards at Bornholmer Strasse crossing, Checkpoint Charlie and several other crossings abandoned all efforts to check credentials, even though the new regulations said East Germans would still need passports and permission to get across. Some guards smiled and took snapshots, assuring passers-by that they were just recording a historic event.

Politburo Announcement

The mass crossing began about two hours after Günter Schabowski, a member of the Politburo, had announced at a press conference that permission to travel or emigrate would be granted quickly and without preconditions, and that East Germans would be allowed to cross at any crossing into West Germany or West Berlin.

"We know this need of citizens to travel or leave the country," Mr. Schabowski said. "Today the decision was taken that makes it possible for all citizens to leave the country through East German crossing points."

Mr. Schabowski also said the decision ended the agreement to let East Germans leave through Czechoslovakia, and a 14-mile-long queue of East German cars was reported Thursday at the Schirnding border crossing on the Czech–West German border. Since September, thousands more have left through Hungary and Poland.

Flag Waving in the West

Once Mr. Schabowski's announcement was read on radio and television, a tentative trickle of East Germans testing the new regulations quickly turned into a jubilant horde, which joined at the border crossings with crowds of flag-waving, cheering West Germans. Thousands of Berliners clambered across the wall at the Brandenburg Gate, passing through the historic arch that for so long had been inaccessible to Berliners of either side.

Similar scenes were reported in Lubeck, the only other East German city touching the border, and at other border crossings along the inter-German frontier.

All through the night and into the early morning, celebrating East Berliners filled the Kurfürstendamm, West Berlin's "great white way," blowing trumpets, dancing, laughing, and absorbing a glittering scene that until now they could glimpse only on television.

Many East Germans said they planned to return home the same night. The Mayor of West Berlin, Walter Momper, toured border crossings in a police radio truck and urged East Berliners to return.

East German radio announced that the uncontrolled crossings would be ended at 8 A.M. today, after which East Germans would be required to obtain a visa.

The extraordinary breach of what had been the most infamous stretch of the iron Curtain marked the culmination of an extraordinary month that has seen the virtual transformation of East Germany under the dual pressures of unceasing flight and continued demonstrations. It also marked a breach of a wall that had become the premier symbol of Stalinist oppression and of the divisions of Europe and Germany into hostile camps after World War II.

The immediate reason for the decision was evidently a recognition by East Germany's embattled authorities that they could not stem the outward tide by opening the door a crack and hoping that rapid liberalization at home would end the urge to flee. They now seemed to hope that an open door would quickly let out those who were determined to leave, and give pause to those who had doubted the sincerity of the Government's pledge of profound change.

The Berlin wall – first raised on Aug. 13, 1961, to halt a vast hemorrhage of East Germans to the West – evolved into a double row of eight-foot high concrete walls with watchtowers, electronic sensors and a no man's land in between. Frequent attempts to breach the barrier often ended in death, and the very sophistication of the wall became a standing indictment of the system that would hold its people only with such extraordinary means.

The decision to allow East Germans to travel freely came on a day when Egon Krenz, the new East German leader, was reported to have called for a law insuring free and democratic elections. In a speech to the Communist Party's Central Committee on Wednesday night that was published today, Mr. Krenz also called for new laws on freedom of assembly, association, and the press. But he gave no details.

Mr. Schabowski's announcement about the unimpeded travel was greeted with an outburst of emotion in West Germany, whose Constitution sustains the hope of a reunited Germany and whose people have seen in the dramatic changes in East Germany the first glimmers of an end to division.

The West German Parliament abandoned a heated debate after learning of the new developments, and ended its session with a spontaneous singing of the national anthem.

"We demand of the responsible people in the German Democratic Republic that they start tomorrow to tear down the wall," declared Friedrich Bohl, the chief whip of the governing Christian Democrats.

In West Berlin, Eberhard Diepgen, the former Mayor, said: "This is a day I have been awaiting since Aug. 13, 1961. With this the wall has lost its function. It can and must be torn down.

Wall Will Not Come Down

Mr. Schabowski, however, said the wall would not be coming down. "There are other factors for the existence of the wall other than traveling," he said, suggesting that its fate depended on broader questions of relations between the two Germanys and between East and West.

In replying to a question, however, Mr. Schabowski abandoned the customary barrier as an "anti-fascist protection wall," and instead called it a "fortified border."

His statement underlined that the new regulations did not change the status of Berlin, which is still formally occupied by the victorious Allies of World War II, with East Berlin as the Soviet zone. There was also no change in the requirements that Westerners obtain visas for East Germany, or day passes to visit East Berlin.

East Germans began almost immediately to test the new measures. One couple crossed into West Berlin at the Bornholmer Strasse crossing with only their identity cards just two hours after Mr. Schabowski spoke. After a gleeful exchange with some West Berliners, they returned to their side of the wall, saying they had only wanted to test the new permeability of the barrier.

West German television showed curious East Germans flocking to crossing points at the wall, with some passing through with their identity cards.

Some Are Skeptical

Other East Berliners were more muted in their reaction, reflecting the skepticism fostered by the dizzying rate of change in East Germany in recent weeks. The Government had already allowed virtually unrestricted emigration to West Germany through Czechoslovakia, and on Monday it published the draft of a new travel law that went far beyond anything granted to before. The measure, however, was roundly condemned because it limited foreign travel to 30 days.

The new measures also raised some questions, including how much currency East Germans would be allowed to change into Western money. The East German mark is not freely convertible, and up to now East Germans have been allowed to exchange just 15 of their marks, about $8 at the official exchange rate.

Hans-Peter Schneider, a member of Democratic Awakening, one of the new opposition groups, said, "At the moment, I doubt that this is a step that will support our efforts to get people to stay in the country."

The official East German press agency, A.D.N said the new measures took effect immediately. They provided that East Germans could apply for trips abroad without giving any reasons, as they had to do in the past, and that permission would be granted on short notice. A.D.N. added that permission would be denied only in exceptional cases, evidently concerning state security.

The new regulations also called on the authorities to grant emigration papers immediately and without conditions.

The main novelty in the new regulations was that permission to travel to the West would be virtually automatic. Though millions of East Germans have traveled to the West in the past, the permission was always conditional and difficult to obtain.

The excitement over so momentous an opening failed to conceal a growing anxiety on both sides of the border over the swelling size of the exodus from East Germany.

More than 50,0000 East Germans fled over only the last weekend. West German estimates have put the figure of East Germans yearning to settle in the West at 1.4 million, out of a population of 16 million.

The huge influx of East Germans and of ethnic Germans from the Soviet Union, Poland and other East European countries has already severely taxed West Germany's capacity.

In Bonn, Interior Minister Wolfgang Schäuble said in Parliament that 225,000 East Germans had crossed into West Germany this year, plus about 300,000 other ethnic Germans. He said would-be migrants should consider the fact that they might be living in worse conditions in the West than they had in the East.

Chancellor Helmut Kohl of West Germany, starting a long-awaited visit to Poland, welcomed the East German decision. But he added: "It is harder to estimate what consequences that this step will have. Our interest must be that our compatriots stay in their homeland."

Mr. Kohl said he was seeking an urgent meeting with Mr. Krenz. The Chancellor has repeatedly declared that he will give extensive aid to East Germany once it grants its citizens free elections.

The leader of the West German Social Democratic Party, Hans-Jochem Vogel, went on East German television to declare that he supported a public appeal made yesterday by Christa Wolf, a prominent East German writer, for East Germans to stay home.

Marked 40th Anniversary

The announcement of the travel measures was the latest in an extraordinary chain of events that has profoundly transformed East Germany since it marked its 40th anniversary on Oct. 7.

Shocked into action by the mass flights that gathered pace all through the summer, hundreds of thousands of East Germans have taken to the streets in the last months to press with increasing urgency for profound change in their society, which under Erich Honecker ranked among the most iron-clad Communist strongholds in Eastern Europe.

The double pressure of the mass exodus and mass demonstrations has sent the Communist Party into headlong retreat. Mr. Honecker was ousted Oct. 18, and at the start of the extraordinary Central Committee session now under way, the entire Politburo resigned to enable Mr. Krenz, the new leader, to select a smaller and younger panel, including only five of the former members.

The Government had already resigned, and the presidium of the legislature announced on Thursday that it would call the full Parliament into session on Monday. Mr. Schabowski announced that the Central Committee would call a party conference on Dec. 15.

Source: *The New York Times*, November 10, 1989, pp. A1, A14.

Suggested Questions for Discussion:

1. What immediate events precipitated the opening of the Berlin Wall?
2. Why was this event such a transformative moment?
3. What kind of future expectations did this moment create?

4 President George H. W. Bush and Soviet Chairman Mikhail Gorbachev, the End of the Cold War, 1989

After almost a year of transition to a new administration, in December 1989 President George H.W. Bush met with Mikhail Gorbachev in the rough seas off the coast of Malta. The two leaders pledged to continue and expand the cooperation between their countries. Stating the obvious, they affirmed the end of the Cold War. Their statements revealed a sincere commitment to a new relationship between the superpowers; their statements also revealed that events on the ground, particularly in Europe, were moving ahead of leaders. Bush and Gorbachev were struggling to catch up with and control the dizzying changes around them.[4]

---

[4] See Derek Chollet and James Goldgeier, *America Between the Wars: From 11/9 to 9/11* (New York: Public Affairs, 2008); Hal Brands, *From Berlin to Baghdad: America's Search for Purpose in the Post-Cold War World* (Lexington, KT: University Press of Kentucky, 2008); Michael R. Beschloss and Strobe Talbott, *At the Highest Levels: The Inside Story of the End of the Cold War* (Boston, MA: Little, Brown, 1993).

Remarks of President George H. W. Bush and Soviet Chairman Mikhail Gorbachev, and a Question-and-Answer Session With Reporters, in Malta, December 3, 1989

The President. Ladies and gentlemen, President Gorbachev has graciously suggested I go first. And I don't think anyone can say that the saltwater get-together was anything other than adventure – at least out in the harbor here,

First, I want to thank Prime Minister Adami and the people of Malta and others for their warm and gracious hospitality. I want to thank the captain and crew of *Belknap* for the great support that they have given us, I think they were wondering if I was about to become a permanent guest. And a special thanks to the captain and crew of *Gorky* for their hospitality, and also thanks to the captain and crew of *Slava*, who have been so hospitable to many on the American side.

I first approached Chairman Gorbachev about an informal meeting of this kind after my trip to Europe last July. Amazing changes that I witnessed in Poland and in Hungary – hopeful changes – led me to believe that it was time to sit down with Chairman Gorbachev face to face to see what he and I could do to seize the opportunities before us to move this relationship forward. He agreed with that concept of a meeting, and so, we got rapid agreement. And I think that the extraordinary developments in Europe since the time that the meeting was proposed only reinforce the importance of our getting together.

And so, I'm especially glad we had this meeting. And we did gain a deeper understanding of each other's views. We set the stage for progress across a broad range of issues. And while it is not for the United States and the Soviet Union to design the future for Europeans or for any other people, I am convinced that a cooperative US–Soviet relationship can, indeed, make the future safer and brighter. And there is virtually no problem in the world, and certainly no problem in Europe, that improvement in the US–Soviet relationship will not help to ameliorate. A better U.S–Soviet relationship is to be valued in and of itself, but it also should be an instrument of positive change for the world.

For 40 years, the Western alliance has stood together in the cause of freedom. And now, with reform underway in the Soviet Union, we stand at the threshold of a brand-new era of U.S–Soviet relations. And it is within our grasp to contribute, each in our own way, to overcoming the division of Europe and ending the military confrontation there. We've got to do more to ameliorate the violence and suffering that afflicts so many regions in the world and to remove common threats to our future: the deterioration of the environment, the spread of nuclear and chemical weapons, ballistic missile technology, the narcotics trade. And our discussions here will give greater impetus to make real progress in these areas.

There's also a great potential to develop common opportunities. For example, the Soviet Union now seeks greater engagement with the international market economy, a step that certainly I'm prepared to encourage in every way I can.

As I leave Malta for Brussels and a meeting with our NATO allies, I am optimistic that as the West works patiently together and increasingly cooperates with the Soviet Union, we can realize a lasting peace and transform the East–West relationship to one of enduring cooperation. And that is a future that's worthy of our peoples. And that's the future that I want to help in creating. And that's the future that Chairman Gorbachev and I began right here in Malta.

Thank you, sir, for your hospitality.

The Chairman. Ladies and gentlemen, comrades, there are many symbolic things about this meeting, and one of them – it has never been in the history that the leaders of our two countries hold a joint press conference. This is also an important symbol. I share the view voiced by President Bush that we are satisfied, in general, with the results of the meeting.

We regard this informal meeting – the idea of it was an informal meeting, and the idea belongs to President Bush. And I supported it – that we would have this informal meeting without restricting it to any formal agenda, to have a free exchange of views – because the time makes great demands to our countries, and this increases the responsibility and the role of our two countries. And I can assure you that in all our discussions – and our discussions lasted for 8 hours, in general – this responsibility on both sides was present.

Our meeting was characterized by openness, by a full scope of the exchange of views. Today it is even difficult, and perhaps there is no sense, to explain the entire range of issues that we have discussed. I wish to say right away, nevertheless, that on all the major issues we attempted in a frank manner, using each side's arguments, to explain our own positions, both with regard to the assessment of the situation and the current changes in the world and Europe and as it regards disarmament issues. We addressed the Geneva negotiating process, the Vienna process, and also negotiations on the elaboration of the convention on chemical weapons ban. All those questions were considered thoroughly.

The President and I myself also felt it necessary to exchange views on our perception, both from Moscow and Washington, of the hot points on our planet. And this exchange of views was very significant and thorough. We reaffirmed our former positions that all those acute issues must be resolved by political methods, and I consider that this was a very important statement of fact.

We not only discussed problems and explained our positions. I think that both sides had many elements which, if they are taken into account in our future activities – activities of both governments – then we can count on progress. This concerns the subject of the reduction of strategic offensive arms by 50 percent, and we have an optimistic assessment of the possibility to move even next year to the conclusion of the Vienna treaty. We both are in favor, and this is our position – naturally, we can be responsible only for our position – we are in favor of signing this document at the summit meeting.

This time we discussed much bilateral relations; and I, on my part, would like to note many positive elements and points which were contained in statements and words by President Bush. Thus, I would say that in all directions of the political dialog of our discussion, including bilateral relations, we not only confirmed the consistency of our political course, the continuity of our political course – and I should say it although we had an informal meeting, we met only for the first time with President Bush in his capacity, and the confirmation of the continuity of the course is an important element. What is also important is that during this informal meeting, we have laid the foundation for increasing this capital. And I believe that, in the first place, it serves the interests of our both countries and also the interests of the entire world community.

Well, we have made our contact, a good contact. The atmosphere was friendly, straightforward, open; and this enabled us to make good work. In our position, the most dangerous thing is to exaggerate. And it is always that we should preserve elements of cautiousness, and I use the favorite word by President Bush. [Laughter] Our world and our relations are at a crucial juncture. We should be highly responsible to face up to the challenges of today's world. And the leaders of our two countries cannot act as a fire brigade, although fire brigades are very useful. We have to keep it in mind also. This element was also present.

I would like once again to thank the President for the idea of holding this meeting with which we are satisfied, I hope. And I would like to thank the people and the Government of Malta and to express the words of appreciation and gratitude for the hospitality. Thank you, Mr. President, for your cooperation.

The President. Thank you.

The Cold War

Q: Chairman Gorbachev, President Bush called on you to end the cold war once and for all. Do you think that has been done now?

THE CHAIRMAN: In the first place, I assured the President of the United States that the Soviet Union would never start hot war against the United States of America, and we would like our relations to develop in such a way that they would open greater possibilities for cooperation. Naturally, the President and I had a wide discussion – rather, we sought the answer to the question where we stand now. We stated, both of us, that the world leaves one epoch of cold war and enters another epoch. This is just the beginning. We're just at the very beginning of our long road to a long-lasting peaceful period.

Thus, we were unanimous in concluding about the special responsibility of such countries as the United States and the Soviet Union. Naturally, we had a rather long discussion, but this is not for the press conference; that is, we shouldn't explain that discussion regarding the fact that the new era calls for a new approach, And thus, many things that were characteristic of the cold war should be abandoned, both the – [inaudible] – in force, the arms race, mistrust, psychological and ideological struggle, and all that. All that should be things of the past.

Source: *Public Papers of President George Bush, 1989*, vol. II (Washington, DC: US Government Printing Office), pp. 1625–7.

Suggested Questions for Discussion:

1. Why did George H. W. Bush and Mikhail Gorbachev believe the Cold War was over?
2. How did they characterize their new relationship?
3. What did they expect for the future?

Chapter 9   After the Cold War

1 President George H. W. Bush, the Iraqi Invasion of Kuwait, 1990

> *On August 2, 1990 Iraqi military forces invaded Kuwait, quickly overrunning the country and seizing its oil reserves. This was the first post-Cold War crisis. President George H. W. Bush responded immediately by condemning the invasion and forming a broad coalition of countries. The coalition included the Soviet Union and various Arab states. Bush was careful to avoid a rush to war, but after August 2, 1990 he slowly prepared the ground for a multinational, US-led, liberation of Kuwait.[1]*

President George H. W. Bush's News Conference, August 2, 1990

THE PRESIDENT. Let me make a brief statement here about recent events. The United States strongly condemns the Iraqi military invasion of Kuwait. We call for the immediate and unconditional withdrawal of all the Iraqi forces, There is no place for this sort of naked aggression in today's world, and I've taken a number of steps to indicate the deep concern that I feel over the events that have taken place.

Last night I instructed our Ambassador at the United Nations, Tom Pickering, to work with Kuwait in convening an emergency meeting of

---

[1] Derek Chollet and James Goldgeier, *America Between the Wars: From 11/9 to 9/11* (New York: Public Affairs, 2008); Hal Brands, *From Berlin to Baghdad: America's Search for Purpose in the Post-Cold War World* (Lexington, KT: University Press of Kentucky, 2008); Richard N. Haass, *War of Necessity, War of Choice: A Memoir of Two Iraq Wars* (New York: Simon and Schuster, 2009).

the Security Council. It was convened, and I am grateful for that quick, overwhelming vote condemning the Iraqi action and calling for immediate and unconditional withdrawal. Tom Pickering will be here in a bit, and we are contemplating with him further United Nations action,

Second, consistent with my authority under the International Emergency Economic Powers Act, I've signed an Executive order early this morning freezing Iraqi assets in this country and prohibiting transactions with Iraq. I've also signed an Executive order freezing Kuwaiti assets. That's to ensure that those assets are not interfered with by the illegitimate authority that is now occupying Kuwait. We call upon other governments to take similar action,

Third, the Department of State has been in touch with governments around the world urging that they, too, condemn the Iraqi aggression and consult to determine what measures should be taken to bring an end to this totally unjustified act. It is important that the international community act together to ensure that Iraqi forces depart Kuwait immediately.

Needless to say, we view the situation with the utmost gravity. We remain committed to take whatever steps are necessary to defend our longstanding, vital interests in the Gulf, and I'm meeting this morning with my senior advisors here to consider all possible options available to us. I've talked to Secretary Baker just now; General Scowcroft and I were on the phone with him. And after this meeting, will proceed to deliver a longstanding speech. I will have consultations – short ones – there in Aspen with Prime Minister Thatcher, and I will be returning home this evening, and I'll be here in Washington tomorrow....

Q.   Mr. President?

THE PRESIDENT. Yes, Helen [Helen Thomas, United Press International]?

Q.   Do you contemplate intervention as one of your options?

THE PRESIDENT. We're not discussing intervention. I would not discuss any military options even if we'd agreed upon them. But one of the things I want to do at this meeting is hear from our Secretary of Defense, our Chairman, and others. But I'm not contemplating such action.

Q.   You're not contemplating any intervention or sending troops?

THE PRESIDENT. I'm not contemplating such action, and I again would not discuss it if I were.

Q.   What is the likely impact on US oil supplies and prices?

THE PRESIDENT. This is a matter that concerns us, and I don't know yet. Again, I'm going to hear from our experts now. Our Secretary of Energy is here, if you'll note, and others who understand this situation very well indeed – our Secretary of Defense. And we'll be discussing that. But this is a matter of considerable concern, and not just to the United States, I might add.

Q.   Are you planning to break relations?

THE PRESIDENT. You've heard me say over and over again, however, that we are dependent for close to 50 percent of our energy requirements on the Middle East. And this is one of the reasons I felt that we have to not let our guard down around the world

Q.   Are you contemplating breaking diplomatic relations?

THE PRESIDENT. I'm discussing this matter with our top advisors here in just a minute.

Q.   Is this action in your view limited to Kuwait?

THE PRESIDENT. There's no evidence to the contrary. But what I want to do is have it limited back to Iraq and have this invasion be reversed and have them get out of Kuwait.

Q.   Do you think Saudi Arabia is threatened or any of the other Emirates?

THE PRESIDENT. I think Saudi Arabia is very concerned; and I want to hear from our top officials here, our Director of Intelligence and others, as to the worldwide implications of this legal action that has been condemned by the United Nations.

Q.   And you were taken by surprise?

THE PRESIDENT Not totally by surprise because we have good intelligence, and our intelligence has had me concerned for some time here about what action might be taken.

Thank you all very much. And I expect I will say something further because I'm having a joint press meeting with Margaret Thatcher and, at that time, I might be able to take a few more questions on this subject. But the main thing I want to do now is hear from our advisors, and then we will go forth from this meeting all on the same wavelength. I'm sure there will be a lot of frenzied diplomatic activity. I plan to participate in some of that myself, because at this time it is important to stay in touch with our many friends around the world, and it's important that we work in concert with our friends around the world.

Q.   Gorbachev?

THE PRESIDENT. Thank you very much. Obviously – Helen, you might be interested – this matter has been discussed at very high level between Secretary Baker and the Foreign Minister of the Soviet Union. And so far I've been pleased with the Soviet reaction.

Source: *Public Papers of Presidents: George Bush, 1990*, vol. II (Washington, DC: US Government Printing Office), pp. 1083–4.

Suggested Questions for Discussion:

1. Why did President George H. W. Bush condemn the Iraqi invasion of Kuwait?
2. How did he define American interests in the region?
3. What were his initial responses to the crisis?

2 Deputy Secretary of Defense, John Deutch, Genocide in Rwanda, 1994

> *Between April and July 1994 para-military groups in Rwanda composed of ethnic Hutus murdered more than 800,000 ethnic Tutsi residents of the country. This was a premeditated genocide, designed to eliminate an entire group of people. By mid-July, Tutsi forces, organized as the Rwandan Patriotic Front, launched retaliatory military actions that created a new crisis as approximately two million Hutus became refugees in neighboring Zaire, Burundi, Uganda, and Tanzania. Fearful of calls for the United States to intervene in the region, President Bill Clinton refused to acknowledge the genocide in Rwanda, despite widespread media reports. This document reveals that as late as July 20, 1994 – three months after the genocide began – the White House was barely organized for limited refugee relief around Rwanda.*[2]

Memorandum for the National Security, Anthony Lake, July 20, 1994

FROM: Deputy Secretary of Defense John Deutch
SUBJECT: Department of Defense Support for Humanitarian Efforts in Rwanda (U)

(U) Last night, prior to my "Nightline" taping, we met to discuss Department of Defense support to ameliorating the horrendous conditions in Rwanda. Dick Clarke and Doug Bennett joined Walt Slocombe, Admiral Owens and an array of OSD and Joint Staff representatives in the meeting. Let me offer you a synopsis.

(C) During the next 24–48 hours we plan to move on several fronts. First, USCINCEUR will deploy a survey team to Goma in Zaire. The team, to

[2]   See Philip Gourevitch, *We Wish to Inform You that Tomorrow We will be Killed with Our Families: Stories from Rwanda* (New York: Farrar, Straus, and Giroux, 1998); Samantha Power, *A Problem from Hell: America and the Age of Genocide* (New York: Basic Books, 2002).

include experts in logistics, health and sanitation, engineering and transportation, will have two functions: to assess possible Department of Defense assistance and to start helping UN and French authorities in areas of our expertise such as flight scheduling, airfield throughput operations, onward movement of supplies, security, communications support, and health services. Second, we will dispatch another team to France to facilitate coordination with their MFA and MOD. Third, we will offer to augment the UNHCR [United Nations Refugee Agency] with a logistic planning cell in Geneva.

(C) After our deployed experts feed us back some analysis, we are willing to consider further steps. Here is a list of some possible responses:

– Deploy runway repair team
– Provide night capability at Goma airfield
– Deploy an airlift control element
– Provide excess medical supplies
– Deploy preventative medicine elements
– Provide water distribution equipment, bladders, ROWPUs [Reverse Osmosis Water Purification Units]
– Provide trucks
– Provide rations
– Deploy Special Forces Teams or a Group
– Deploy PSYOP [Psychological Operations] unit(s)
– Provide civil affairs personnel to assist in the UN relief operation
– Provide additional airlift

(U) Funding: Approximately $8M of the $15M Department of Defense humanitarian assistance funds identified for transportation support remain. State is passing $19M to the UN which may be helpful as we work in concert with UNHCR; perhaps State and other agencies can offer other similar contributions. Beyond that we see two possibilities. The first is a Presidential drawdown under section 506a2, but that isn't cash and would mean pulling goods and services out of serving Army units, with possible impact on readiness. We would also be willing to pursue an emergency Department of Defense reprogramming.

(C) As we begin to immerse ourselves more deeply, two factors are critical. First, we will be playing a supportive role to the UN and the French, nothing more. Second, while we work to save lives in Zaire, the international community must find a way to convince Rwandan refugees to return home as soon as possible.

(C) Currently, Hutu refugees prefer the uncertainties of Goma to what they see as almost certain death at the hands of avenging Tutsis. Security in

Rwanda is key to bringing the refugees back. UNAMIR [United Nations Assistance Mission for Rwanda] forces in Rwanda must provide this security; working in tandem with UNHCR, they must become a "magnet" to draw Hutus home as US forces helped draw Kurds back to northern Iraq. As I told Ted Koppel last night, our model is not Somalia but Provide Comfort [United States relief assistance for Kurds in Northern Iraq].

(C) Your staff is working with State and USUN [US Mission to the United Nations] to try to reconfigure UNAMIR from a heavy mostly African force to a light force with a substantial component of First World militaries with the logistical skills to assist in refugee repatriation and humanitarian assistance inside of Rwanda. Walt alerted Bob Hunter yesterday that we and the UN may be calling on our NATO allies in this regard. At the same time, we must continue to facilitate political reconciliation through international and bilateral channels. State is working this and of course we stand by to help.

cc: Strobe Talbott [Deputy Secretary of State]
General Shalikashvili [Chairman of the Joint Chiefs of Staff]

Source: http://www.gwu.edu/~nsarchiv/NSAEBB/NSAEBB117/index.htm (accessed August 20, 2008).

Suggested Questions for Discussion:

1. How did American leaders define the nature of the crisis in Rwanda?
2. How did they define American interests?
3. What role did the media play?

3 President Bill Clinton, the Kosovo Crisis, 1999

The end of the Cold War marked the beginning of a new series of wars in Yugoslavia. Between 1991 and 1999 this mixed ethnic and religious state, created at the end of the First World War, fragmented in a fire of violence and hatred. The leaders of both Serbia and Croatia supported brutal "ethnic cleansing" policies that forcibly moved populations, appropriated property, and murdered large groups. Slobodan Milošević, the leader of Serbia, played a particularly powerful role in encouraging Serbian para-military groups to "cleanse" towns and villages of Croats and Bosnians. In 1998 Milošević extended the killing into the province of Kosovo, populated in part by ethnic Albanians. Eight years of failed peace efforts by European and American representatives, and the evidence of this extension of the conflict, motivated

President Bill Clinton to push for NATO air strikes against Serbia. The NATO allies approved this move, but the United Nations did not. Clinton was careful to justify the air strikes, but renounce the use of foreign ground troops in Serbia under hostile conditions. The NATO bombing campaign in Serbia lasted from March 24, 1999 until Milošević agreed to withdraw his forces from Kosovo on June 11, 1999.[3]

President Bill Clinton's Address to the Nation, March 24, 1999

My fellow Americans, today our Armed Forces joined our NATO Allies in airstrikes against Serbian forces responsible for the brutality in Kosovo. We have acted with resolve for several reasons.

We act to protect thousands of innocent people in Kosovo from a mounting military offensive. We act to prevent a wider war, to defuse a powder keg at the heart of Europe that has exploded twice before in this century with catastrophic results. And we act to stand united with our allies for peace. By acting now, we are upholding our values, protecting our interests, and advancing the cause of peace.

Tonight I want to speak to you about the tragedy in Kosovo and why it matters to America that we work with our allies to end it. First, let me explain what it is we are responding to. Kosovo is a province of Serbia, in the middle of southeastern Europe, about 160 miles east of Italy. That's less than the distance between Washington and New York and only about 70 miles north of Greece. Its people are mostly ethnic Albanian and mostly Muslim.

In 1989 Serbia's leader, Slobodan Milošević, the same leader who started the wars in Bosnia and Croatia and moved against Slovenia in the last decade, stripped Kosovo of the constitutional autonomy its people enjoyed, thus denying them their right to speak their language, run their schools, shape their daily lives. For years, Kosovars struggled peacefully to get their rights back. When President Milošević sent his troops and police to crush them, the struggle grew violent.

Last fall our diplomacy, backed by the threat of force form our NATO Alliance, stopped the fighting for a while and rescued tens of thousands of people from freezing and starvation in the hills where they had fled to save their lives. And last month, with our allies and Russia, we proposed a peace agreement to end the fighting for good. The Kosovar leaders signed that

---

[3] See Tim Judah, *Kosovo: War and Revenge* (New Haven, CT: Yale University Press, 2000); Misha Glenny, *The Fall of Yugoslavia* (New York: Penguin, 1996); Samantha Power, *A Problem from Hell: America and the Age of Genocide* (New York: Basic Books, 2002).

agreement last week. Even though it does not give them all they want, even though their people were still being savaged, they saw that a just peace is better than a long and unwinnable war.

The Serbian leaders, on the other hand, refused even to discuss key elements of the peace agreement. As the Kosovars were saying yes to peace, Serbia stationed 40,000 troops in and around Kosovo in preparation for a major offensive – and in clear violation of the commitments they had made.

Now they've started moving from village to village, shelling civilians and torching their houses. We've seen innocent people taken from their homes, forced to kneel in the dirt, and sprayed with bullets; Kosovar men dragged from their families, fathers and sons together, lined up and shot in cold blood. This is not war in the traditional sense. It is an attack by tanks and artillery on a largely defenseless people whose leaders already have agreed to peace.

Ending this tragedy is a moral imperative. It is also important to America's national interest. Take a look at this map. Kosovo is a small place, but it sits on a major fault line between Europe, Asia, and the Middle East, at the meeting place of Islam and both the Western and Orthodox branches of Christianity. To the south are our allies Greece and Turkey; to the north, our new democratic allies in central Europe. And all around Kosovo, there are other small countries struggling with their own economic and political challenges, countries that could be overwhelmed by a large, new wave of refugees from Kosovo. All the ingredients for a major war are there: ancient grievances; struggling democracies; and in the center of it all, a dictator in Serbia who has done nothing since the cold war ended but start new wars and pour gasoline on the flames of ethnic and religious division.

Sarajevo, the capital of neighboring Bosnia, is where World War I began. World War II and the Holocaust engulfed this region. In both wars, Europe was slow to recognize the dangers and the United States waited even longer to enter the conflicts. Just imagine if leaders back then had acted wisely and early enough, how many lives would have been saved, how many Americans would not have had to die.

We learned some of the same lessons in Bosnia just a few years ago. The world did not act early enough to stop that war, either. And let's not forget what happened: innocent people herded into concentration camps, children gunned down by snipers on their way to school, soccer fields and parks turned into cemeteries, a quarter of a million people killed, not because of anything they have done but because of who they were. Two million Bosnians became refugees. This was genocide in the heart of Europe, not in 1945 but in 1995; not in some grainy newsreel from our parents' and grandparents' time but in our own time, testing our humanity and our resolve.

At the time, many people believed nothing could be done to end the bloodshed in Bosnia. They said, "Well, that's just the way those people in the Balkans are." But when we and our allies joined with courageous Bosnians to stand up to the aggressors, we helped to end the war. We learned that in the Balkans, inaction in the face of brutality simply invites more brutality, but firmness can stop armies and save lives. We must apply that lesson in Kosovo before what happened in Bosnia happens there, too.

Over the last few months we have done everything we possibly could to solve this problem peacefully. Secretary Albright has worked tirelessly for a negotiated agreement. Mr. Milošević has refused. On Sunday I sent Ambassador [Richard] Dick Holbrooke to Serbia to make clear to him again, on behalf of the United States and our NATO Allies, that he must honor his own commitments and stop his repression, or face military action. Again, he refused.

Today we and our 18 NATO Allies agreed to do what we said we would do, what we must do to restore the peace. Our mission is clear: to demonstrate the seriousness of NATO's purpose so that the Serbian leaders understand the imperative of reversing course; to deter an even bloodier offensive against innocent civilians in Kosovo; and, if necessary, to seriously damage the Serbian military's capacity to harm the people of Kosovo. In short, if President Milošević will not make peace, we will limit his ability to make war.

Now, I want to be clear with you, there are risks in this military action, risks to our pilots and the people on the ground. Serbia's air defenses are strong. It could decide to intensify its assault on Kosovo or to seek to harm us or our allies elsewhere. If it does, we will deliver a forceful response.

Hopefully, Mr. Milošević will realize his present course is self-destructive and unsustainable. If he decides to accept the peace agreement and demilitarize Kosovo, NATO has agreed to help implement it with a peacekeeping force. If NATO is invited to do so, our troops should take part in that mission to keep the peace. But I do not intend to put our troops in Kosovo to fight a war.

Do our interests in Kosovo justify the dangers to our Armed Forces? I've thought long and hard about that question. I am convinced that the dangers of acting are far outweighed by the dangers of not acting – dangers to defenseless people and to our national interests. If we and our allies were to allow this war to continue with no response, President Milošević would read our hesitation as a license to kill. There would be many more massacres, tens of thousands more refugees, more victims crying out for revenge.

Right now our firmness is the only hope the people of Kosovo have to be able to live in their own country without having to fear for their own lives. Remember, we asked them to accept peace, and they did. We asked them to promise to lay down their arms, and they agreed. We pledged that we, the United States and the other 18 nations of NATO, would stick by them if they did the right thing. We cannot let them down now.

Imagine what would happen if we and our allies instead decided just to look the other way, as these people were massacred on NATO's doorstep. That would discredit NATO, the cornerstone on which our security has rested for 50 years now.

We must also remember that this is a conflict with no natural national boundaries. Let me ask you to look again at a map. The red dots are towns the Serbs have attacked. The arrows show the movement of refugees north, east, and south. Already, this movement is threatening the young democracy in Macedonia, which has its own Albanian minority and a Turkish minority. Already, Serbian forces have made forays into Albania from which Kosovars have drawn support. Albania has a Greek minority. Let a fire burn here in this area, and the flames will spread. Eventually, key US allies could be drawn into a wider conflict, a war we could be forced to confront later, only at far greater risk and greater cost.

I have a responsibility as President to deal with problems such as this before they do permanent harm to our national interests. America has a responsibility to stand with our allies when they are trying to save innocent lives and preserve peace, freedom, and stability in Europe. That is what we are doing in Kosovo.

If we've learned anything from the century drawing to a close, it is that if America is going to be prosperous and secure, we need a Europe that is prosperous, secure, undivided, and free. We need a Europe that is coming together, not falling apart, a Europe that shares our values and shares the burdens of leadership. That is the foundation on which the security of our children will depend.

That is why I have supported the political and economic unification of Europe. That is why we brought Poland, Hungary, and the Czech Republic into NATO, and redefined its missions, and reached out to Russia and Ukraine for new partnerships.

Now, what are the challenges to that vision of a peaceful, secure, united, stable Europe? The challenge of strengthening a partnership with a democratic Russia that, despite our disagreements, is a constructive partner in the work of building peace; the challenge of resolving the tension between Greece and Turkey and building bridges with the Islamic world; and finally, the challenge of ending instability in the Balkans so that these bitter ethnic problems in Europe are resolved by the force of argument, not the force of arms, so that future generations of Americans do not have to cross the Atlantic to fight another terrible war.

It is this challenge that we and our allies are facing in Kosovo. That is why we have acted now: because we care about saving innocent lives; because we have an interest in avoiding an even crueler and costlier war; and because our children need and deserve a peaceful, stable, free Europe.

Our thoughts and prayers tonight must be with the men and women of our Armed Forces who are undertaking this mission for the sake of our values and our children's future.

May God bless them, and may God bless America. . . .

President Bill Clinton's News Conference, March 25, 1999

Q.   What is the exit strategy?

THE PRESIDENT. The exit strategy is what it is in a military operation. It's when the mission is completed.

Q.   Do you believe the Kosovars can be safe without the intervention of ground troops from NATO? Can your goals be achieved just through airstrikes?

THE PRESIDENT. I do. I believe we can create a situation in which we have limited their ability to make war and thereby increase the prospects that they can protect themselves better. I do believe that. . . .

Q.   Are you concerned that the American people aren't more strongly behind you on this?

THE PRESIDENT. No. I believe that many Americans really had not thought a lot about this until the last 2 days. I hope that a lot of them heard my presentation last night. I did my very best to explain what we were doing and why, and I believe that a majority of them will support what we're trying to do here. I also believe very strongly that it is my responsibility to make this judgment based on what I think is in the long-term interests of the American people.

Source: *Public Papers of President William J. Clinton, 1999*, vol. 1 (Washington, DC: US Government Printing Office), pp. 451–4.

Suggested Questions for Discussion:

1.   How did President Bill Clinton define the crisis in the former Yugoslavia?
2.   How did Clinton define American interests in the region?
3.   Why did Clinton advocate the use of air power, but reject the deployment of ground troops in hostile territory?

Chapter 10   The War on Terror

1 The Terrorist Attacks of September 11, 2001

On the clear and sunny morning of September 11, 2001 a small group of foreign terrorists carried out the worst attack on American territory since 1941. They boarded four jet aircraft, seized control of them, and flew them into major public buildings: two World Center buildings in New York, and the Pentagon in Washington DC. The fourth aircraft crashed in rural Pennsylvania, when the passengers on board overpowered the terrorists. The National Commission on Terrorist Attacks Upon the United States (the "9/11 Commission") reconstructed a detailed history of these horrible events.[1]

Boarding the Flights

Boston: American 11 and United 175

Atta and Omari boarded a 6:00 A.M. flight from Portland to Boston's Logan International Airport.

When he checked in for his flight to Boston, Atta was selected by a computerized prescreening system known as CAPPS (Computer Assisted Passenger Prescreening System), created to identify passengers who should be subject to special security measures. Under security rules in place at the

[1] See *Final Report of the National Commission on Terrorist Attacks Upon the United States (The 9/11 Commission Report)*, http://www.gpoaccess.gov/911/ (accessed August 20, 2008); Philip Shenon, *The Commission: The Uncensored History of the 9/11 Investigation* (New York: Hachette Books, 2008).

time, the only consequence of Atta's selection by CAPPS was that his checked bags were held off the plane until it was confirmed that he had boarded the aircraft. This did not hinder Atta's plans.

Atta and Omari arrived in Boston at 6:45. Seven minutes later, Atta apparently took a call from Marwan al Shehhi, a longtime colleague who was at another terminal at Logan Airport. They spoke for three minutes. It would be their final conversation.

Between 6:45 and 7:40, Atta and Omari, along with Satam al Suqami, Wail al Shehri, and Waleed al Shehri, checked in and boarded American Airlines Flight 11, bound for Los Angeles. The flight was scheduled to depart at 7:45.

In another Logan terminal, Shehhi, joined by Fayez Banihammad, Mohand al Shehri, Ahmed al Ghamdi, and Hamza al Ghamdi, checked in for United Airlines Flight 175, also bound for Los Angeles. A couple of Shehhi's colleagues were obviously unused to travel; according to the United ticket agent, they had trouble understanding the standard security questions, and she had to go over them slowly until they gave the routine, reassuring answers. Their flight was scheduled to depart at 8:00.

The security checkpoints through which passengers, including Atta and his colleagues, gained access to the American 11 gate were operated by Globe Security under a contract with American Airlines. In a different terminal, the single checkpoint through which passengers for United 175 passed was controlled by United Airlines, which had contracted with Huntleigh USA to perform the screening.

In passing through these checkpoints, each of the hijackers would have been screened by a walk-through metal detector calibrated to detect items with at least the metal content of a .22-caliber handgun. Anyone who might have set off that detector would have been screened with a hand wand – a procedure requiring the screener to identify the metal item or items that caused the alarm. In addition, an X-ray machine would have screened the hijackers' carry-on belongings. The screening was in place to identify and confiscate weapons and other items prohibited from being carried onto a commercial flight. None of the checkpoint supervisors recalled the hijackers or reported anything suspicious regarding their screening.

While Atta had been selected by CAPPS in Portland, three members of his hijacking team – Suqami, Wail al Shehri, and Waleed al Shehri – were selected in Boston. Their selection affected only the handling of their checked bags, not their screening at the checkpoint. All five men cleared the checkpoint and made their way to the gate for American 11. Atta, Omari, and Suqami took their seats in business class (seats 8D, 8G, and 10B, respectively). The Shehri brothers had adjacent seats in row 2 (Wail in 2A, Waleed in 2B), in the first-class cabin. They boarded American 11 between 7:31 and 7:40. The aircraft pushed back from the gate at 7:40.

Shehhi and his team, none of whom had been selected by CAPPS, boarded United 175 between 7:23 and 7:28 (Banihammad in 2A, Shehri in 2B, Shehhi in 6C, Hamza al Ghamdi in 9C, and Ahmed al Ghamdi in 9D). Their aircraft pushed back from the gate just before 8:00. . . .

Newark: United 93

Between 7:03 and 7:39, Saeed al Ghamdi, Ahmed al Nami, Ahmad al Haznawi, and Ziad Jarrah checked in at the United Airlines ticket counter for Flight 93, going to Los Angeles. Two checked bags; two did not. Haznawi was selected by CAPPS. His checked bag was screened for explosives and then loaded on the plane.

The four men passed through the security checkpoint, owned by United Airlines and operated under contract by Argenbright Security. Like the checkpoints in Boston, it lacked closed-circuit television surveillance so there is no documentary evidence to indicate when the hijackers passed through the checkpoint, what alarms may have been triggered, or what security procedures were administered. The FAA interviewed the screeners later; none recalled anything unusual or suspicious.

The four men boarded the plane between 7:39 and 7:48. All four had seats in the first-class cabin; their plane had no business-class section. Jarrah was in seat 1B, closest to the cockpit; Nami was in 3C, Ghamdi in 3D, and Haznawi in 6B.

The 19 men were aboard four transcontinental flights. They were planning to hijack these planes and turn them into large guided missiles, loaded with up to 11,400 gallons of jet fuel. By 8:00 A.M. on the morning of Tuesday, September 11, 2001, they had defeated all the security layers that America's civil aviation security system then had in place to prevent a hijacking.

The Hijacking of American 11

American Airlines Flight 11 provided nonstop service from Boston to Los Angeles. On September 11, Captain John Ogonowski and First Officer Thomas McGuinness piloted the Boeing 767. It carried its full capacity of nine flight attendants. Eighty-one passengers boarded the flight with them (including the five terrorists).

The plane took off at 7:59. Just before 8:14, it had climbed to 26,000 feet, not quite its initial assigned cruising altitude of 29,000 feet. All communications and flight profile data were normal. About this time the "Fasten Seatbelt" sign would usually have been turned off and the flight attendants would have begun preparing for cabin service.

At that same time, American 11 had its last routine communication with the ground when it acknowledged navigational instructions from the FAA's air traffic control (ATC) center in Boston. Sixteen seconds after that transmission, ATC instructed the aircraft's pilots to climb to 35,000 feet. That message and all subsequent attempts to contact the flight were not acknowledged. From this and other evidence, we believe the hijacking began at 8:14 or shortly thereafter.

Reports from two flight attendants in the coach cabin, Betty Ong and Madeline "Amy" Sweeney, tell us most of what we know about how the hijacking happened. As it began, some of the hijackers – most likely Wail al Shehri and Waleed al Shehri, who were seated in row 2 in first class – stabbed the two unarmed flight attendants who would have been preparing for cabin service.

We do not know exactly how the hijackers gained access to the cockpit; FAA rules required that the doors remain closed and locked during flight. Ong speculated that they had "jammed their way" in. Perhaps the terrorists stabbed the flight attendants to get a cockpit key, to force one of them to open the cockpit door, or to lure the captain or first officer out of the cockpit. Or the flight attendants may just have been in their way.

At the same time or shortly thereafter, Atta – the only terrorist on board trained to fly a jet – would have moved to the cockpit from his business-class seat, possibly accompanied by Omari. As this was happening, passenger Daniel Lewin, who was seated in the row just behind Atta and Omari, was stabbed by one of the hijackers – probably Satam al Suqami, who was seated directly behind Lewin. Lewin had served four years as an officer in the Israeli military. He may have made an attempt to stop the hijackers in front of him, not realizing that another was sitting behind him.

The hijackers quickly gained control and sprayed Mace, pepper spray, or some other irritant in the first-class cabin, in order to force the passengers and flight attendants toward the rear of the plane. They claimed they had a bomb.

About five minutes after the hijacking began, Betty Ong contacted the American Airlines Southeastern Reservations Office in Cary, North Carolina, via an AT&T airphone to report an emergency aboard the flight. This was the first of several occasions on 9/11 when flight attendants took action outside the scope of their training, which emphasized that in a hijacking, they were to communicate with the cockpit crew. The emergency call lasted approximately 25 minutes, as Ong calmly and professionally relayed information about events taking place aboard the airplane to authorities on the ground.

At 8:19, Ong reported: "The cockpit is not answering, somebody's stabbed in business class – and I think there's Mace – that we can't breathe – I don't know, I think we're getting hijacked." She then told of the stabbings of the two flight attendants.

At 8:21, one of the American employees receiving Ong's call in North Carolina, Nydia Gonzalez, alerted the American Airlines operations center in Fort Worth, Texas, reaching Craig Marquis, the manager on duty. Marquis soon realized this was an emergency and instructed the airline's dispatcher responsible for the flight to contact the cockpit. At 8:23, the dispatcher tried unsuccessfully to contact the aircraft. Six minutes later, the air traffic control specialist in American's operations center contacted the FAA's Boston Air Traffic Control Center about the flight. The center was already aware of the problem.

Boston Center knew of a problem on the flight in part because just before 8:25 the hijackers had attempted to communicate with the passengers. The microphone was keyed, and immediately one of the hijackers said, "Nobody move. Everything will be okay. If you try to make any moves, you'll endanger yourself and the airplane. Just stay quiet." Air traffic controllers heard the transmission; Ong did not. The hijackers probably did not know how to operate the cockpit radio communication system correctly, and thus inadvertently broadcast their message over the air traffic control channel instead of the cabin public-address channel. Also at 8:25, and again at 8:29, Amy Sweeney got through to the American Flight Services Office in Boston but was cut off after she reported someone was hurt aboard the flight. Three minutes later, Sweeney was reconnected to the office and began relaying updates to the manager, Michael Woodward.

At 8:26, Ong reported that the plane was "flying erratically." A minute later, Flight 11 turned south. American also began getting identifications of the hijackers, as Ong and then Sweeney passed on some of the seat numbers of those who had gained unauthorized access to the cockpit.

Sweeney calmly reported on her line that the plane had been hijacked; a man in first class had his throat slashed; two flight attendants had been stabbed – one was seriously hurt and was on oxygen while the other's wounds seemed minor; a doctor had been requested; the flight attendants were unable to contact the cockpit; and there was a bomb in the cockpit. Sweeney told Woodward that she and Ong were trying to relay as much information as they could to people on the ground.

At 8:38, Ong told Gonzalez that the plane was flying erratically again. Around this time Sweeney told Woodward that the hijackers were Middle

Easterners, naming three of their seat numbers. One spoke very little English and one spoke excellent English. The hijackers had gained entry to the cockpit, and she did not know how. The aircraft was in a rapid descent.

At 8:41, Sweeney told Woodward that passengers in coach were under the impression that there was a routine medical emergency in first class. Other flight attendants were busy at duties such as getting medical supplies while Ong and Sweeney were reporting the events.

At 8:41, in American's operations center, a colleague told Marquis that the air traffic controllers declared Flight 11 a hijacking and "think he's [American 11] headed toward Kennedy [airport in New York City]. They're moving everybody out of the way. They seem to have him on a primary radar. They seem to think that he is descending"

At 8:44, Gonzalez reported losing phone contact with Ong. About this same time Sweeney reported to Woodward, "Something is wrong. We are in a rapid descent ... we are all over the place." Woodward asked Sweeney to look out the window to see if she could determine where they were. Sweeney responded: "We are flying low. We are flying very, very low. We are flying way too low." Seconds later she said, "Oh my God we are way too low." The phone call ended.

At 8:46:40, American 11 crashed into the North Tower of the World Trade Center in New York City. All on board, along with an unknown number of people in the tower, were killed instantly.

The Battle for United 93

At 8:42, United Airlines Flight 93 took off from Newark (New Jersey) Liberty International Airport bound for San Francisco. The aircraft was piloted by Captain Jason Dahl and First Officer Leroy Homer, and there were five flight attendants. Thirty-seven passengers, including the hijackers, boarded the plane. Scheduled to depart the gate at 8:00, the Boeing 757's takeoff was delayed because of the airport's typically heavy morning traffic.

The hijackers had planned to take flights scheduled to depart at 7:45 (American 11), 8:00 (United 175 and United 93), and 8:10 (American 77). Three of the flights had actually taken off within 10 to 15 minutes of their planned departure times. United 93 would ordinarily have taken off about 15 minutes after pulling away from the gate. When it left the ground at 8:42, the flight was running more than 25 minutes late.

As United 93 left Newark, the flight's crew members were unaware of the hijacking of American 11. Around 9:00, the FAA, American, and United were facing the staggering realization of apparent multiple hijackings. At 9:03, they would see another aircraft strike the World Trade Center. Crisis managers at the FAA and the airlines did not yet act to warn other aircraft. At the same time, Boston Center realized that a message transmitted just before 8:25 by the hijacker pilot of American 11 included the phrase, "We have some planes."

No one at the FAA or the airlines that day had ever dealt with multiple hijackings. Such a plot had not been carried out anywhere in the world in more than 30 years, and never in the United States. As news of the hijackings filtered through the FAA and the airlines, it does not seem to have occurred to their leadership that they needed to alert other aircraft in the air that they too might be at risk.

United 175 was hijacked between 8:42 and 8:46, and awareness of that hijacking began to spread after 8:51. American 77 was hijacked between 8:51 and 8:54. By 9:00, FAA and airline officials began to comprehend that attackers were going after multiple aircraft. American Airlines' nationwide ground stop between 9:05 and 9:10 was followed by a United Airlines ground stop. FAA controllers at Boston Center, which had tracked the first two hijackings, requested at 9:07 that Herndon Command Center "get messages to airborne aircraft to increase security for the cockpit." There is no evidence that Herndon took such action. Boston Center immediately began speculating about other aircraft that might be in danger, leading them to worry about a transcontinental flight – Delta 1989 – that in fact was not hijacked. At 9:19, the FAA's New England regional office called Herndon and asked that Cleveland Center advise Delta 1989 to use extra cockpit security.

Several FAA air traffic control officials told us it was the air carriers' responsibility to notify their planes of security problems. One senior FAA air traffic control manager said that it was simply not the FAA's place to order the airlines what to tell their pilots. We believe such statements do not reflect an adequate appreciation of the FAA's responsibility for the safety and security of civil aviation.

The airlines bore responsibility, too. They were facing an escalating number of conflicting and, for the most part, erroneous reports about other flights, as well as a continuing lack of vital information from the FAA about the hijacked flights. We found no evidence, however, that American Airlines sent any cockpit warnings to its aircraft on 9/11. United's first decisive action to notify its airborne aircraft to take defensive action did not come until 9:19, when a United flight dispatcher, Ed Ballinger, took the initiative to begin transmitting warnings to his 16 transcontinental flights: "Beware any cockpit intrusion – Two a/c [aircraft] hit World Trade Center." One of the flights that received the warning was United 93. Because Ballinger was still responsible for his other flights as well as Flight 175, his warning message was not transmitted to Flight 93 until 9:23.

By all accounts, the first 46 minutes of Flight 93's cross-country trip proceeded routinely. Radio communications from the plane were normal. Heading, speed, and altitude ran according to plan. At 9:24, Ballinger's warning to United 93 was received in the cockpit. Within two minutes, at 9:26, the pilot, Jason Dahl, responded with a note of puzzlement: "Ed, confirm latest mssg plz – Jason."

The hijackers attacked at 9:28. While traveling 35,000 feet above eastern Ohio, United 93 suddenly dropped 700 feet. Eleven seconds into the descent, the FAA's air traffic control center in Cleveland received the first of two radio transmissions from the aircraft. During the first broadcast, the captain or first officer could be heard declaring "Mayday" amid the sounds of a physical struggle in the cockpit. The second radio transmission, 35 seconds later, indicated that the fight was continuing. The captain or first officer could be heard shouting: "Hey get out of here – get out of here – get out of here."

On the morning of 9/11, there were only 37 passengers on United 93 – 33 in addition to the 4 hijackers. This was below the norm for Tuesday mornings during the summer of 2001. But there is no evidence that the hijackers manipulated passenger levels or purchased additional seats to facilitate their operation.

The terrorists who hijacked three other commercial flights on 9/11 operated in five man teams. They initiated their cockpit takeover within 30 minutes of takeoff. On Flight 93, however, the takeover took place 46 minutes after takeoff and there were only four hijackers. The operative likely intended to round out the team for this flight, Mohamed al Kahtani, had been refused entry by a suspicious immigration inspector at Florida's Orlando International Airport in August.

Because several passengers on United 93 described three hijackers on the plane, not four, some have wondered whether one of the hijackers had been able to use the cockpit jump seat from the outset of the flight. FAA rules allow use of this seat by documented and approved individuals, usually air carrier or FAA personnel. We have found no evidence indicating that one of the hijackers, or anyone else, sat there on this flight. All the hijackers had assigned seats in first class, and they seem to have used them. We believe it is more likely that Jarrah, the crucial pilot-trained member of their team, remained seated and inconspicuous until after the cockpit was seized; and once inside, he would not have been visible to the passengers.

At 9:32, a hijacker, probably Jarrah, made or attempted to make the following announcement to the passengers of Flight 93: "Ladies and Gentlemen: Here the captain, please sit down keep remaining sitting. We have a bomb on board. So, sit." The flight data recorder (also recovered) indicates that Jarrah then instructed the plane's autopilot to turn the aircraft around and head east.

The cockpit voice recorder data indicate that a woman, most likely a flight attendant, was being held captive in the cockpit. She struggled with one of the hijackers who killed or otherwise silenced her.

Shortly thereafter, the passengers and flight crew began a series of calls from GTE airphones and cellular phones. These calls between family, friends, and colleagues took place until the end of the flight and provided those on the ground with firsthand accounts. They enabled the passengers to gain critical information, including the news that two aircraft had slammed into the World Trade Center.

At 9:39, the FAA's Cleveland Air Route Traffic Control Center overheard a second announcement indicating that there was a bomb on board, that the plane was returning to the airport, and that they should remain seated. While it apparently was not heard by the passengers, this announcement, like those on Flight 11 and Flight 77, was intended to deceive them. Jarrah, like Atta earlier, may have inadvertently broadcast the message because he did not know how to operate the radio and the intercom. To our knowledge none of them had ever flown an actual airliner before.

At least two callers from the flight reported that the hijackers knew that passengers were making calls but did not seem to care. It is quite possible Jarrah knew of the success of the assault on the World Trade Center. He could have learned of this from messages being sent by United Airlines to the cockpits of its transcontinental flights, including Flight 93, warning of cockpit intrusion and telling of the New York attacks. But even without them, he would certainly have understood that the attacks on the World Trade Center would already have unfolded, given Flight 93's tardy departure from Newark. If Jarrah did know that the passengers were making calls, it might not have occurred to him that they were certain to learn what had happened in New York, thereby defeating his attempts at deception.

At least ten passengers and two crew members shared vital information with family, friends, colleagues, or others on the ground. All understood the plane had been hijacked. They said the hijackers wielded knives and claimed to have a bomb. The hijackers were wearing red bandanas, and they forced the passengers to the back of the aircraft.

Callers reported that a passenger had been stabbed and that two people were lying on the floor of the cabin, injured or dead – possibly the captain and first officer. One caller reported that a flight attendant had been killed.

One of the callers from United 93 also reported that he thought the hijackers might possess a gun. But none of the other callers reported the presence of a firearm. One recipient of a call from the aircraft recounted specifically asking her caller whether the hijackers had guns. The passenger replied that he did not see one. No evidence of firearms or of their identifiable remains was found at the aircraft's crash site, and the cockpit voice recorder gives no indication of a gun being fired or mentioned at any time. We believe that if the hijackers had possessed a gun, they would have used it in the flight's last minutes as the passengers fought back.

Passengers on three flights reported the hijackers' claim of having a bomb. The FBI told us they found no trace of explosives at the crash sites. One of the passengers who mentioned a bomb expressed his belief that it was not real. Lacking any evidence that the hijackers attempted to smuggle such illegal items past the security screening checkpoints, we believe the bombs were probably fake.

During at least five of the passengers' phone calls, information was shared about the attacks that had occurred earlier that morning at the World Trade Center. Five calls described the intent of passengers and surviving crew members to revolt against the hijackers. According to one call, they voted on whether to rush the terrorists in an attempt to retake the plane. They decided, and acted.

At 9:57, the passenger assault began. Several passengers had terminated phone calls with loved ones in order to join the revolt. One of the callers ended her message as follows: "Everyone's running up to first class, I've got to go. Bye."

The cockpit voice recorder captured the sounds of the passenger assault muffled by the intervening cockpit door. Some family members who listened to the recording report that they can hear the voice of a loved one among the din. We cannot identify whose voices can be heard. But the assault was sustained. In response, Jarrah immediately began to roll the airplane to the left and right, attempting to knock the passengers off balance. At 9:58:57, Jarrah told another hijacker in the cockpit to block the door. Jarrah continued to roll the airplane sharply left and right, but the assault continued. At 9:59:52, Jarrah changed tactics and pitched the nose of the airplane up and down to disrupt the assault. The recorder captured the sounds of loud thumps, crashes, shouts, and breaking glasses and plates. At 10:00:03, Jarrah stabilized the airplane.

Five seconds later, Jarrah asked, "Is that it? Shall we finish it off?" A hijacker responded, "No. Not yet. When they all come, we finish it off." The sounds of fighting continued outside the cockpit. Again, Jarrah pitched the nose of the aircraft up and down. At 10:00:26, a passenger in the background said, "In the cockpit. If we don't we'll die!" Sixteen seconds later, a passenger yelled, "Roll it!" Jarrah stopped the violent maneuvers at about 10:01:00 and said, "Allah is the greatest! Allah is the greatest!" He then asked another hijacker in the cockpit, "Is that it? I mean, shall we put it down?" to which the other replied, "Yes, put it in it, and pull it down."

The passengers continued their assault and at 10:02:23, a hijacker said, "Pull it down! Pull it down!" The hijackers remained at the controls but must have judged that the passengers were only seconds from overcoming them. The airplane headed down; the control wheel was turned hard to the right. The airplane rolled onto its back, and one of the hijackers began shouting "Allah is the greatest. Allah is the greatest." With the sounds of the passenger counterattack continuing, the aircraft plowed into an empty field in Shanksville, Pennsylvania, at 580 miles per hour, about 20 minutes' flying time from Washington, D.C.

Jarrah's objective was to crash his airliner into symbols of the American Republic, the Capitol or the White House. He was defeated by the alerted, unarmed passengers of United 93.

Source: *Final Report of the National Commission on Terrorist Attacks Upon the United States (The 9/11 Commission Report)*, pp. 1–14, available at: http://www.gpoaccess.gov/911 (accessed August 20, 2008).

Suggested Questions for Discussion:

1. How did the terrorists seize control of the aircraft?
2. Why weren't they stopped?
3. What were the consequences of these events?

2 *The New York Times,* the Public Horror of September 11, 2001

> *Americans and citizens around the world reacted to the events of September 11, 2001 with a mix of horror, uncertainty, and disorientation. They were uncertain how to react. They looked for leadership, and perhaps easy answers.[2]*

---

[2] See *Final Report of the National Commission on Terrorist Attacks on the United States (The 9/11 Commission Report)*, available at: http://www.gpoaccess.gov/911/ (accessed August 20, 2008); Ron Suskind, *The One Percent Doctrine: Deep Inside America's Pursuit of its Enemies since 9/11* (New York: Simon & Schuster, 2006).

Maureen Dowd, "A Grave Silence"

If you called yesterday afternoon to the White House switchboard, that famously efficient Washington institution, you would hear a brief recording saying to hold for an operator and then the line would go dead.

For many hours, the most eerie thing about the American capital, under attack for the first time since the British burned the White House in the War of 1812, was the stillness at the center of the city.

New York was a clamorous inferno of pain, confusion and fear, with Mayor Rudolph Giuliani on the scene in the rubble of the World Trade Center towers and on TV trying to reassure residents about schools and transportation and hospitals.

Manhattan had the noise of the grave. Washington had the silence of the grave. Downtown you could smell the smoke and see the plume rising from a Pentagon full of carnage and fire and see the flag over the emptied White House flying at half-staff.

But until the nation's leaders reappeared on television after nightfall to speak of what President Bush called their "quiet, unyielding anger," no one understood what had happened. No one knew what might happen next. Would there be a gas attack? Would the White House blow up? Would another plane crash into the Capitol?

People were so hungry for clues that they gathered, as their parents did after Pearl Harbor, around radios, huddled in small groups a block from a cordoned-off White House.

A doctor, Mark Cinnamon, 54, held up a radio broadcasting Peter Jennings interviewing Gov. George Pataki, while 15 strangers leaned in to listen. "We're just sharing, with an old battery-operated radio some guy handed me," he said.

On a gorgeous blue fall day, terrorism had turned into war. The city that leads the world took on a weird neutron-bomb quality. No one even tried to pretend, as we are supposed to, that no matter what, terrorists cannot disrupt our government.

For much of the day we weren't sure where the president was. There were statements floating in from him from various secure zones in the air or underground. The vice president was out of sight. We didn't know where the first lady was.

The secretary of state was in the air somewhere. The Capitol had been evacuated. Congressional leaders had gone off to a bunker somewhere. The Joint Chiefs of Staff could not be immediately accounted for. The C.I.A. and F.B.I. were stunned. Most vividly at his post was Donald Rumsfeld, who helped rescue victims at the Pentagon and stayed all day in the smoky command center.

White House officials had fled the building five minutes after the plane crashed into the Pentagon at 9:45 a.m., streaming out with some men screaming and some women barefoot and carrying their high heels.

"That floored me," said one federal official, stranded at a bus stop. "This is supposed to be the most secure place in the world. I said, 'Why are you running? You can leave but just slow down a little.'"

Federal buildings were evacuated, coffee shops shuttered, dress shops barred. A few tourists wandered around in shorts looking confused as military planes patrolled above. D.C. police carried rifles, and Secret Service agents in black Mustangs and green Luminas blocked off the streets adjacent to the White House.

The country cannot be completely protected from fanatics willing to die. And yet, it was chilling to see how unprepared those in charge of planning seemed, after years of warnings about just such an attack. The top Congressional leaders were calling each other, unsure whether to stay or go, or where to go.

"There was some confusion; no alarm bells went off," said Mitch Daniels, the Bush budget director, about the scene in the Old Executive Office Building, adding that people had decided to go "by word of mouth."

Even the president didn't seem sure of where to go.

"He is at the very top of the United States": said Tammie Owens, a subway supervisor in a bright yellow uniform, who felt that a president, like the British royal family during the blitz, needed to reassure people with his presence. "And the White House is where he should be."

David McCullough, the historian who wrote the biographies of Harry Truman and John Adams, disagreed. Mr. McCullough happened to be in town for a Laura Bush book festival and had just volunteered to give blood at a hospital. "All presidents do what they're told on matters of security" he said. "The most important thing is that the president is alive and safe and knows what's going on. We haven't seen this level of destruction on our home ground since the Civil War. This isn't the 'Titanic' movie. It's real."

Source: *The New York Times* (late edition (East Coast)), September 12, 2001, p. A2.

Suggested Questions for Discussion:

1. How did Americans begin to make sense of the September 11, 2001 attacks in their immediate aftermath?
2. What were the dominant emotions?
3. What were the expectations for the future?

3 President George W. Bush, the Bush Doctrine, 2002

*The terrorist attacks of September 11, 2001 sent a jolt through American
society and the foreign policy community, in particular. Within less than a
year, President George W. Bush announced a new radical doctrine for
combating threats to the United States. Bush emphasized a number of key
points: the proliferation of threats from non-state actors, the possibilities of
grave destruction, failures of deterrence and containment, the need for strong
preemptive military action, and the importance of building new authority
structures around American values. The Bush Doctrine was an aggressive
conceptualization of American force for what the White House began calling a
global "war on terror." Many observers later criticized the unilateral,
militaristic, and over-reaching elements of the Bush Doctrine, but in the
months after September 11, 2001 it shaped the political debate in the United
States.[3]*

---

*President George W. Bush, Address at the United States Military
Academy in West Point, New York, June 1, 2002*

... History has also issued its call to your generation. In your last year,
America was attacked by a ruthless and resourceful enemy. You graduate
from this Academy in a time of war, taking your place in an American
military that is powerful and is honorable. Our war on terror is only begun,
but in Afghanistan it was begun well.

I am proud of the men and women who have fought on my orders.
America is profoundly grateful for all who serve that the cause of freedom
and for all who have given their lives in its defense. This Nation respects and
trusts our military, and we are confident in your victories to come.

This war will take many turns we cannot predict. Yet, I am certain of this:
Wherever we carry it, the American flag will stand not only for our power
but for freedom. Our Nation's cause has always been larger than our
Nation's defense. We fight, as we always fight, for a just peace, a peace
that favors human liberty. We will defend the peace against threats from
terrorists and tyrants. We will preserve the peace by building good relations

---

[3] See John Lewis Gaddis, *Surprise, Security, and the American Experience* (Cambridge, MA:
Harvard University Press, 2004); Ivo Daalder and James Lindsay, *America Unbound: The Bush
Revolution in Foreign Policy* (Washington DC: Brookings Institution Press, 2003); Melvyn
P. Leffler and Jeffrey W. Legro, *To Lead the World: American Strategy after the Bush Doctrine*
(New York: Oxford University Press, 2008).

among the great powers. And we will extend the peace by encouraging free and open societies on every continent.

Building this just peace is America's opportunity and America's duty. From this day forward, it is your challenge as well, and we will meet this challenge together. You will wear the uniform of a great and unique country. America has no empire to extend or utopia to establish. We wish for others only what we wish for ourselves, safety from violence, the rewards of liberty and the hope for a better life.

In defending the peace, we face a threat with no precedent. Enemies in the past needed great armies and great industrial capabilities to endanger the American people and our Nation. The attacks of September the 11th required a few hundred thousand dollars in the hands of a few dozen evil and deluded men. All of the chaos and suffering they caused came at much less than the cost of a single tank. The dangers have not passed. This government and the American people are on watch. We are ready, because we know the terrorists have more money and more men and more plans.

The gravest danger to freedom lies at the perilous crossroads of radicalism and technology. When the spread of chemical and biological and nuclear weapons, along with ballistic missile technology – when that occurs, even weak states and small groups could attain a catastrophic power to strike great nations. Our enemies have declared this very intention and have been caught seeking these terrible weapons. They want the capability to blackmail us or to harm us or to harm our fiends, and we will oppose them with all our power.

For much of the last century, America's defense relied on the cold war doctrines of deterrence and containment. In some cases, those strategies still apply, but new threats also require new thinking. Deterrence – the promise of massive retaliation against nations – means nothing against shadowy terrorist networks with no nation or citizen to defend. Containment is not possible when unbalanced dictators with weapons of mass destruction can deliver those weapons on missiles or secretly provided them to terrorist allies. We cannot defend America and our friends by hoping for the best. We cannot put our faith in the word of tyrants who solemnly sign nonproliferation treaties and then systemically break them. If we wait for threats to fully materialize, we will have to wait too long.

Homeland defense and missile defense are part of stronger security; they're essential priorities for America. Yet the war on terror will not be won on the defensive. We must take the battle to the enemy, disrupt his plans, and confront the worst threats before they emerge. In the world we have entered, the only path to safety is the path of action, and this Nation will act.

Our security will require the best intelligence to reveal threats hidden in caves and growing in laboratories. Our security will require modernizing domestic agencies such as the FBI, so they're prepared to act and act quickly against danger. Our security will require transforming the military you will lead, a military that must be ready to strike at a moment's notice in any dark corner of the world. And our security will require all Americans to be forward-looking and resolute, to be ready for preemptive action when necessary to defend our liberty and to defend our lives.

The work ahead is difficult. The choices we will face are complex. We must uncover terror cells in 60 or more countries using every tool of finance, intelligence, and law enforcement. Along with our friends and allies, we must oppose proliferation and confront regimes that sponsor terror, as each case requires. Some nations need military training to fight terror, and we'll provide it. Other nations oppose terror but tolerate the hatred that leads to terror, and that must change. We will send diplomats where they are needed, and we will send you, our soldiers, where you're needed.

All nations that decide for aggression and terror will pay a price. We will not leave the safety of America and the peace of the planet at the mercy of a few mad terrorists and tyrants. We will lift this dark threat from our country and from the world.

Because the war on terror will require resolve and patience, it will also require firm moral purpose. In this way our struggle is similar to the cold war. Now, as then, our enemies are totalitarians, holding a creed of power with no place for human dignity. Now, as then, they seek to impose a joyless conformity, to control every life and all of life....

The 20th century ended with a single surviving model of human progress, based on nonnegotiable demands of human dignity, the rule of law, limits on the power of the state, respect for women, and private property and free speech and equal justice and religious tolerance. America cannot impose this vision, yet we can support and reward governments that make the right choices for their own people. In our development aid, in our diplomatic efforts, in our international broadcasting, and in our educational assistance, the United States will promote moderation and tolerance and human rights. And we will defend the peace that makes all progress possible.

When it comes to the common rights and needs of men and women, there is no clash of civilizations. The requirements of freedom apply fully to Africa and Latin America and the entire Islamic world. The peoples of the Islamic nations want and deserve the same freedoms and opportunities as people in every nation. And their governments should listen to their hopes.

A truly strong nation will permit legal avenues of dissent for all groups that pursue their aspirations without violence. An advancing nation will pursue economic reform, to unleash the great entrepreneurial energy of its people. A thriving nation will respect the rights of women, because no society can prosper while denying opportunity to half its citizens. Mothers and fathers and children across the Islamic world and all the world share the same fears and aspirations: In poverty, they struggle; in tyranny, they suffer; and as we saw in Afghanistan, in liberation, they celebrate.

America has a greater objective than controlling threats and containing resentment. We will work for a just and peaceful world beyond the war on terror.

Source: *Public Papers of President George W. Bush, 2002*, vol. 1 (Washington, DC: US Government Printing Office), pp. 917–21.

Suggested Questions for Discussion:

1. How did President George W. Bush define the threats to the United States?
2. Which responses did he advocate?
3. Why were these words so persuasive at the time?

4 George Packer, the Iraq War, 2005

George Packer was one of many American journalists to cover the early weeks and years of the American-led occupation of Iraq. His account is sympathetic to the aims and actions of American soldiers, but also highly critical of their inability to understand the reactions of local Iraqis. Packer shows how an unprepared American occupation Army contributed to the rise of a destructive Iraqi insurgency.[4]

Shortly after the fall of Baghdad, CNN aired footage of a Marine, confronted with a crowd of angry Iraqis, who shouts at them, "We're here for your fucking freedom! Now *back up*!"

When the war of liberation turned into an occupation, tens of thousands of soldiers who thought they would be home by June saw their rotations out postponed, and then again, and again. They soon became the occupation's

[4] See George Packer, *The Assassin's Gate: America in Iraq* (New York: Farrar, Straus, and Giroux, 2005); Thomas E. Ricks, *Fiasco: The American Military Adventure in Iraq* (New York: Penguin, 2006); Rajiv Chandrasekaran, *Imperial Life in the Emerald City: Inside Iraq's Green Zone* (New York: Alfred Knopf, 2006).

most visible face. Combat engineers trained to blow up minefields sat through meetings of the Baghdad water department; airborne troops used to jumping in and out of missions in a matter of days spent months setting up the Kirkuk police department; soldiers of the Third Infantry Division who spearheaded the invasion passed out textbooks in a Baghdad girls' school. The peacekeeping missions in the Balkans had given some of them a certain amount of preparation, but there was never any training for the massive project that fell on the shoulders of soldiers in Iraq. The CPA [Coalition Provisional Authority] was months away from setting up provincial offices. Ray Salvatore Jennings, a consultant to USAID, who wrote one of the forecasts on postconflict Iraq that ended up on Bremer's desk, kept coming across young officers trying to establish government in mid-sized cities who told him, "I'm doing the best I can but I don't know how to do this, I don't have a manual. You got a manual? Anything you can offer me I'd be profoundly grateful for." A civil affairs captain asked Jennings's colleague Albert Cevallos for training in Robert's Rules of Order IOI. Donald Rumsfeld's nightmare of an army of nation builders came to pass all over Iraq.

A rifle company commander named Captain John Prior showed me his war log for the spring of 2003. After Charlie Company of the Second Battalion, Sixth Infantry Regiment, First Armored Division had fought its way up from Kuwait to Baghdad airport, Captain Prior's unit began an odyssey around central Iraq that lasted the better part of three months, before finally arriving at its permanent location in south Baghdad. Prior's war log tells one story of soldiers coming to realize that what President Bush, on May 1, called the end of "major combat operations" was only the beginning.

Prior was a twenty-nine-year-old from Indiana, six feet tall and stringy (he lost twenty-five pounds in his first five months in Iraq). He had joined the Reserve Officers' Training Corps at a small engineering college in Indiana, then decided to make the military his career. His undergraduate's face, deadpan sarcasm, and bouncy slew-footed stride did not prepare you for his toughness. "Some people are just born to do something," Prior said. By his own account, he loved Army life, the taking and giving of orders. "The sappy reasons people say they're in the military, and people say, 'Nah, they can't be' – those are the reasons I'm in the military. When Peace Corps can't quite get it done and diplomacy fails and McDonald's can't build enough franchises to win Baghdad over, that's when the military comes in."

Charlie Company's first mission after the fall of Baghdad sent Prior west to the city of Ramadi, to evacuate the body of an Argentinian journalist named Veronica Cabrera who had been killed in a highway accident. Prior and his soldiers were the first conventional forces to enter Ramadi, which was already – in late April – becoming a center of Baathist resistance. They were asked by Special Forces and the CIA to stay on for a few days and help patrol the town. As Prior's convoy of Bradleys, Humvees, and armored personnel carriers drove down the main east–west road, a mosque began blaring anti-American rhetoric, and soon a crowd of three or four hundred Iraqis gathered. Prior and his soldiers found themselves in the middle of a riot, with insults, fruit, shoes, two-by-fours, rocks, and finally chunks of concrete flying at them and their vehicles. The Americans didn't shoot and no one was seriously injured; in his log Prior commends his soldiers for their restraint. That night, Prior sent out another patrol along the same route, "to show the population of Ramadi that we are tougher and more resilient than they are and that we are here to stay." This patrol came under small-arms fire from dark alleyways, but the shooters melted away before the Americans could find them.

In the following days in Ramadi, and then in nearby Falluja, Prior records a series of raids on houses and weapons markets. "Our soldiers are becoming experienced enough to know the difference between being nice and cordial to people and when it is time to not be nice and throw people to the ground." Charlie Company is making the difficult transition from combat to stability operations – from Phase III to Phase IV – and Prior is pleased with his soldiers' resourcefulness. Then something new and strange enters the margins of his account: Iraqis.

In Ramadi, a man who speaks broken English among other Iraqis suddenly pulls Prior to the side, cups his hands around the captain's ear, and whispers in flawless English, "I am an American, take me with you." When Prior tries to learn more, the man slips back into broken English and then clams up. On another day, another man, accompanied by his wife and small child, approaches a soldier at the gate of the university. Speaking perfect English with a British accent, he tells the soldier his story: He went to school in England, returned to Iraq in 1987, and has been unable to get out ever since. The man warns the soldier not to trust Iraqis, that things are not what they seem. Suddenly, a white truck pulls up and seven well-dressed men get out. The man at the gate quickly disappears with his wife and child before the Iraqis can speak to him. Prior and his first sergeant, Mark Lahan, track him down at home to find out whether he and his family are in danger. Now using broken English, the man tells them that everything is fine.

In another mysterious incident, an Iraqi approaches Lahan on a night patrol and bluntly asks, "How are things in Baghdad? Have there been any suicide bombings? Have any Americans been killed?" When Lahan replies that nothing of the sort has happened, the man looks surprised. Prior notes in his log, "It is interesting to see that here, after the bulk of the fighting is done in this country, the disinformation campaign by Iraqi hard-liners is still in effect, it will be a long time coming to get these people to be able to trust [one] another again and to understand how a government and law and order is supposed to work." In fact, it isn't disinformation from regime diehards. The guerrilla war is about to begin.

"The entire situation seemed very weird," Prior writes on April 26, after five days in Ramadi. "It is clear now that they are not as happy as they say that we are here. For the first time in awhile, I felt extremely nervous being in such close proximity to Iraqi nationals. I do not trust them." In another entry, from Falluja, he writes: "The Iraqis are an interesting people. None of them have weapons, none of them know where weapons are, all the bad people have left Falluja, and they only want life to be normal again. Unfortunately, our compound was hit by RPG fire today so I am not inclined to believe them."

Ramadi and Falluja are the major cities of Anbar province, a vast western desert region of conservative Sunni Arabs, home to large numbers of Iraqi military and intelligence officers. Anbar was the last province to fall to coalition forces, and it did so without a shot being fired. By the time American soldiers arrived, local leaders had taken control of the towns and prevented looting. Anbar is where the insurgency began, and tribal sheikhs later told me that it had all been unnecessary. The province was ready to cooperate with the coalition. If only the Americans had remained outside the cities, then crowds wouldn't have gathered to protest, and soldiers wouldn't have fired on the crowds, as they did in Falluja on April 28 and 30, killing eighteen civilians, and Iraqis wouldn't have retaliated with grenades and automatic weapons, and the second war wouldn't have begun.

There is a bit of truth to this account. The American units that took control of Ramadi and Falluja – the Third Armored Cavalry Regiment and the Eighty-second Airborne Division, respectively – were ill-suited to urban operations, didn't want to be there, and overreacted when they were provoked. "I was not impressed with the 3rd ACR's operations in Ramadi," Prior wrote, "they did not seem to have any idea what was going on, there was no sense of urgency, no one knew what the situation was anywhere in sector, none of the senior leadership could provide any guidance or answers." Having arrived in Iraq too late for the war, amid sand and heat and unfriendly locals, the regiment seemed unable or unwilling to adjust to Phase IV: "They did not appear to be ready for nor understand the urban/peace operations mission they had been assigned. Their attitude in terms of Rules of Engagement suggested to me that they had not made the change from combat operations to stability operations." Nor did it help that the house of a tribal leader in Ramadi, who had been cooperating with the CIA for years, was hit by an American air strike that killed him and seventeen members of his family. The Eighty-second in Falluja, clueless about Arab culture and lacking any civilian expertise (the CPA didn't come to Anbar until August), refused to compensate the families of the dead from the late April killings. By the time the Marines took control of Falluja in early 2004 and belatedly offered blood money, half the families refused it.

But Prior's log also shows that Anbar was set up for American failure. The CIA agents and Special Forces that first entered Falluja found no one to work with. "The local clerics, sheikhs, and government leaders have been complaining for some time that they need help to clear out the bad elements of their city," Prior wrote, "this has been their major reason for not providing more assistance or why they have been dragging their feet on getting anything done." But when the American agents summoned a small infantry unit for support, it was met with a riot, and the Eighty-second Airborne had to be called in to take control. Some American military analysts would later say that the problem in Anbar wasn't too much force but too little, and too late. The calibrations had to be finer than even the best-prepared units could make, and then each mistake played its part in deepening the ill-will and hastening the insurgency.

Prior's soldiers drove a vehicle through a gate and smashed down a garden wall on their way to raiding the wrong house; when they hit the right house, which was next door, they picked up only two of the five brothers they were looking for. Prior recorded the raid as a success. But a few days earlier, he noted that professors at the bleak, sand-blown university in Ramadi, who had protected the property themselves with their own weapons, blamed the Americans for breaching the perimeter wire and inadvertently allowing looters in. No one was using the phrase "hearts and minds" yet, but Prior, unlike some of his superiors in Qatar and Washington, knew that it was a missed chance: "The university people seem neutral to the American cause and appear to be the typical university types, liberal, not appreciative of the military and looking to play both sides of the equation. The impression I got was that they did not care if Americans were there or if Fedayeen were there, they just do not want the university looted any more. Their loyalties appear to be able to be purchased for the protection of their university."

Prior was among the first soldiers to encounter the hidden nature of things in an Iraq that was neither at war nor at peace. Nothing was as it seemed. Firepower and good intentions would be less important than learning to read the signs. Prior saw himself as a liberator, but there were people out there whose support remained to be won or lost, and nothing would come easily, and every judgment he made would have its small effect on the outcome. Iraqis, no longer the cheering crowds that had greeted the company on its way up to Baghdad, were now going to play an intimate role in Prior's life.

The raids in Ramadi and Falluja lasted almost a month; then Charlie Company was recalled to Baghdad. There Captain Prior's log ends. "We put trouble down, we left," he told me later, "trouble came again."

Source: George Packer, *The Assassin's Gate: America in Iraq* (New York: Farrar, Straus, and Giroux, 2005), pp. 219–24.

Suggested Questions for Discussion:

1. What did American soldiers expect in Iraq?
2. How did Iraqi citizens view the American Army?
3. How did American actions contribute to the rise of the Iraqi insurgency?

5 Torture at Abu Ghraib Prison, 2004

In the spring of 2004 photographs from the digital cameras of American soldiers surfaced, showing that US servicemen and women had engaged in the systematic and sadistic torture of Iraqi prisoners held at Baghdad Central Prison, also known as Abu Ghraib. Investigations by the military and various journalists confirmed the widespread use of torture to extract information, but also to humiliate prisoners. The Bush administration denied any direct culpability for these acts of what the President deemed a few misguided and disorderly soldiers. Nonetheless, the graphic evidence of American inhumanity undermined the moralistic claims of the United States in Iraq. This particular photograph shows a Pakistani protester – one of thousands around the world – shaming the United States with the visual evidence of American cruelty toward defenseless Muslim prisoners.[5]

---

[5] See Karen J. Greenberg and Joshua L. Dratel (eds.), *The Torture Papers: The Road to Abu Ghraib* (Cambridge: Cambridge University Press, 2005); Alfred W. McCoy, *A Question of Torture: CIA Interrogation, from the Cold War to the War on Terror* (New York: Metropolitan Books, 2006); Mark Danner, *Torture and Truth: America, Abu Ghraib, and the War on Terror* (New York: New York Review of Books, 2004).

Figure 10.1   *Pakistani supporters of the Citizens Peace Committee, a non-government organization, hold placards during an anti-US demonstration in Islamabad on May 26, 2004. Photo © Mian Khursheed/Reuters/Corbis*

Source: info in figure log http://pro.corbis.com/Enlargement/Enlargement.aspx? id=DWF15–733927&caller=search.

Suggested Questions for Discussion:

1. Why were the photographs from Abu Ghraib so disturbing?
2. How did they challenge American moral and political claims in the Middle East and other parts of the world?
3. Did these photographs undermine the War on Terror?

Select Bibliography

War, Imperialism, and Anti-Imperialism

Beisner, Robert, *From the Old Diplomacy to the New, 1865–1900* (New York: Crowell, 1975).

Cohen, Warren, *America's Response to China* (New York: Columbia University Press, 2000).

Ferrer, Ada, *Insurgent Cuba: Race, Nation, and Revolution, 1868–1898* (Chapel Hill, NC: University of North Carolina Press, 1999).

Iriye, Akira, *Cultural Internationalism and World Order* (Baltimore, MD: Johns Hopkins University Press, 1997).

Hoganson, Kristen, *Fighting for American Manhood* (New Haven, CT: Yale University Press, 1998).

LaFeber, Walter, *The New Empire: An Interpretation of American Expansion, 1865–1898* (Ithaca, NY: Cornell University Press, 1998).

Pérez, Louis A., *Cuba Under the Platt Amendment, 1902–1934* (Pittsburg, PA: University of Pittsburgh Press, 1986).

Williams, William Appleman, *The Tragedy of American Diplomacy*, enlarged edn. (New York: W. W. Norton, 1972).

The Great War to World War II

Borgwardt, Elizabeth, *New Deal for the World: America's Vision for Human Rights* (Cambridge, MA: Belknap Press of Harvard University Press, 2005).

Cohen, Warren, *Empire Without Tears: American Foreign Relations, 1921–1933* (New York: Knopf Press, 1987).

Cooper, John Milton, *Breaking the Heart of the World: Woodrow Wilson and the Fight for the League of Nations* (New York: Cambridge University Press, 2001).

Costigliola, Frank, *Awkward Dominion: American Political, Cultural, and Economic Relations with Europe, 1919–1933* (Ithaca, NY: Cornell University Press, 1984).

Dower, John, *Embracing Defeat: Japan in the Wake of World War II* (New York: W. W. Norton, 1999).

Iriye, Akira, *The Origins of the Second World War in Asia and the Pacific* (New York: Longman, 1987).

Knock, Thomas, *To End All Wars: Woodrow Wilson and the Quest for a New World Order* (New York: Oxford University Press, 1992).

Lauren, Paul Gordon, *Power and Prejudice: The Politics and Diplomacy of Racial Discrimination* (Boulder, CO: Westview Press, 1996).

Leffler, Melvyn, *Specter of Communism: The United States and the Origins of the Cold War, 1917–1953* (New York: Hill and Wang, 1994).

Rosenberg, Emily S., *Spreading the American Dream: American Economic and Cultural Expansion, 1890–1945* (New York: Hill and Wang, 1982).

The Early Cold War

Anderson, Carol, *Eyes off the Prize: The United Nations and the African American Struggle for Human Rights, 1944–1955* (New York: Cambridge University Press, 2003).

Boyer, Paul, *By the Bomb's Early Light: American Thought and Culture at the Dawn of the Atomic Age* (Chapel Hill, NC: University of North Carolina Press, 1994).

Chang, Gordon, *Friends and Enemies: the United States, China, and the Soviet Union, 1948–1972* (Stanford, CA: Stanford University Press, 1990).

Gaddis, John Lewis, *Strategies of Containment: A Critical Appraisal of American National Security Policy during the Cold War*, rev. edn. (New York: Oxford University Press, 2005).

Hogan, Michael J., *A Cross of Iron: Harry S. Truman and the Origins of the National Security State, 1945–1954* (New York: Cambridge University Press, 1998).

Leffler, Melvyn, *A Preponderance of Power: National Security, the Truman Administration, and the Cold War* (Stanford, CA: Stanford University Press, 1992).

McMahon, Robert, *Cold War on the Periphery: the United States, India, and Pakistan* (New York: Columbia University Press, 1994).

Zubok, Vladislav and Constantine Pleshakov, *Inside the Kremlin's Cold War: from Stalin to Khrushchev* (Cambridge, MA: Harvard University Press, 1996).

Rebellions Against the Cold War

Borstelmann, Thomas, *The Cold War and the Color Line: American Race Relations in the Global Arena* (Cambridge, MA: Harvard University Press, 2001).

Bradley, Mark, *Imagining Vietnam and America: The Making of Postcolonial Vietnam, 1919–1950* (Chapel Hill, NC: University of North Carolina Press, 2000).

Gardner, Lloyd, *Pay Any Price: Lyndon Johnson and the Wars for Vietnam* (Chicago, IL: Elephant Paperbacks, 1997).

Logevall, Fredrik, *Choosing War: the Lost Chance for Peace and the Escalation of War in Vietnam* (Berkeley, CA: University of California Press, 1999).

McPherson, Alan, *Yankee No! Anti-Imperialism in U.S.–Latin American Relations* (Cambridge, MA: Harvard University Press, 2003).

Suri, Jeremi, *Power and Protest: Global Revolution and the Rise of Détente* (Cambridge, MA: Harvard University Press, 2003).

Von Eschen, Penny, *Race Against Empire: Black Americans and Anticolonialism, 1937–1957* (Ithaca, NY: Cornell University Press, 1997).

Westad, Odd Arne, *The Global Cold War: Third World Interventions and the Making of Our Times* (New York: Cambridge University Press, 2005).

Young, Marilyn, *The Vietnam Wars, 1945–1990* (New York: HarperCollins, 1991).

Détente, Human Rights, and the Continuation of the Cold War

Leffler, Melvyn, *For the Soul of Mankind: the United States, the Soviet Union, and the Cold War* (New York: Hill and Wang, 2007).

Leogrande, William M., *Our Own Backyard: The United States in Central America, 1977–1992* (Chapel Hill, NC: University of North Carolina Press, 1998).

Power, Samantha, *A Problem from Hell: America and the Age of Genocide* (New York: Perennial, 2003).

Sikkink, Kathryn, *Mixed Signals: U.S. Human Rights Policy and Latin America* (Ithaca, NY: Cornell University Press, 2004).

Smith, Gaddis, *Morality, Reason, and Power: American Diplomacy in the Carter Years* (New York: Hill and Wang, 1986).

Suri, Jeremi, *Henry Kissinger and the American Century* (Cambridge, MA: Belknap Press of Harvard University Press, 2007).

The End of the Cold War

Gaddis, John Lewis, *The Cold War: A New History* (New York: Penguin, 2005).

Hogan, Michael J. (ed.), *The End of the Cold War: Its Meaning and Implications* (New York: Cambridge University Press, 1992).

Mann, James, *Rise of the Vulcans: History of Bush's War Cabinet* (New York: Viking, 2004).

Oberdofer, Don, *The Turn: From the Cold War to a New Era: The United States and the Soviet Union, 1983–1991* (New York: Poseidon Press, 1991).

Into the Twenty-First Century

Bacevich, Andrew, *American Empire: the Realities and Consequences of U.S. Diplomacy* (Cambridge, MA: Harvard University Press, 2002).

Clark, Wesley, *Waging Modern War: Bosnia, Kosovo, and the Future of Combat* (New York: Public Affairs, 2001).

Halberstam, David, *War in a Time of Peace: Bush, Clinton, and the General* (New York: Scribner, 2001).

Packer, George, *Assassin's Gate: America in Iraq* (New York: Farrar, Straus, and Giroux, 2005).

Ricks, Thomas, *Fiasco: The American Military Adventure in Iraq* (New York: Penguin Press, 2007).

Ricks, Thomas, *The Gamble: General David Petraeus and the American Military Adventure in Iraq, 2006–2008* (New York: Penguin Press, 2009).

Index